FORT LEAVENWORTH ■ • Independence • **St. Louis**

Pueblo •

Bent's Fort

KEARNY

Raton Pass

MISSOURI

Jaos

KY.

Santa Fé

Las Vegas

DONIPHAN

FORT SMITH ■

ARKANSAS R.

TENN.

RED R.

ARKANSAS

LOUISIANA

MISSISSIPPI RIVER

Socorro •
Valverde •

Grand Ecore •

FT. JESUP ■ • **Natchitoches**

SABINE R.

Baton Rouge •

El Paso del Norte •

PECOS R.

COLORADO R.

BRAZOS R.

New Orleans •

RIO GRANDE

NUECES R.

Austin •

San Antonio •

Goliad •

TAYLOR

Chihuahua •

DONIPHAN

WOOL

RIO GRANDE

Corpus Christi

SCOTT

TAYLOR

Monclova •

Mier •

FORT BROWN ■

Gulf of Mexico

Camargo •

TAYLOR

Parras •

Monterrey •

Saltillo •

Matamoros

Victoria •

PATTERSON

Mazatlan •

San Luis Potosí •

Tampico

SCOTT

Perote •

Mexico City • ← **Jalapa** •

Vera Cruz

Puebla •

Tabasco

Acapulco • **Oaxaca**

barbara long

The
Mexican War

A Compact History

1846-1848

The
Mexican War

A Compact History

1846-1848

by Charles L. Dufour

Maps by Barbara Long

Hawthorn Books, Inc.   Publishers   New York

First Edition: 1968

Contents

For
Marie Jeanne Dufour
who "sat out" the
Battle of Buena Vista

Foreword

In 1846, the United States went to war with Mexico, and, after an unbroken succession of victories, ended with territorial acquisitions which completed the nation's sweep to the Pacific.

Was it a just war or an unjust one? There were Americans at the time who held contrary opinions.

Was it Manifest Destiny, the plan of Divine Providence for America's eventual greatness? Or was it an aggressive grab of a neighbor's land? American opinion was divided on these questions, too, in 1846-1848, when the poorly led Mexicans were vanquished by Zachary Taylor and Winfield Scott.

Was General Taylor inept, but lucky? Was Winfield Scott sabotaged by President James K. Polk, as he believed? Was Polk, the zealous Democrat, reluctant to let Whig generals win the war?

This book does not attempt to support or approve any of the various positions on the Mexican War. Rather it tries to tell in narrative form the story of the conflict, drawing almost entirely on the printed record as represented in official reports, eyewitness accounts in books and articles, and published diaries and letters.

The author acknowledges a debt to earlier chroniclers of the Mexican War, specifically Justin H. Smith, Alfred Hoyt Bill, W. S. Henry, and Otis Singletary.

To all who assisted go grateful thanks, particularly to Connie Griffith, Dorothea Whittemore, Betty Maihles, and Bill Nañas of Tulane University's Howard-Tilton Library for research assistance; to Congressman F. Edward Herbert of Louisiana for his continuing help; to Charles Ferguson of the *States-Item* for a critical reading of the manuscript; and to Polly Le Beuf for typing the manuscript and contributing valuable suggestions while doing so. The author also acknowledges, with gratitude, the notable contribution Barbara Long has made with her excellent maps.

Finally, the author must thank Colonel R. E. Dupuy, editor of the Miltary History of the United States, for his excellent suggestions and generous cooperation in reading the manuscript as it progressed.

Any errors which exist are solely the author's.

CHARLES L. DUFOUR

The
Mexican War

A Compact History

1846-1848

1

The President's Message

The news reached the White House about 6 P.M. on May 9, 1846. Just minutes earlier, dispatches had arrived from General Zachary Taylor to the War Department, and Adjutant General of the Army Roger Jones himself had brought them to President Polk.

"Hostilities may now be considered as commenced," reported Old Zach, under date of April 26, and he stated that a force of sixty-three dragoons, commanded by Captain Seth B. Thornton, had been ambushed by Mexican cavalry. Sixteen American soldiers had been killed and the others had been captured.

President Polk immediately called his cabinet into session for the second time that day. But what had been only "the Mexican question" at the first meeting was now a matter of war. Polk knew exactly what steps he now had to take.

At the first cabinet meeting that May Saturday, the opinion was unanimous that if Mexican forces committed any acts of hostility against Taylor's little army, which had been ordered to the Rio Grande shortly after Texas was admitted to the Union, President Polk should send a message to Congress recommending an immediate declaration of war.

On the previous night, Polk's Minister to Mexico, John Slidell, had called at the White House to report on his fruitless mission. Slidell was closeted with the President for about an hour and Polk agreed with him that the time had come for the United States to "redress . . . the wrongs and injuries" perpetrated by Mexico, and "to act with promptness and energy." A few days earlier, the President had told Senator Thomas Hart Benton that "we had ample cause of war," but Polk had stressed his desire "to avoid it if it could be done honorably."

During the first discussion with his cabinet, Polk had pointed out that the situation in Texas was a delicate one and that a provocative

11

incident could come any time. Polk repeated what he had told Senator Benton and he expressed an unwillingness to remain silent any longer. His duty, the President told the cabinet, dictated that he send a message to Congress with recommendations of definite measures. The President suggested that he prepare such a message by Tuesday—just three days off—because the nation was excited over the Mexican crisis and growing impatient.

"I then propounded the distinct question to the cabinet, and took their opinions individually, whether I should make a message to Congress on Tuesday, and whether in that message I should recommend a declaration of war against Mexico," Polk recorded in his diary. "All except the Secretary of the Navy [George Bancroft] gave their advice in the affirmative. Mr. Bancroft dissented but said if any act of hostility should be committed by the Mexican forces he was then in favour of immediate war."

The cabinet, on the President's hurried call, reassembled for the second meeting at seven-thirty at the White House. With the reading of General Taylor's dispatch, Secretary Bancroft had the "act of hostility" that he needed to vote for war. After a thorough discussion of the Mexican crisis, there was unanimous agreement that the President should send a war message to Congress on Monday. The meeting adjourned at 10 P.M., and barely had the cabinet members filed out than James Knox Polk sat down at his desk and began to write.

The next morning, Sunday, President Polk returned to his message. At 9:30 A.M., he was joined by Secretary Bancroft, who assisted with the draft until 11 A.M., when the President put down his pen and left for church with Mrs. Polk and his niece and nephew. Upon his return at 1 P.M., he worked on the message until dinner and he continued to write after dinner and throughout the afternoon. The draft finally finished, the President, who had remained unavailable to visitors all day, received a stream of Senators and Congressmen until 10:30 P.M. When the last departed, the weary Chief Executive retired for the night.

Early Monday, President Polk carefully revised his message and at noon he sent it to both Houses of Congress. In the first two thirds of the war message, Polk sketched the diplomatic background to the Mexican crisis and related events down to the ambuscade of Taylor's detachment of Dragoons on April 24. Then he got to the heart of the message:

.... We have tried every effort at reconciliation. The cup of forebearance had been exhausted, even before the recent information from the frontier. ... But now after reiterated menaces, Mexico has passed the boundary of the United States, has invaded our territory, and shed American blood upon the American soil. She has proclaimed that hostilities have commenced, and that the two nations are now at war.

As war exists, and, notwithstanding all our efforts to avoid it, exists by the act of Mexico herself, we are called upon by every consideration of duty and patriotism to vindicate with decision the honor, the rights and interest of our country.

.... I invoke the prompt action of Congress to recognize the existence of the war, and to place at the disposition of the Executive the means of prosecuting the war with vigor, and thus hastening the restoration of peace.

For more than five hours the President waited impatiently in the White House for word of Congressional action. "It was a day of great anxiety for me," he recorded in his diary. "Between five and six o'clock P.M., Mr. Slidell . . . called and informed me that the House of Representatives had passed a bill carrying out all the recommendations of the message by a vote of 173 ayes to 14 noes, and that the Senate had adjourned after a debate without coming to any decision."

Despite the overwhelming vote in the House, there had been opposition to the bill "to authorize the President of the United States, under certain contingencies therein named, to accept the service of volunteers, and for other purposes." This opposition resulted from a preamble which a Democratic member of the Committee on Military Affairs had tacked onto the bill. The preamble read: "Whereas, by the act of the Republic of Mexico, a state of war exists between the United States and that Republic." Whigs and unconvinced Democrats found themselves in the peculiar position of either voting for the bill and thus endorsing Polk's contention that Mexico was to blame for hostilities, or rejecting the bill and thus subjecting themselves to the charge that they had sacrificed American troops on the Rio Grande.

The "haughty and dominating majority," as a Whig, Garrett Davis of Kentucky, characterized the pro-war House members, had effectively gagged debate. The reading of the voluminous docu-

ments the President had sent with the message—they fill 144 printed
pages in the records—would have taken all day, so selected documents were read by the House clerk. In vain did Whig members
ask for a day to examine the documents, piled high on the Speaker's
desk. The pro-war majority pushed for immediate action as "Whigs,
on rising to the floor, became invisible to the Speaker." In the end,
when the vote was taken, thirty-five members—twenty-two Democrats and thirteen Whigs—abstained from voting.

That night, Senator Benton called at the White House, and President Polk's diary reveals what was on his mind:

> Col. Benton said that the House of Representatives had
> passed a bill . . . declaring war in two hours, and that one and
> a half hours of that time had been occupied in reading the
> documents which accompanied my message, and that in his
> opinion in the nineteenth century war should not be declared
> without full discussion and much more consideration than
> had been given to it in the House of Representatives . . . Mr.
> Buchanan, Mr. [Secretary of War William L.] Marcy and my-
> self were perfectly satisfied that he would oppose the bill which
> had passed the House today, and that if the Whigs on party
> grounds acted with him the bill might be defeated.

It was with considerable concern that the President met with
his cabinet the next day, May 12. All present expressed doubts that
the Senate would pass the war bill which the House had so overwhelmingly voted. The day was a long and anxious one for the
President. But at 7:30 P.M., Polk's private secretary arrived hurriedly
from the Capitol with the glad tidings: the formal declaration of
war against Mexico had passed the Senate by a 40 to 2 vote.

The feared opposition in the Senate was never mustered, but
criticism of the bill came not only from Polk's avowed enemies,
the Whigs, but also from the great South Carolinian and Democratic leader, John C. Calhoun. As it was with many of the minority
Senators, the preamble of the bill was the stumbling block to Calhoun. The South Carolinian thought the war could have been
avoided, and he objected vehemently to placing the blame for hostilities upon Mexico. It was just as impossible for him to vote for
that preamble as it was for him to plunge a dagger into his own
heart, and more so, Calhoun declared. When the vote was called,
Calhoun abstained.

Members of both Houses had challenged Polk's thesis "that American blood had been spilled upon the American soil." The dissident Congressmen doubted that the Mexicans had violated an American boundary or had invaded American territory. Senator John J. Crittenden, Kentucky Whig, had asserted that few members of Congress, when the annexation of Texas was voted, believed that the Rio Grande was the boundary. Representative Garrett Davis had flatly insisted the territory between the Nueces and Rio Grande rivers was Mexican. Others held the area was, at best, debatable territory and that in sending Taylor's army into it, President Polk had committed an act of aggression.

Nevertheless, when the vote came, Davis voted "aye" for the war bill he had bitterly denounced, and Crittenden, along with another Whig, voted "aye, except the preamble." The two negative votes in the Senate were cast by Thomas Clayton of Delaware and John Davis of Massachusetts. Several days later, Calhoun wrote a friend that if time had been given to examine the documents, less than ten percent of Congress would have voted for the war bill. To another friend, still later, Calhoun asserted that if there had been the deliberation of a single day and if a single Democrat of standing had come to his side, the Mexican War would have been averted.

But the war was not averted and President Polk, accepting his private secretary's appraisal of the action in Congress, recorded it in his diary as "a great triumph for the administration."

On May 13, shortly after 1 P.M., a committee of Congress waited on the President, delivering to him the act recognizing the existence of a state of war with Mexico. Polk read it in the committee's presence and immediately signed it. The President was authorized to raise an army of 50,000 volunteers and $10,000,000 were voted for the prosecution of what administrative critics would soon call "Mr. Polk's War."

There were no doubts as to what Mr. Polk's war aims were. He recorded them that very night, after talking with Secretary of State Buchanan. In his diary, the President wrote:

I told him that though we had not gone to war for conquest, yet it was clear that in making peace we would if practicable obtain California and such other portions of the Mexican territory as would be sufficient to indemnify our claimants on Mexico and to defray the expense of war which that power by her long continued wrongs and injuries had forced us to wage.

I told him it was well known that the Mexican government had not other means to indemnifying us.

Yet, the very next day, May 14, Buchanan piously declared:

We go to War with Mexico solely for the purpose of conquering an honorable and just peace. Whilst we intend to prosecute the War with vigor, both by land and by sea, we shall bear the olive branch in one hand, and the sword in the other; and whenever she will accept the former, we shall sheath the latter.

2

Background to War

To Aaron Burr on his deathbed in 1836 came the news that Texas had declared its independence of Mexico. "I was thirty years too soon," murmured the old man.

Was Burr's fantastic adventure of 1806–1807 aimed at the conquest of Mexico? Whatever may have been his designs on the western states and territories, was Burr's real purpose the invasion of Texas, the "liberation"of Mexico?

When Burr visited New Orleans in June, 1805, he found there an organization known as the Mexican Association, with about three hundred members. Its aim was the revolutionizing of Mexico. Burr was lavishly entertained by Daniel Clark and Edward Livingston and others in the group. Later, Burr told Harman Blennerhassett, his Ohio Valley ally, that on his visit to New Orleans the Mexican Association had asked him to be its leader. That Burr and the Mexican Association were working together with the idea of eventually invading Mexico cannot be doubted. Matthew L. Davis, to whom Burr confided his private papers, wrote in his *Memoirs of Aaron Burr*: "The great object of Burr was the conquest of Mexico."

And so, four decades before what Mexican historians still call "the unjust North American invasion," citizens of the United States were already casting covetous eyes upon Mexican territory, especially the vast expanse between the Sabine and the Rio Grande, known as Texas.

The vagueness in the definition of the boundaries of the Louisiana Purchase in 1803 ultimately gave rise to disputed claims to Texas between the United States and Spain. At the same time, the United States claimed that West Florida, as far east as the Perdido River, was part of the Purchase. When, in 1810, a group of Americans rose against Spain, captured Baton Rouge, and established the Republic of West Florida, Governor William C. C. Claiborne, of the Territory of Orleans, on the orders of President Madison, quickly marched in and annexed the short-lived republic to the Territory.

Early in 1819, Secretary of State John Quincy Adams negotiated a treaty with Spain whereby the latter gave up both Florida and West Florida and the United States relinquished its claim to Texas and assumed, at the same time, $5,000,000 in American citizens' claims against Spain. Thus, the United States accepted the Sabine River as the boundary between Louisiana and the Mexican province of Texas.

When Adams became President, the United States Minister, Joel R. Poinsett, was instructed, in 1827, to offer Mexico, which meanwhile had declared its independence from Spain, $1,000,000 for the territory between the Sabine and the Rio Grande, and half that amount for the area east of the Colorado River. Informal conversations with Mexican leaders indicated that such a transaction would never pass the Mexican Congress, so Poinsett made no official attempt to purchase Texas in whole or in part.

During Mexico's struggle for independence, both financial and moral assistance was provided the revolutionists by influential Americans. And once it had established itself the new Mexican Republic was eager to attract settlers to Texas. Generous grants of land were made in an effort to encourage colonization, and land-hungry Americans flocked into the region. Soon, they far outnumbered the Europeans and native Mexicans who had moved into Texas. This pattern of settlement was a cause of considerable concern to the Mexican Government and in 1828 a fact-finding commission was sent to Texas to study the situation. The commission's report was an alarming one, for it revealed that in Texas, the American frontiersman was employing his traditional custom of merging his interests with those of the United States. In a warning to the Mexican Congress, Secretary of Foreign Relations Lucas Alamán said, in part:

They commence by introducing themselves into the territory which they covet, upon pretence of commercial negotiations, or of the establishment of colonies, with or without the assent of the government to which it belongs. These colonies grow, multiply, become the predominant party in the population; and as soon as support is found in this manner, they begin to set up rights which it is impossible to sustain . . . These pioneers excite, by degrees, movements which disturb the political state of the country . . . and then follow discontents and dissatisfaction, calculated to fatigue the patience of the legitimate owner, and to diminish the usefulness of the administration and of the exercise of authority. When things have come to this pass, which is precisely the present state of things in Texas . . . they proceed, upon the most extraordinary pretexts, to make themselves masters of the country . . . leaving the question to be decided afterwards as to the legality of the possession, which force alone could take from them.

It was about this time that President Andrew Jackson made a serious effort to buy Texas from Mexico. On August 12, 1829, Jackson directed that Poinsett be instructed to negotiate for its purchase with authority to offer as high as $5,000,000. But before Poinsett could implement these instructions, he was recalled at Mexico's request. To Poinsett's successor in Mexico, Anthony Butler, President Jackson wrote on October 10, 1829: "The acquisition of that territory [Texas] is becoming every day an object of more importance to us," and on October 19, Jackson underscored this: ". . . The purchase of Texas . . . is very important to the harmony and peace of the two republics."

When the Texas Revolution broke out in 1835, the official position of the United States was one of strict neutrality. However, this did not prevent Americans from forming committees to collect money, arms, clothing, and supplies for the Texans. The Mexican minister in Washington protested bitterly to the State Department over "the notorious cooperation of the citizens of Louisiana with the colonial insurgents of Texas, whose cause they have espoused, and with whom they act as auxiliaries." The minister also complained that the Texans "were daily obtaining from New Orleans assistance of all kinds in men, munitions, and arms, in silver and soldiers . . ."

Stephen F. Austin secured loans of more than $300,000 in New Orleans, where, he wrote, "the cause of liberty and Texas stands high." Austin's success with individuals and groups of Americans was not matched, however, in Washington. In a circular to President Jackson and high ranking members of the administration, he appealed not only to national interest, but to humanitarianism as well. "This is a war of barbarism against civilization, of despotism against liberty, of Mexicans against Americans," Austin declared. He urged the President and Congress to recognize that the war in Texas is a "national war" and "thus responds to the noble feelings of the American people . . . Let the administration and Congress take this position *at once,* and the butcheries in Texas will cease, humanity will no longer be outraged by a war against liberty . . ."

President Jackson penned the following endorsement on Austin's impassioned plea:

> The writer does not reflect that we have a treaty with Mexico, and our national faith is pledged to support it. The Texians before they took the step to declare themselves independent, which has aroused and united all Mexico against them, ought to have pondered well, it was a rash and premature act, our neutrality must be faithfully maintained.

Despite the position of official Washington, the American people were in full sympathy with their compatriots in Texas. They were outraged by the Mexican atrocities at San Antonio and Goliad, and "Remember the Alamo" became on the Western Frontier almost as much of a battle cry as it was in Texas. When Texas independence was established by Sam Houston's victory over Santa Anna in the Battle of San Jacinto, April 21, 1836, many Americans looked to an early annexation of Texas by the United States. So indeed did the Texans, who had in the same year voted overwhelmingly to enter the Union.

Both Jackson and his successor in the White House, Martin Van Buren, were aloof to Texas proposals of annexation. However, the former made official the recognition of Texas, voted by Congress in July, 1836, when he signed on March 3, 1837, a bill providing a salary for a chargé d'affaires to the Republic of Texas when the President judged it expedient to appoint one.

During the years leading up to the Presidential election of 1844, resentment and ill-feeling were nurtured on both sides of the Rio Grande. Mexican hatred of the insurgents never flagged and this was reciprocated even more strongly by the Texans. The hostility of the Mexicans extended to the United States which it saw as a rapacious neighbor about to launch an aggressive program of expansion at its expense.

That, in many American minds, Mexico was considered vulnerable to Manifest Destiny cannot be doubted. William Bollaert, an English traveler, sensed this in New Orleans in 1842, when he wrote in his journal:

> New Orleans . . . having been and was even then the hot bed for all operations regarding Texas. . . . At every emergency there were always found parties in N.O. to assist in widening the breach in every possible way between the New Republic and Mexico . . . It may be asked what was New Orleans to reap from Texas: In the first place, the belligerent excitement was in accordance with the feeling of the southern population. . . . The occupation of Texas by the white race would open the door to the rich natural production of Mexico and doubtless there were some aspiring minds who did not consider it as very problematical to see the whole of the Great Empire of the Montezumas divided into a number of states and forming part of the Union. Onward, was and is their cry, and it is very difficult to say when or how it is to be arrested—or if such is not the natural course of events—which cannot be stopped by human means.

Mexico's fear and resentment of American expansionism were as understandable as was American hostility engendered by Mexican cruelties in Texas. A modern historian, Otis A. Singletary, has neatly summed up the interplay of geography and emotionalism in the deterioration of American-Mexican relations:

> By virtue of her geographic proximity to the United States, Mexico was an inevitable target for her acquisitive northern neighbor, and it was only natural that her nationals should be deeply offended by this tendency to absorb her territory . . .
> The Mexican resentment was, however, a pale thing compared to the hostility many Americans felt towards Mexico . . . A series of excesses and cruelties running like a red thread through the history of the 1830's and '40's gave rise to this hostility against Mexicans . . .

The stage, then, was set for war between the United States and

Mexico. All that was needed was a spark to ignite the tinderbox which mutual distrust had prepared. The annexation of Texas provided the spark; it was the immediate cause of the Mexican War.

When the American voters in the Presidential election of 1844 chose James K. Polk over Henry Clay, it was accurately interpreted as their approval of the annexation of Texas. The Democratic platform on which Polk was elected was unequivocal in calling the reoccupation of Oregon and the "reannexation" of Texas "great American measures, which the convention recommends to the cordial support of the Democracy of the Union." The implication in *reannexation* was that Texas was a part of the Louisiana Purchase and that John Quincy Adams had bartered it away.

More than six months before the election, Polk had published a letter in the Washington *Globe* calling for the annexation of both Texas and the Oregon Territory. About the same time, Clay published a letter opposing annexation without Mexico's consent. Later in the campaign, Clay modified his position, declaring he had no objection to the annexation of Texas provided it was done "without dishonor, without war."

Meanwhile, in April, 1844, President Tyler had submitted to the Senate a treaty of annexation whereby Texas would enter the Union as a territory. However, on June 8, the Texas Annexation Treaty was rejected by the Senate by a 35 to 16 vote. Within a month of Polk's election, Tyler, in his final annual message to Congress, recommended a joint resolution by the House and Senate, offering annexation as a state to Texas.

On March 1, 1845, just three days before the inauguration of Polk, Congress passed the joint resolution and Tyler signed it the same day. General Juan N. Almonte, Mexican Minister, demanded his passports and left Washington, assailing bitterly "the greatest injustice recorded in the annals of modern history . . . despoiling a friendly nation . . . of a considerable part of its territory." Several weeks later, United States Minister Wilson Shannon was invited to leave Mexico, and diplomatic relations between the two nations were completely severed.

President Polk thus inherited two international problems when he entered the White House—one with Great Britain over the Oregon border and the other the long-smoldering crisis with Mexico over Texas. In the early days of his administration, Polk told George Bancroft, his Secretary of the Navy: "There are four great measures which are to be the measures of my administration: one, a reduction of the tariff; another the independent treasury; a third, the settlement of the Oregon boundary question; and lastly, the acquisition of California."

By the summer of 1846, Polk had achieved three of his aims: On June 15, the Oregon Treaty with Great Britain was signed, establishing the Oregon border along the forty-ninth parallel. On July 30, the Walker Tariff Act was passed. And on August 6, Congress reestablished an independent Treasury.

But before the President reached his fourth goal—the acquisition of California—the Mexican War had to be fought. And events in 1845 hurried the two nations to the brink of open conflict:

June 15—The protection of the United States was promised Texas by Secretary of State Buchanan if Texas accepted the annexation terms. In anticipation of the expected acceptance of annexation by Texas, Brigadier General Zachary Taylor was ordered by the War Department to move his little army from Fort Jessup, Louisiana, "to the mouth of the Sabine, or to such other point on the Gulf of Mexico, or its navigable waters, as in your judgment may be most convenient for an embarkation at the proper time for the Western Frontier of Texas."

June 23—The Texas Congress approved annexation.

July 4—A convention of Texans at Austin accepted the terms of annexation.

July 21—President Herrera asked the Mexican Congress for a declaration of war to take effect at the time of annexation or invasion of Texas.

July 31—General Taylor established his camp at Corpus Christi, on the western bank of the Nueces River.

August 27—The Texas Convention framed a state constitution.

October 13—The people of Texas ratified both annexation and the state constitution in a special election.

The die was now cast for war. Two years earlier, J. M. Bocanegra, Mexican Foreign Minister, had warned American Minister Waddy Thompson, that "the Mexican Government will consider equivalent to a declaration of war against the Mexican Republic the passage of an act for the incorporation of Texas with the territory of the United States; the certainty of the fact being sufficent for the immediate proclamation of war." And, also in 1843, General Almonte, in a note to the State Department on the possible annexation of Texas, said: "The Mexican Government is resolved to declare war as soon as it receives information of such an act."

But Mexico did not make a formal declaration of war against the United States. Bocanegra's statement to Waddy Thompson, which had been repeated, had never been withdrawn. In Mexican eyes, the United States had launched an aggressive war, first by annexing Texas, and then by invading it.

President Polk decided to make one last diplomatic effort to avoid the war which his election in 1844 on an expansionist platform had made all but inevitable.

3

Failure of a Mission

Historians are divided as to the validity of President Polk's charges concerning "the long-continued and unredressed wrongs and injuries committed by the Mexican Government on citizens of the United States," alleged in his war message to Congress on May 11, 1846.

Nor is there agreement among historians on Polk's "strong desire to establish peace with Mexico on liberal and honorable terms" and his expressed readiness "to regulate and adjust our boundary, and other causes of difference with that power, on such fair and equitable principles as would lead to permanent relations of the most friendly nature."

The thesis of the Whigs, Polk's political enemies, that he was responsible for the Mexican War, was echoed by James Ford Rhodes, who charged that "open hostilities would have been avoided had the conduct of the administration been honorable. Mexico was actually goaded on to the war." And Hubert H. Bancroft was no less condemnatory: "It was a premeditated and predetermined affair, the war of the United States on Mexico; it was the result of a deliberately calculated scheme of robbery on the part of the superior power."

On the other hand, Justin H. Smith flatly blames the Mexican people and their leaders for the war: "The press clamored for war; the government was deeply committed to that policy; and the great majority of those who counted for anything . . . were passionately determined that no fair adjustment of the pending difficulties should be made." Samuel F. Bemis also rallied to Polk's support: "James K. Polk allowed Mexico to begin the war, and this, too, without any dishonorable action on his part to precipitate it . . . It would be well-nigh impossible today to find a citizen of the United States who would desire to undo President Polk's diplomacy, President Polk's war . . ."

In mid-September, 1845, dispatches from a confidential agent of the United States in Mexico, Dr. William S. Parrott, indicated that the Mexican Government was desirous of reestablishing diplomatic relations with the United States and that a minister would be received. Concurrence in Parrott's opinion by John Black and F. M. Dimond, American consuls at Mexico City and Vera Cruz, prompted the unanimous agreement of the cabinet that President Polk should reopen diplomatic relations with Mexico. A secret mission was planned to prevent any possible steps the British, French, and other foreign ministers at Washington, might take to thwart or defeat the object. Polk, in consultation with the cabinet, selected John Slidell of New Orleans, who spoke Spanish fluently and who was otherwise well qualified, for the mission. "One great object of the mission," President Polk recorded, "would be to adjust a permanent boundary between Mexico and the United States, and that in doing this the Minister would be instructed to purchase for a pecuniary consideration Upper California and New Mexico . . . A better boundary would be the Del Norte [Rio Grande] from its mouth to the Passo [El Paso] . . . and thence to the Pacific Ocean, Mexico ceding to the United States all the country east and north of these lines." Polk believed that to obtain such a boundary, the amount to be paid would be of "small importance," even as much as $15,000,000 or $20,000,000. Indeed, the President was so set on securing California he was prepared to pay $40,000,000.

The next day, September 17, Secretary Buchanan wrote Consul Black "to ascertain from the Mexican Government whether they would receive an envoy from the United States, entrusted with full powers to adjust all the questions in dispute between the two governments."

A month later Black replied that in an exchange of letters with Manuel de la Peña y Peña, the Mexican Minister of Foreign Relations, he had received assurances that an envoy—Peña y Peña employed the term "commissioner"—would be received if the American flotilla, then cruising off Vera Cruz, was recalled. "Its presence," the Minister told Black, "would degrade Mexico, while she is receiving the commissioner, and would justly subject the United States to the imputation of contradicting by acts the vehement desire of conciliation, peace and friendship, which is professed and asserted by words."

Now reassured that an envoy would be received by Mexico, President Polk issued John Slidell his commission as envoy extraordinary and minister plenipotentiary on November 10. Slidell reached Vera Cruz on November 29 and pushed on immediately for Mexico City which, after several days delay, he reached on December 6. Meanwhile, news of the arrival of an American envoy at Vera Cruz had reached Peña y Peña, who protested to Consul Black that the government did not expect the envoy until January; that it was not prepared to receive him; that he desired, if possible, that the envoy not come to the capital because his presence at this time might prove destructive to the government and thus defeat the whole affair.

The truth was that the administration of President José Herrera was tottering. A revolution was brewing and General Mariano Paredes, at the head of the army, was awaiting the propitious moment to tumble Herrera from office and assume the presidency himself. Black summed up for Secretary Buchanan the predicament in which Herrera found himself as Slidell approached Mexico City:

> He [Peña y Peña] said that the government itself was well disposed, and ready to proceed with negotiations, but that if the affair were commenced now, it would endanger its existence: that . . . by January . . . they would be able to proceed in the affair with more security; that the government were afraid that the appearance of the envoy at this time would produce a revolution against it, which might terminate in its destruction.

Slidell addressed a brief note to Peña y Peña on December 8, advising him of his appointment as envoy extraordinary and minister plenipotentiary, and of his arrival in the capital. He requested the time and place at which he might present his letter of credence, a copy of which he enclosed, to President Herrera.

Having received no reply at the end of a week—he received a memorandum from Black relating two informal talks the Consul had had with Peña y Peña, in which the latter raised difficulties—Slidell addressed the Minister a second time on December 15, inquiring as to when he might expect an answer to his note of December 8. The next day, Peña y Peña replied that the delays in Slidell's reception and in responding to his first note were occasioned "solely from certain difficulties occasioned by the nature of

[Slidell's] credentials, as compared with the proposition made by the United States . . . to treat peacefully upon the affairs of Texas." Accordingly, the credentials were submitted to the council of government for its opinion, and Peña y Peña promised that the result would be communicated to Slidell "without loss of time." The Minister closed by assuring Slidell that "the government of Mexico is ready to proceed agreeably to what it proposed in its answer on the subject."

Three days later, on December 20, Peña y Peña informed Slidell that President Herrera would not receive him, because "Mr. Slidell does not come . . . with . . . credentials authorizing him expressly and exclusively to settle the questions which have disturbed the harmony and good understanding between the two republics, and which will bring war between them unless such settlements be effected in a satisfactory manner . . ."

Slidell's reply, dated December 24, was a step by step review of the informal negotiations between Peña y Peña and Consul John Black, which led to his mission to Mexico—it is more than five thousand words in length and occupies almost ten printed pages in the House records—and it was prefaced by ill-disguised indignation. Fearful of overstepping "the bounds which courtesy and the usages of diplomatic intercourse prescribe," Slidell declared he was abstaining "from the full expression of the feelings of astonishment and dissatisfaction" he had derived from the Mexican note. However, Slidell stated "he should be recreant alike to the character, dignity, and interests of the government which he has the honor to represent," if he failed to point out to Peña y Peña and through him to the people of the United States and Mexico, "the misstatements (and he begs to be understood that he uses this in no invidious sense) which the communication of your excellency contains of the correspondence which induced the appointment of the undersigned."

Having thus diplomatically called Peña y Peña a liar, Slidell moved to the task of refuting the reasoning by which the Mexican Government refused to receive him and to warn the Minister "of the very grave consequences to which a persistence in that refusal will probably lead." Near the end of this lengthy, sharp note, Slidell declared that if war came, "the fault will not be with the United States; the sole responsibility of such a calamity, with all its consequences, must rest with the Mexican Republic."

In reporting to Secretary Buchanan on Peña y Peña's "most extraordinary document," Slidell conceded that in his anxiety "to preserve that tone of forbearance . . . so strongly inculcated upon me by your instructions" he may have failed in his reply "to animadvert with becoming spirit on its unparalleled bad faith, its gross falsification of the correspondence which led to my appointment, and the utter futility of the miserable sophistry by which it attempts to justify its conduct."

The long-expected revolution against José Herrera's government came on December 29—ironically, the day on which Texas entered the Union—and General Paredes assumed power. Slidell's report to Buchanan on the change of administrations gave a graphic picture of the internal instability in Mexico, a fact that had rendered his mission virtually fruitless from the beginning:

> . . . General Herrera, satisfied that he could make no effectual resistance, resigned the presidency. The ringing of bells and firing of cannons announced the success of the revolutionists and the overthrow of the government. When it is recollected that the civil authorities throughout the country, with [a] single exception . . . were opposed to the movement of Paredes; that most of them had made loud protestations of their intention to resist it at all hazards; that both branches of Congress had unanimously declared their abhorrence of his treachery, and denounced his "plan" as an undisguised military despotism; and that, after all this war of manifestoes and resolutions, not a shot has been fired in defense of constitutional government . . .

On January 28, 1846, Secretary Buchanan, assuming but not knowing, that "a new administration of some kind or other at this moment controls that unfortunate country," instructed Slidell "to act with such prudence and firmness that it may appear manifest to the people of the United States, and to the world, that a rupture could not be honorably avoided." Buchanan told Slidell that President Polk is "sincerely desirous to preserve peace with Mexico" both by "inclination and policy," but if the Mexican Government continued to refuse to receive him, "the cup of forebearance will then have been exhausted." In this case, Slidell should demand his passport. "It will then become the duty of the President to submit the whole case to Congress," Buchanan stated, "and call upon the nation to assert its just rights, and avenge its injured honor."

Upon receipt of this letter, Slidell, who had left Mexico City for Jalapa to await developments, dispatched a note on March 1, to Joaquín Castillo y Lanzas, successor to Peña y Peña:

> The destinies of the Mexican Republic . . . having since been committed to other hands, the President is unwilling to take a course which would inevitably result in war, without making another effort to avert so great a calamity. He wishes, by exhausting every honorable means of conciliation, to demonstrate to the civilized world that, if its peace shall be disturbed, the responsibility must fall upon Mexico alone . . . It would be idle to repeat the arguments which the undersigned had the honor to present in his notes [to Peña y Peña]. He has nothing to add to them but is instructed again to present them to the consideration of the President ad Interim of the Mexican Republic, General Mariano Paredes y Arrillago.

On March 12, Castillo y Lanzas wrote Slidell—the American Minister received the letter three days later in Jalapa—that "the Mexican Government cannot receive him," and added several thousand words in denouncing American expansionism at Mexico's expense.

Slidell immediately asked for his passport, but he could not let Castillo y Lanzas' attack on American policy go unchallenged. He said, in part:

> The Mexican Government cannot shift the responsibility of war upon the United States, by assuming that they are the aggressors. A plain, unanswerable fact responds to all the subtleties and sophistries by which it is attempted to obscure the real question; that fact, is the presence in Mexico of a minister of the United States, clothed with full powers to settle all the questions in dispute between the two nations, and among them, that of Texas.

Slidell sailed from Vera Cruz for New Orleans on the USS *Mississippi* and the last dispatch of his mission was written at sea and dated April 2. On May 8, Slidell reported in person to President Polk and urged him "to act with promptness and energy."

4

Old Zach and His Army

Zachary Taylor looked more like a frontier farmer than a military man. After thirty-seven years in the United States Army, the sixty-one-year-old brevet brigadier general hated the traditional "spit-and-polish" that went with rank. Soldiering on the frontier and fighting Indians was a question of comfort with him, and much of the time he went about post and camp in old civilian clothes, with no semblance of insignia, and often a broad-brimmed straw hat on his head.

Heavily set on a frame of medium height, Taylor's short legs and corpulence tended to make him appear short. To one Texas volunteer, Old Zach was "a plain old farmer-looking man—no particular indications of smartness or intellect," while another volunteer wrote home that his commanding general was "an ordinary-looking old man." A young Illinois lieutenant summed him up for the home folks: "Taylor is short and very heavy, with pronounced face lines and gray hair, wears an old oilcloth cap, a dusty green coat, a frightful pair of trousers and on horseback looks like a toad." Gideon Pillow, one of the Mexican War's political generals, summed Taylor up for his wife as "a frank and manly old gentleman about the size of myself except that he is quite fat."

Taylor's rough appearance and unassuming manner and speech once caused great embarrassment to two young brevet second lieutenants, newly graduated from West Point, who joined Old Zach's command at Fort Smith, Arkansas. Encountering an amiable old hayseed, the two "bandbox" soldiers decided to have some fun.

"Good morning, old fellow!" they greeted him.

"Good morning."

"How's crops?"

"Purty good."

"Come on, take a drink with us."

The old man joined them, but probably did not accept their hospitality. For some time he provided them much amusement and when he left to go, one of the lieutenants said: "Give our love to the old woman and the gals."

Later that day, decked in full-dress finery, the young officers called on General Taylor to pay their respects. To their astonished dismay they found themselves saluting the old "farmer" at whom they had poked fun that morning. Acknowledging the youngsters' embarrassed salutes with proper military dignity, General Taylor then presented Mrs. Taylor and his teen-age daughter Betty.

"Here," said the General, "are the old woman and the gal."

Later, during the Mexican War, when military protocol called for him to receive a visit from Commodore David Conner, United States Naval Commander, Taylor made the supreme effort. He dug out of his military chest his finest, most glittering uniform in which to greet the Commodore. But Conner, knowing Taylor's penchant for old clothes, had, as the perfect visitor, dressed in civilian clothes for the occasion. Taylor promptly stowed away his dress uniform for the duration of the war.

Simplicity, amiability, and accessibility made Old Zach an easy commander under whom to serve, and officers and men in the ranks alike respected his common sense, his stubborn determination, and his courage under fire. It was not for nothing that Zachary Taylor had won the nom de guerre of "Old Rough and Ready." A wounded sergeant, home from battle, described Taylor as approachable by his soldiers at all hours: "He will sit and talk with the commonest soldier in the most affable manner . . . enter minutely into the private affairs of the soldiers under his command, give them advice when asked, as it frequently is . . ."

In the spring of 1845, Taylor was commander of the First Department, with headquarters at Fort Jessup, Louisiana, a few miles west of Natchitoches and not many miles from the Sabine River, the border between Louisiana and the Republic of Texas. Almost a quarter of a century earlier, in 1822, Taylor had established Fort Jessup. Except for his service in the Second Seminole War in 1837–1838, when his victory over the Indians in Florida at Okeechobee led to his promotion to brevet brigadier general, Taylor's military experience was all gained on the Western Frontier.

Commissioned a first lieutenant in 1808, and promoted to captain in 1810, Taylor's conspicuous bravery in defending Fort Harrison in Indiana Territory in the War of 1812 gained him the brevet of major. At the end of the war he was awarded the full rank of major. During the next twenty years, Taylor served in Michigan Territory, Mississippi, Louisiana, Minnesota, and in the Black Hawk War. At the age of forty-eight, when he had attained the rank of colonel, he went to Florida to fight the Seminoles. Promoted to brevet brigadier general, Taylor next commanded the Second Department, Western Division, with headquarters at Fort Smith, Arkansas. In 1844, General Taylor took command at Fort Jessup, where a force of less than 1,500 troops was stationed.

On May 28, 1845, Secretary of War William L. Marcy sent instructions to General Taylor to place his command "into a position where they may most promptly and efficiently act in defense of Texas," should such a necessity arise. The Secretary of War stated that just as soon as Texas accepted the terms of annexation, "Texas will then be regarded . . . so far a part of the United States as to be entitled from this government to defense and protection from foreign invasion and Indian incursions."

Less than three weeks later, Taylor got his orders to move. Acting for Marcy, Secretary of the Navy Bancroft instructed Taylor on June 15, as follows:

> On the 4th day of July . . . Texas will probably accept . . . annexation. That . . . will constitute Texas an integral portion of our country.
>
> In anticipation of that event, you will forthwith make a forward movement with the troops under your command, and advance to the mouth of the Sabine, or to such other points on the Gulf of Mexico . . . as in your judgment may be most convenient for an embarkation at the proper time for the Western Frontier of Texas . . . It is intended that you choose the most expeditious [route], having due regard to the health and efficiency of the troops, on reaching the point of destination.
>
> . . . The point of your ultimate destination is the Western Frontier of Texas, where you will select and occupy, on or near the Rio Grande del Norte, such a site as will be consistent with the health of the troops, and will be best adapted to repel invasion, and to protect what, in the event of annexation, will be our western border. You will limit yourself to the defense

of the Territory of Texas, unless Mexico should declare war against the United States.

Taylor's command consisted of seven companies of the Second Dragoons, commanded by Colonel David E. Twiggs; the Third Infantry, commanded by Lieutenant Colonel Ethan Allen Hitchcock; and the Fourth Infantry, commanded by Colonel Josiah H. Vose. In the aggregate, Old Zach had about 600 dragoons and about 800 infantry.

Taylor wasted no time in implementing his orders. On July 2, eight companies of the Fourth Infantry marched to Grand Ecore on the Red River and embarked for New Orleans, which Taylor had selected as the staging area for his little Army of Observation. Upon arrival, the Fourth Infantry went into camp at Jackson Barracks, on the lower edge of the city. On July 10, the Third Infantry reached New Orleans and was quartered in a large cotton press. "At $100 a day—pretty costly," recorded Lieutenant Colonel Ethan Allen Hitchcock in his journal.

General Taylor, who had remained at Fort Jessup to see Twiggs's Second Dragoons take off on their cross-country ride to San Antonio, joined his infantry troops in New Orleans on July 15. Several days later, Lieutenant Braxton Bragg's company of the Third Artillery joined the command, and within a week, Taylor was ready to move. Before departure, the little force suffered its first casualty when Colonel Vose of the Fourth Infantry collapsed after a drill. "Nothing could exceed the heat of the weather during the few days we spent in New Orleans," an officer observed. "Few of us will forget the melting heat we endured while marching . . ." Colonel Vose, this same officer recorded, "was on drill within a few minutes of his death. He fell back on the porch of his quarters in a fit and died before medical aid could be of any avail. . . . We could not but be impressed with so melancholy a commencement of the campaign."

By July 22, the steamship *Alabama* was ready to receive Taylor's troops and Old Zach went aboard before midnight. The Third Infantry—two companies remained in New Orleans for a later transport—formed at 11 P.M. in the street outside the cotton press and at the order, the foot-soldiers "wheeled into column, and, to the soul-inspiring air of their regimental quick-step, marched through the streets, thence to their transports." At least one officer in the regiment thought it a sufficiently memorable moment to note it in his journal. Captain William S. Henry wrote:

Many curious heads were seen protruding from half-opened doors and windows, to know what all the fuss could be about; and many an old veteran had the dormant feelings of the 8th of January rekindled by the "ear-piercing fife" and "spirit-stirring drum." The moon was just rising as we marched out, gilding the domes and house-tops, and caused our bayonets to glisten in the mellow light. The deep shadows on one side of the street, the bright moonlight upon the other, solemn quiet of the sleeping city, disturbed so harshly by the martial music of the column, formed a scene which touched one's feelings, and will not be easily forgotten.

The *Alabama* steamed out of the harbor of New Orleans at 3 A.M. on July 23, its destination Corpus Christi, on the western bank of the Nueces River. But although the *Alabama* "made a very favorable run from New Orleans," as Taylor reported, and reached St. Joseph's Island early on the morning of July 26, sandbars prevented the steamer from approaching the mainland. General Taylor was anxious to get the troops ashore, but shallow-draft lighters and small boats were scarce. "The difficulties of effecting a debarkation on this coast, and of establishing depots for supplying the army, are much greater than I anticipated, and will render our operations at once embarrassing and expensive," Taylor reported.

Despite high winds and rough seas, Lieutenant Colonel Hitchcock was able to land three companies with their mess-chests on St. Joseph's Island. But first, at 9 A.M., Hitchcock sent Lieutenant Chandler ashore to plant the American flag on one of the highest sand hills, "the first Stars and Stripes," he observed, "ever raised in Texas by authority."

Captain Henry led the first company ashore in small boats and his men "made a real frolic of it," when "seventy-five yards distant from the shore," they "had to jump overboard into the roaring surf."

By July 28, Hitchcock had completed the landing of the Third Infantry, which established a camp strung out along the length of the island for about three miles. After the sultry heat of New Orleans, the troops found St. Joseph's Island a paradise, with abundant game and fish to suit the most fastidious palate as well as plenty of fresh, if unpleasant-tasting water to drink.

So while General Taylor fussed and fumed—"he was quite beside himself with anxiety, fatigue, and passion," said Hitchcock—because of delays in establishing himself at Corpus Christi, the troops delighted in their enforced stay on the island. Hitchcock, whose journal ill-conceals his high estimate of his own undoubted substantial talents, declared that the ultimate safe landing on the mainland was "little short of a miracle . . . attributable to the mere accident of the bay being tolerably calm." Taylor had ignored Hitchcock's suggestion that the troops remain on St. Joseph's Island until a strong southwest wind provided high water across the bars. Instead, he ordered his quartermaster to hire all the fishing boats that had flocked to the island from curiosity, and to transfer the men and supplies to them. "I undertook to tell him that the troops would be very comfortable on St. Joseph's Island . . . but he would not listen to me and was exceedingly impatient to have the companies off," complained Hitchcock.

At sundown on July 31 the landing of two companies of the Third Infantry was completed, seven small boats having transferred them across the flats. Taylor himself remained at St. Joseph's Island until August 15, where, as Captain Henry recorded it, "with his usual energy [he pushed] forward his troops and supplies, with the contemptible means he has at his command." Lieutenant Colonel Hitchcock, who was suffering an annoying indisposition, however, was unimpressed by the operation. "My sickness," he wrote, "is partly disgust at the state of things here—the haste and ignorance displayed in this movement. The government has actually no information of the coast, harbors, bars, etc., and as little of the interior."

Corpus Christi was a village of less than thirty houses, and locally was known as Kinney's Ranch. It was established in 1838 by a "Colonel" H. L. Kinney as a trading post, where contraband commerce with the Mexicans flourished. Hitchcock described the proprietor succinctly: "Kinney seems to have a government of his own here, and to be alternately the friend and foe of Mexicans, Texans, Americans and Indians, sometimes defying them and meeting them with force and sometimes bribing and wheedling them. He lives by smuggling goods across the line."

As August neared its end, Taylor had in camp at Corpus Christi all the infantry with which he had left Fort Jessup, and reinforcements to his little army were on the way. Concern for the whereabouts of Colonel Twiggs's Second Dragoons was dispelled when Taylor, riding out himself on a reconnaissance, met the Dragoons at San Patricio, about twenty-five miles north of the camp. Taylor was pleased with their "efficient condition" and noted with satisfaction that the horses were "in excellent flesh."

The Second Dragoons were hurrying forward to the "relief" of Taylor's force when the General came upon them. On August 24, before noon, a frightful thunderstorm, accompanied by drenching rain and high wind, descended upon the camp at Corpus Christi. One of Lieutenant Bragg's Negro boys was killed instantly by lightning and another seriously injured. "The crash was tremendous, and was felt throughout the camp," wrote Henry. ". . . The whole air was impregnated with a smell of sulphur." To Hitchcock, the rolling thunder sounded like an "incessant cannonade." And so, too, did it to Colonel Twiggs and the Second Dragoons, then about twenty miles away from San Patricio. Convinced that Taylor was under strong attack at Corpus Christi, Twiggs ordered "To horse" to be sounded, and the command hurried forward to Old Zach's relief.

On August 26, in a report to the War Department, General Taylor summed up his position at Corpus Christi:

Judging from the best information I can obtain as to the future wants of the service on this frontier, looking more particularly to the possibility of an invasion of the soil of Texas by Mexican troops, I deem the force soon to be under my orders, *Viz:* four batteries of field artillery, one regiment of cavalry, and five regiments of infantry, to be fully adequate to meet any crisis that may arise. The ordnance and ordnance stores already shipped are ample for all our purposes, unless it should be necessary to invest Matamoros, in which case a battering train of heavier calibre would be required. A moderate supply of pontons and ponton wagons might greatly facilitate any operations in this country, where it is next to impossible to bridge the streams, owing to the scarcity of timber.

In this same report, Taylor regretted the "most false and exaggerated rumors . . . in New Orleans in relation to reported disasters encountered by this command." Such rumors, he said, not only cause "pain and anxiety in the community," but "entail a heavy and needless expense" on the government in mustering in volunteers. "I beg you to understand that, even with the small force originally under my command, I have had too much confidence in my officers and men to feel any apprehension of serious disaster."

5

The Army of Occupation

Has there ever been an army—Xerxes', Hannibal's, Caesar's, Napoleon's, Zachary Taylor's—in which rumors of the wildest sort did not spread rapidly?

At the very time that Taylor was consolidating his position at Corpus Christi, rumor had it in the camp that Old Zach was getting ready to quit and retire to his plantation.

Lieutenant George Gordon Meade heard the rumor the very day he reported to Taylor in mid-September, 1845. He found the General, he wrote his wife, "a plain, sensible old man" who "thinks there is not the remotest probability of there being any war." Meade added:

> He is said to be very tired of this country, and the duty assigned to him, and it is supposed will return on the arrival of General [William J.] Worth, who is expected daily, and who will then assume command.
>
> General Taylor, so says rumor, is a staunch Whig, and opposed *in toto* to the Texas annexation, and therefore does not enter heart and soul in his present duties; all this, however, is mere rumor . . .

Lieutenant Colonel Hitchcock, on the other hand, found Taylor speaking more and more about marching to the Rio Grande and he noted this as "singular language from one who originally and till very lately denounced annexation as both injudicious in policy and wicked in fact." About the time that Meade made his observation to his wife, Hitchcock recorded in his diary:

> General Taylor came into my tent this morning and again, as frequently of late, he introduced the subject of moving upon

the Rio Grande. I discovered this time more clearly than ever that the General is instigated by ambition—or so it appears to me. He seems quite to have lost all respect for Mexican rights and willing to be an instrument of Mr. Polk for pushing our boundary as far west as possible. When I told him that, if he suggested a movement (which he told me he intended), Mr. Polk would seize upon it and throw the responsibility on him, he at once said he would take it, and added that if the President instructed him to use his discretion, he would ask no orders, but would go upon the Rio Grande as soon as he could get transportation. I think the General wants an additional brevet, and would strain a point to get it.

Far from not having his heart in the operation at Corpus Christi, as Lieutenant Meade suggested, General Taylor had a multiplicity of things that demanded his routine attention and these were augmented by unusual circumstances that developed as more troops arrived to join the Army of Occupation. Drill and discipline were, or should have been, according to Lieutenant Colonel Hitchcock, Taylor's prime preoccupation. But Hitchcock claimed that neither General Taylor nor Colonel William Whistler could form a brigade into line and Colonel Twiggs could do so only "after a fashion of his own. As for manoeuvering, not one of them can move it a step." Fortunately, the camp at Corpus Christi was not devoid of a talented drillmaster, as Hitchcock hastened to add: "Egotism or no egotism, I am the only field officer who could change a single position of the troops according to any but a militia mode." As for discipline in the camp, the arrival of the Second Dragoons was the signal for what Hitchcock called "disgraceful brawls and quarrels, to say nothing of drunken frolics." The Dragoons' conduct he characterized as a "public scandal," and noted that one captain resigned to escape trial while two others had "a dirty brawl." On New Year's Day, 1846, Hitchcock wrote in his diary: ". . . The day will go as other days—drinking, horse-racing, gambling, theatrical amusements . . . There are no ladies here and very few women." On the other hand, Lieutenant Meade told his wife: "I have seen nothing like dissipation, except in some very few instance," but obviously Meade was speaking of the officers. Corpus Christi's population had mushroomed from about a hundred souls when the army arrived to more than 2,000 by the end of 1845, and

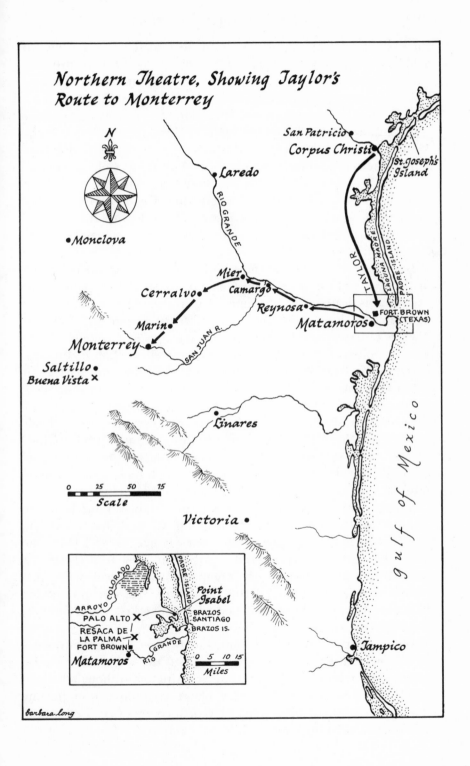

Northern Theatre, Showing Taylor's
Route to Monterrey

N

Laredo

RIO GRANDE

Monclova

Mier

Cerralvo

Camargo

Reynosa

Matamoros

San Patricio

Corpus Christi

St. Joseph's
Island

TAGUNA MADRE

PADRE ISLAND

TAYLOR

FORT BROWN
(TEXAS)

Marin

Monterrey

SAN JUAN R.

Saltillo
Buena Vista ✕

Linares

0 25 50 15
Scale

Victoria

Gulf of Mexico

ARROYO COLORADO

PADRE ISLAND

Point
Isabel

PALO ALTO ✕

RESACA DE
LA PALMA ✕
FORT BROWN ■

Matamoros

RIO GRANDE

BRAZOS
SANTIAGO
BRAZOS IS.

0 5 10 15
Miles

Tampico

barbara long

the greater part of the arrivals were dedicated to separating the soldier from his hard-earned $7 a month pay. Opportunities to gamble or quench the thirst were plentiful. One officer described the place as "the most murderous, thieving, gambling, cutthroat, God-forsaken hole in the 'Lone Star State.'"

Shortly after the arrival in camp of Brevet Brigadier General William J. Worth on October 13, 1845, General Taylor found himself in the middle of a feud between Worth and Colonel Twiggs over the question of brevet rank. Both were veterans of the War of 1812 and were the ranking officers after Taylor, Worth as commander of the First Brigade, made up of the Eighth Infantry and twelve companies of artillery, and Twiggs as commander of the Second Dragoons.

But who ranked whom? And who would succeed to the command of the Army of Occupation in General Taylor's absence or in the event of his death? Worth claimed that his brevet rank of brigadier general gave him precedence over Twiggs, despite the fact that Twiggs ranked Worth in their permanent grade of colonel. There was, obviously, a clash of personalities as well as clash of interests between the two officers. Worth, who had a trim and martial air about him, was characterized by Lieutenant U. S. Grant as "nervous, impatient and restless on the march, or when important or responsible duty confronted him." Lieutenant George Gordon Meade considered Worth "a most excellent officer in some respects [but] has the great misfortune of being most rash and impetuous, and of constantly doing things which cooler reflection causes him to repent."

Twiggs had the reputation as a stern disciplinarian. His men called him "Old Davey, the Bengal Tiger," and didn't seem to mind when he "cursed them right out of their boots." One who knew Twiggs nearly two decades earlier in Wisconsin Territory, recalled him as "a large, portly, pompous man and had the reputation of being an arbitrary, overbearing officer." He was an imposing figure at Corpus Christi, big-bodied, bull-necked, pink-cheeked, white-haired, and profanely eloquent.

When the two contending commanders brought the controversy to Taylor, himself only a line colonel with the brevet of brigadier general, he referred the matter to Washington, although he personally agreed with nearly every officer in camp in supporting Twiggs's position. A biographer of Worth charges that Taylor "unmanfully ducked the issue," while a biographer of Old Zach asserts he "had the good judgment and good taste to refrain from taking a personal part in the dispute."

But, apparently, Taylor failed to exercise good judgment when he scheduled a review of the troops and announced Colonel Twiggs as commander. Naturally, Worth protested vehemently, and Taylor decided to call off the review rather than to aggravate an already deplorable situation.

Taylor at this time was engaged in a feud of his own with General Thomas Jesup, Quartermaster General, with whom he had been on intimate terms for more than twenty-five years. Whether Jesup was to blame, or whether the burden rested with his staff or subordinates in New Orleans and Texas, the result was repeated delays in the forwarding of supplies. Badly needed tents, when they finally arrived, proved of shoddy workmanship with sievelike texture through which rain poured. In his disgust, Taylor in a private letter complained "the Qr Masters dep is on crutches." The General, himself, was not completely blameless, and there was some justice in Jesup's later charge that Taylor failed to anticipate his needs and when he made his requisitions he expected them filled on short notice. But, generally, Taylor's opinion of the Quartermaster Department was concurred in by his officers. Within a few weeks after joining Taylor, young Lieutenant George Brinton McClellan concluded "that the Quartermaster's Department is most woefully conducted—never trust anything to that Department which you can do for yourself."

As more troops arrived to swell the Army of Occupation to about 4,000 men, the health of his forces became a major problem for Taylor. Certainly, by modern standards, the General did not have either knowledge or appreciation of even rudimentary sanitation. "The whole army," a surgeon noted, ". . . might be considered a vast hospital . . . Hundreds were affected who were never entered on sick report." Perhaps it was this that prompted General Worth's comment in a family letter: "Whether an idea strategic, or of any description, has had the rudeness to invade the mind or imagination of our chief is a matter of doubt. We are literally a huge body without a head."

One of Taylor's biographers, Holman Hamilton, takes the General to task on the question of sanitation and health:

> . . . Taylor was patently culpable . . . for even in an age when medical science was still in its infancy sanitary conditions could

scarcely have been more primitive than they were in the Corpus Christi camp. That Taylor tolerated an almost complete lack of sanitation certainly did him little credit. Few soldiers died from disease, but the record shows that diarrhea and dysentery kept an average of ten percent of the officers and thirteen percent of the men bedridden throughout the late autumn and winter months. Actually, in November and December [1845] the number of those affected was even larger.

With this opinion, another biographer of Taylor, Brainerd Dyer, agrees:

Taylor shared the inconveniences and discomforts of his men, but his own health remained good . . . Because of his readiness to put up with such discomforts and his disinclination to waste public funds it is probable that Taylor did not make as adequate provision for the health of his army as he should have. He could have done nothing about the brackish water, but he might have obtained a more adequate fuel supply and, had he ascertained in advance the nature of the winter weather at Corpus Christi, he might have made provisions for more satisfactory shelter . . . Moreover, there is no evidence that Taylor was aware of the necessity for adequate sanitation or that he took any steps to ensure the health of his camp in this regard.

Meanwhile, in Washington, Secretary of War Marcy had turned over the brevet controversy to General Winfield Scott to settle, and the Commanding General of the Army had issued a circular letter favoring the brevet rank. When the circular reached Corpus Christi, the officers were indignant and decided to appeal to Congress over Scott's head. Hitchcock was chosen—"by common consent," he recorded—to draw up a memorial to the President of the Senate, answering Scott's "impertinent interposition between General Taylor and the President." The memorial, in printed form took ten octavo pages and was signed by 158 officers of every rank from colonel to second lieutenant. On December 19, Hitchcock dispatched to the Senate this document "which General Scott will wish he had not provoked."

Throughout the winter of 1845–1846. despite miserable weather and exasperating shortages, despite exposure and sickness, despite the jealous rivalry of his chief subordinates, General Taylor went methodically about the business of molding a tough fighting unit. Lieutenant Meade, as a topographical engineer, was not involved in the daily routine which consisted of "nothing but drill and parades, and your ears are filled all day with drumming and fifeing." Captain William Henry found a review of the troops "quite credit-able" and felt "that a more efficient army, for its size, was never brought into the field." A young lieutenant, who didn't think a better general than Taylor could be found, was convinced that "our army is well drilled and disciplined."

To his daughter Betty, General Taylor confided on December 15, 1845, that homesickness had become a principle disease among his officers, and his letter suggests that Old Zach was not himself immune:

> Since I have been here my time has passed rapidly, having constant employment; the scene too has been quite an impos-ing one: what with instructions, mounting guards, reviews, etc., with between three and four thousand men, & two hun-dred and fifty officers, with five bands & excellent music, has made the time pass tolerably rapidly; but all the pomp & parade of such things are lost on me; I now sigh for peace & quiet with my family around me . . .

Critics of Zachary Taylor have charged that he made no atempt to gain information about the country in which he would operate if war came, or to concern himself about the movements of the Mexicans. "We are quite in the dark," Hitchcock claimed. "The General may have information which he keeps to himself, but I know him too well to believe he has any." And again: "General Arista has been at Mier and the General of the Am. 'Army of oc-cupation' has been in profound ignorance of the fact!"

Taylor, in fact, had sent out many parties. Meade and other topographical engineers explored the Nueces River as well as the Laguna Madre, a passage between Padre Island and the mainland which ended at Point Isabel near the mouth of the Rio Grande. "General Taylor is sending out exploring parties in various direc-tions," Captain Ephraim Kirby Smith wrote his wife, early in November, 1845. ". . . An expedition has gone by water to examine the harbor of Brazos Santiago and the mouth of the Rio Grande, all these explorations are to acquire knowledge upon which to locate the permanent posts." And Taylor was kept well informed of activity on the Rio Grande by Colonel Kinney's "favorite and confidential spy," Chapita. Captain Henry described the spy as "a man in the prime of life, middling height, broad shoulders, muscles like whipcords, a dark, piercing eye, prominent forehead, and bushy eyebrows; having that determined expression of countenance common to one who follows so dangerous an occupation." Devotedly attached to Colonel Kinney, whom he once helped escape from a prison in Matamoros, Chapita was a "loner" in his comings and goings between Corpus Christi and the Rio Grande.

Ultimate failure of John Slidell's diplomatic mission to Mexico was indicated to President Polk on January 12, 1846, when word that the Herrera government had rejected the Minister reached Washington. The next day, Secretary of War Marcy dispatched orders to Zachary Taylor to "advance and occupy, with the troops of your command, positions on or near the east bank of the Rio [Grande] del Norte." Although the Secretary suggested Point Isabel or points opposite Matamoros, Mier, or Laredo as feasible positions for the army, he left it to Taylor's "better knowledge." Marcy asserted the United States' common right with Mexico to navigate the Rio Grande, but he cautioned Taylor not "to enforce this right without further instruction." The Secretary spelled out Taylor's prescribed instructions:

It is not desired, in our present relations with Mexico, that you should treat her as an enemy; but, should she assume that character by a declaration of war, or an open act of hostility towards us, you will not act merely on the defensive, if your relative means enable you to do otherwise.

Taylor received the order to move to the Rio Grande on February 3. "I shall lose no time in making the necessary preparation for carrying out these instructions," he wrote the Adjutant General the next day. But more than a month would pass before he could report on March 8 "that the advance of the army . . . took up the line of march this morning in the direction of Matamoros." In the meantime, Taylor kept Washington informed, both on information available to him and on his operations:

February 4—"I propose to abandon this position entirely, as soon after our march as the stores, hospital, &c., can be transferred to St. Joseph's Island . . . Our supplies will come to Point Isabel direct from New Orleans . . . I have every reason to believe that the people residing on the river are well disposed towards our government."

February 16—"Commodore Conner . . . announces his intention to proceed with the squadron to Vera Cruz, and desires to know in what way he can cooperate with the land force . . . I . . . have desired him to give me the support of one or two small vessels to assist us . . . in taking possession of Brazos Santiago . . . Examinations are now in progress of the two routes to Point Isabel—that by the main land and that by Padre Island . . . I do not believe that our advance to the banks of the Rio Grande will be resisted. The army, however, will go fully prepared for a state of hostilities, should they unfortunately be provoked by the Mexicans."

February 26—"Preparations for a forward movement of this command are now nearly completed . . . By the 25th of March, at the latest, I hope to be in position on the Rio Grande . . . I have [informed] some citizens of Matomoros . . . here with a large number of mules for sale . . . that the United States Government, in occupying the Rio Grande, has no motive of hostility toward Mexico, and that the army will, in no case, go beyond the river unless hostilities should be commenced by the Mexicans themselves; that the Mexicans, living on this side, will not be disturbed in any way by the troops; that they will be protected in all their rights and usages; and, that everything which the army may need, will be purchased from them at fair prices."

For Taylor's little army, the dull monotony of camp life was finally over after seven months and eleven days. Captain Henry, who kept this tally, expressed his pleasure with an exclamation point: "We are off to the Rio Grande!"

6

The March to the River

Zachary Taylor may not have maneuvered troops to suit the meticulous fancy of Colonel Hitchcock and ideas of strategy may not have "intruded" into his mind to a degree to satisfy the self-assured General Worth, but the Commanding General of the little Army of Occupation had more than his share of a rare commodity, common sense.

Old Zach appreciated that a proclamation, outlining his aims and purposes, might be construed by the Mexicans on the Rio Grande as the blustering of an aggressor. Thus, instead of securing for his army a climate of calm and at least the passive cooperation of the people, a proclamation might actually stir up active hostility. So Taylor hit upon the device of presenting, in the form of orders to his own troops, the message which he intended for the Mexicans on the river.

And so, on March 8, as the first elements of the army—Twiggs's Second Dragoons and Major Samuel Ringgold's light artillery, a total of 401 officers and men—took up the march to the Rio Grande, Taylor reported to Washington:

> I have deemed it proper to cause my "orders" No. 30 to be translated into Spanish, and circulated on the Rio Grande. Sixty copies have already been sent in advance of the army to Matamoros, Camargo, and Mier. This form of giving publicity to the spirit which actuates our movement, in occupying the country, I thought preferable to a proclamation.

In Orders No. 30, Taylor stated he was moving to the Rio Grande under orders of the President of the United States and enjoined his command "to observe, with the most scrupulous respect, the rights of all the inhabitants . . . in peaceful prosecution of

48

their respective occupations." The religious and civil rights of the inhabitants were not to be interfered with, "under [any] pretext [or] in any way." And Taylor told his troops—and the Mexicans —that whatever the army needed, "will be bought . . . and paid for at the highest prices." Orders No. 30 concluded with Taylor's expression of confidence "in the patriotism and discipline of . . . his command, and . . . that his orders will be obeyed with the utmost exactness."

This was a master stroke of propaganda, written in the simple, clear, and direct language which, many years later, Lieutenant U. S. Grant, recalled as a particular gift of Old Zach. "Taylor . . . could put his meaning so plainly that there could be no mistaking it," wrote Grant. "He knew how to express what he wanted to say in the fewest well-chosen words, but would not sacrifice meaning to the construction of high-sounding sentences . . . Taylor . . . gave orders . . . without reference to how they read in history."

The "canvas town" of Corpus Christi—so Lieutenant Sam French called it—disappeared even more rapidly than it had sprung up seven months earlier. At 10 A.M., on March 8, Colonel Twiggs started the movement of the army and the three brigades followed the cavalry at intervals of a day. General Worth put the First Brigade into motion on the 9th, having attached to it Captain James Duncan's battery. On the 10th, Lieutenant Colonel James S. McIntosh, an 1812 veteran and only two years Taylor's junior, led forth the Second Brigade. The last to strike their tents were the soldiers of the Third Brigade, commanded by Colonel William Whistler, the oldest old soldier of the lot at sixty-six. The Third Brigade—"We were the first to arrive, the last to leave," wrote Captain Henry—with Bragg's battery attached, marched out on the 11th, and General Taylor and his staff followed. "Corpus Christi looked perfectly deserted; the field of white canvas was no longer visible; and the camp ground looked like desolation itself . . ." observed Henry.

"The roads are in good order," Taylor reported, "the weather fine, and the troops in excellent condition for service."

Despite the heat and the dust, the contrasting, uncomfortable cold at night, and a shortage of drinking water, the Army of Occupation, 3,554 strong with a train of 300 wagons strung along for miles, pushed on steadily through scenery which every diarist in Taylor's army took pains to describe.

"The flowers during today's march were gloriously rich; conspicuous above all were the Texas plume, the Mexican poppy, and the indigo," noted Captain Henry.

"I observed in great abundance the spiderwort, phlox, lupin, fireplant, lobelia inflata, primrose, etc.," wrote Captain Ephraim Kirby Smith.

"The first night out we encamped at a beautiful place covered with blue flowers like the hyacinth," recorded Lieutenant French.

Not only the flora, but also the fauna, were objects to be identified and noted as Taylor's little army plodded on between the Nueces and the Arroyo Colorado.

". . . A herd of antelope . . . dashed away to the verge of the horizon, and proudly looked at the passing column. An immense drove of mustangs . . . galloped towards us to gratify their curiosity," observed Henry.

". . . The advance pickets encountered a herd of wild cattle that all ran away except an old bull that showed fight," declared French.

"Our camp . . . was full of 'varmints.' From one hole a rabbit, a rat, a rattlesnake, and a tarantula were dislodged, these animals, incredible as it may appear, living in common in the same den. I killed with my sword, immediately in rear of my tent, a huge rattler nearly six feet in length," stated Ephraim Kirby Smith.

The army also encountered jack rabbits ("their speed is wonderful; there are few dogs that can catch them"); peccaries ("a fierce animal [bearing] about the same resemblance to a hog that the buffalo does to the common ox"); deer ("I saw more . . . than I supposed existed in all America"); wild geese, wild turkeys, curlew, cranes, ducks, and plover.

Most of the troops saw mirages ("The delusion was perfect") of distant mountains as they marched on, and some of the officers saw something more tangible—an army toughening itself for combat.

"There is a 'physique' and 'morale' about our 'little army' . . ." wrote Captain Henry. "Well clad, well fed, and well armed; moving forward with an enthusiasm and 'sang froid' which carries victory in their face. I feel more and more convinced that we can successfully contend with an immensely superior force." To Captain Ephraim Kirby Smith, the army "presented . . . an imposing spectacle as we moved in parallel columns across the open prairie, with our long baggage train close up in our rear and our scouts far in advance and on our flanks examining every thicket." Even the hypercritical Ethan Allen Hitchcock conceded "the army presented a fine appearance" as it marched four columns abreast across the plains.

However, the best evidence of all that the army was maturing on the march came from an officer, who, in later years, had no superior in evaluating the effectiveness of a military force. "A more efficient army for its number and armament I do not believe ever fought a battle than the one commanded by General Taylor in his first two engagements on Mexican—or Texan soil," wrote General Grant in his *Memoirs*. Second Lieutenant John Sedgwick, writing home at the time had the same opinion: "There never was so fine an American army."

The march, of course, was not without its amusing incidents. Lieutenant Sam French, to keep the sun and wind from making his lips and nose raw, protected himself with a Mexican sombrero.

"When General Taylor comes up you will be put under arrest for wearing that hat," someone told him.

After Taylor overtook the advance units, Lieutenant French, still wearing his sombrero, called on the General while he was at breakfast the next morning. Old Zach's nose was white from the skin peeling off and his lips were raw.

"Good morning, Lieutenant, good morning," greeted Taylor. "Sensible man to wear a hat."

French was pleased, and hastened to tell his friends that he had been commended by Old Zach, not censured "for making myself comfortable."

Lieutenant Grant—they called him Sam Grant in those days— afforded much amusement when he bought an untamed mustang for five dollars and proceeded to break him on the march. "The day we started," Grant later recalled, "was the first time the horse had been under a saddle . . . The first day there were frequent disagreements between us as to which way we should go, and sometimes whether we should go at all. At no time during the day could I choose exactly the part of the column I would march with; but after that I had as tractable a horse as any with the army."

There were some officers in Zachary Taylor's army who were not in full sympathy with the movement to the Rio Grande. Lieutenant Grant was one of them: "I was bitterly opposed to . . . the war . . . as one of the most unjust ever waged by a stronger against a weaker nation . . . We were sent to provoke a fight, but it was essential that Mexico should commence it . . . Mexico showing no willingness to come to the Nueces to drive the invaders from her soil, it became necessary for the 'invaders' to approach within a convenient distance to be struck." Another was Lieutenant Colonel Hitchcock: "As to the right of this movement, I have said from the first that the United States are the aggressors. We have outraged the Mexican Government and people by an arrogance and presumption that deserve to be punished . . . My heart is not in this business; I am against it from the bottom of my soul as a most unholy and unrighteous proceeding; but, as a military man, I am bound to execute orders." To Lieutenant George Deas, "the march to the banks of the Rio Grande was, of itself, an act of hostility."

After marching about a week, the advance guard of Taylor's force began to encounter Mexican patrols, which kept their distance, retiring over the horizon as the column pushed on. On one occasion, when some American cavalrymen rode up to a small pond to water their horses, they encountered some Mexican lancers watering their mounts. After an exchange of brief perfunctory politeness, the Mexicans mounted and rode off. "Once," Lieutenant Sam French recalled, "they set the prairie on fire and we had to drive through the leaping flames with our guns and caissons filled with ammunition."

On March 20, as the army neared the Arroyo Colorado, a deep salt lagoon with steep banks, word traveled through the ranks that the head of the column had been challenged by Mexican cavalry, which announced its determination to dispute the passage of the stream. The Mexican officer, spokesman for General Francisco Mejía, commander at Matamoros, warned that an attempt to cross the Colorado would be regarded as an act of war and it would be resisted.

Troops and horsemen showed themselves at various spots in the chaparral on the Mexican side of the lagoon and bugles, up and down the stream, sounded the advance, while kettledrums and fife were heard in the thickets in front. It appeared, at last, that the peaceful movement across Texas had come to an end. Taylor brushed the Mexican threat aside, deployed his troops to advance, and set his batteries into position to rake the opposite shore. "We will cross immediately," Old Zach informed the Mexican, "and if a single man of you shows his face after my men enter the river, I will open artillery fire on him."

To Captain Ephraim Kirby Smith, it was "one of the most exciting hours" of his life. "All, from the General-in-Chief to the smallest drummer boy, felt mortally certain that we were on the verge of a fierce and bloody conflict," wrote Captain Smith, "yet I saw no one who was not cheerful and apparently eager for the game to begin."

The width of the Colorado at the ford was about eighty yards. The stream had a depth of about four feet, while its banks were between fifteen and twenty feet high. These first had to be cut down for the passage of the wagon train. At half past ten, Taylor gave the order to advance, and Captain C. F. Smith, at the head of four companies of the First Brigade, plunged into the lagoon. The troops followed him into the water in perfect order, holding their muskets and cartridge boxes high as they splashed across. General Worth galloped through the water to the head of the column to lead the charge on the other side.

"We watched them in breathless silence as they deepened in the water, expecting that at every step they would receive a withering fire," wrote Ephraim Kirby Smith. "When they were half way over and not a shot fired the disappointment of the men was shown right to left in muttered curses."

The crossing uneventful, the troops swarmed up the other bank and immediately deployed to the right and left. Twiggs's Dragoons crossed next and within thirty minutes from the order to move, Taylor's entire little army was on the other side. "The men with cheers formed in order of battle, the music struck up 'Yankee Doodle' and we all marched rapidly up the hill," said Ephraim Kirby Smith. "A few Mexicans were seen retreating, and the great battle of Arroyo Colorado was terminated!"

Captain Henry thought that if the Mexicans ever intended to challenge Taylor's advance, the Arroyo Colorado was the spot. "They could have done us great damage, and rendered some desperate fighting necessary," he said. "This presumption is, there were very few men at the river, and they thought to frighten us away by the sound of bugles and big threats." Lieutenant Colonel Hitchcock estimated the Mexican force at 300. The Commanding General, in his report to Washington, agreed with Captain Henry: "It would have formed a serious obstruction to our march had the enemy chosen to occupy its right bank, even with a small force."

Taylor pushed on a few miles and then went into camp to await the arrival of his wagons. On March 23, the march to Matamoros, about twenty-eight miles away, was resumed, and on the next day, the road from Point Isabel to Matamoros was struck. Instructing Worth to advance toward Matamoros with the infantry brigades, Taylor, with Twiggs's cavalry, took the road to the coast. At Point Isabel, Taylor was delighted to find the transports from Corpus Christi in the harbor and several naval vessels dispatched to his support by Commodore David Conner. Taylor remained only long enough to give orders to fortify the supply depot and then he and Twiggs's Dragoons rode out of Port Isabel to rejoin Worth.

March 28 was, Captain Henry noted in his diary, "a day not easily forgotten." As the army, moving over good roads in level country, neared the river it came upon clusters of huts and large cultivated fields. "The poor devils at their cottage doors appeared pleased at our arrival," Henry noted, "and saluted us as we passed."

"At half past ten," wrote Captain Ephraim Kirby Smith, "we were marching upon the banks of the Rio Grande immediately in front and in full view of Matamoros, our colors flying and music playing." To Captain Henry, who set the arrival at the river at 11 o'clock, "the city of Matamoros rose like a fairy vision before our enraptured eyes." Lieutenant Sam French welcomed "as the promised land," the city across the river, "embowered in green foliage, with tropical plants around the white houses."

The Mexican flag flew from several buildings in the town, the main portion of which was set back from the river about a mile. Curious Mexicans—Henry says "some two hundred," while Smith limits the crowd to "a few men and women walking about carelessly"—lined the opposite shore. Sentries, of course, were posted at regular intervals on the Mexican side of the river.

A flagstaff was procured and within two hours after Taylor had reached the river "the flag of our country . . . was seen floating over the Rio Grande, proclaiming in a silent but impressive manner that 'the area of freedom' was again extended." So thought Captain Henry, who felt, despite the playing of the "Star-Spangled Banner" and "Yankee Doodle," that "there was not ceremony enough raising it."

7

"War Has Commenced"

On the day of his arrival on the Rio Grande, General Taylor dispatched General Worth to General Francisco Mejía to assure the Mexican commander that the American mission was a pacific one. Mejía refused to receive Taylor's second-in-command, but delegated a subordinate, General Rómolo Díaz de La Vega, to confer with Worth. Each general, the American with his splendid military bearing, and the Mexican with his courtly politeness, impressed the other favorably, but their interview, conducted in three languages, did nothing more than to establish, formally, Mexican hostility to American troops on the Rio Grande and Zachary Taylor's determination to remain there.

With Lieutenant Knowlton translating Worth's English into French and La Vega's aide translating the French into Spanish, and vice versa, the interview opened with the Mexican's protest that "the march of the United States troops through a part of the Mexican territory was considered as an act of war."

General Worth replied that "it was not so considered by his government" and that the army having been ordered there, "there it would remain" until the matter was settled by the two governments. Worth chilled La Vega's disposition to argue the merits of the case by declaring "that he came to state facts, not to argue them."

Worth then stated that since General Mejía had not received him, he could not therefore deliver to him the dispatch with which he was entrusted. He read the dispatch to La Vega as a matter of courtesy and then declared: "I now state that I withdraw this dispatch." Worth added that if General Mejía wished to communicate further with General Taylor, either in person or through a subordinate, "they would be received with becoming courtesy and hospitality." When La Vega returned to the question of the rights of territory, Worth changed the subject.

Worth—"Is the American consul in arrest, or in prison?"
La Vega—"No."
Worth—"Is he now in the exercise of his proper functions?"
La Vega—"He is."
Worth—"Then, as an American officer, in the name of my government and my commanding general I *demand* an interview with the consul of my country."
La Vega—No reply.
Worth—"Has Mexico declared war against the United States?"
La Vega—"No."
Worth—"Are the two countries still at peace."
La Vega—"Yes."
Worth—"Then I again demand an interview with the consul of my government . . ."
Here the interview was suspended while a civil official with General La Vega submitted Worth's "demand" to General Mejía. Fifteen minutes later he returned with an unfavorable reply.
La Vega—"Is it the intention of General Taylor to remain with his army on the left bank of the Rio Grande?"
Worth—"Most assuredly, and there to remain until directed otherwise by his government."
Worth reiterated his demand to see the American consul, and La Vega, without waiting for the interpreter to translate, answered quickly: "No! No!" Before breaking off the interview and recrossing the river, Worth, in unmistakable terms, declared the American position as of that moment:

I have now to state that a refusal of my demand to see the American consul is regarded as a belligerent act; and, in conclusion, I have to add, the commanding general of the American forces on the left bank of the river will regard the passage of any armed party of Mexicans in hostile array across the Rio Grande as an act of war, and pursue it accordingly.

Curiosity reigned on both sides of the Rio Grande. Mexicans in Matamoros stood or walked along the right bank watching the *Americanos* in their camp activities or in the erection of batteries. Taylor's officers and troops, on their part, were just as curious about Mexican fortifications and activities in Matamoros. The attention of the Americans was often seized by extra-military incidents, such, for instance, as the young girls Captain Ephraim Kirby Smith described as swimming, unashamedly, in the nude, "regardless of the numerous spectators on either bank." Some American officers swam toward them, but the Mexican sentries prevented their coming nearer than the middle of the river.

Another amenity during this "cold war" period on the Rio Grande was the mutual serenading by the army bands on either side of the river. The American bands "played 'Yankee Doodle,' because it made a loud noise, the 'Star-Spangled Banner' because it waved over us, 'Hail Columbia' because it was inspiriting, and the sweetest airs from the operas," Lieutenant Sam French remembered. "The music from the other side I cannot recall now, only it rose with a 'voluptuous swell' that floated over the water and died away softly in the distance . . ." Captain Henry agreed that the Mexicans had "excellent music." Captain Philip N. Barbour took delight in "the exquisite music of their fine bands. It surpassed anything I have heard from a military band."

Work on a field fortification opposite Matamoros, ordered by Taylor on arrival at the Rio Grande, was pushed forward under the energetic direction of Captain Joseph K. F. Mansfield. It was, Taylor reported to the War Department, "a strong bastioned field fort, for a garrison of 500 men," [which] "will enable a brigade to maintain this position against any Mexican odds, and will leave me free to dispose of the other corps as considerations of health and convenience may render desirable." By April 4, four eighteen-pound siege guns had arrived from the Point Isabel depot, and were duly installed. "These guns," Taylor reported, "bear directly upon the public square of Matamoros, and within good range of demolishing the town."

Confidence pervaded Taylor's army, from Old Zach down. "Our brigades," Taylor reported on April 1, "occupy strong positions, beyond reach of fire from the town, and can hold themselves against many times their number of Mexican troops. In the meantime, our defences here and at Point Isabel are daily gaining strength." To his daughter Betty, Old Zach was more explicit: "Their force . . . is equal if not greater than ours, but very inferior in quality & equipment, & should we come to blows there can not be a doubt as to the result. We must beat them." Lieutenant Meade approved of six-sided Fort Texas, as the field fortification had been named, and of its armament. "We have such superiority in artillery," he wrote, "that it is impossible for them with any force to drive us from here."

General Pedro de Ampudia arrived at Matamoros on April 11, and relieved Mejía in command. He was accompanied by 200 cavalry, while behind him marched reinforcements variously estimated at between 2,000 and 3,000 troops. Ampudia's coming did not inspire the people of Matamoros. According to a contemporary Mexican history: "The news . . . was received with positive regret . . . by many persons who had a decided hatred to the man. Some thought he was actuated at all times by sordid and interested views, and others deemed him incapable . . ."

The next day, in a note that was insolent in tone, Ampudia gave Taylor twenty-four hours "to break up your camp and retire to the other bank of the Nueces River, while our governments are regulating the pending question in relation to Texas." Taylor's polite reply stated unmistakably that he had no thought of leaving the Rio Grande. The words, however, were a bit stuffy, more like his adjutant, Captain William W. S. Bliss, than Old Zach: "The instructions under which I am acting will not permit me to retrograde from the position I now occupy."

Lieutenant Sam French admired Old Zach's spunk. "I do not believe that Taylor was much acquainted with fear," he wrote, "because . . . he had the audacity to remain just where he was until the twenty-four hours had expired, and long after." Moreover, in answer to Ampudia's bombastic threats, Taylor that day wrote to Commodore Conner, requesting a naval blockade of the mouth of the Rio Grande, through which supplies for Matamoros came.

Meanwhile, on April 2, official word reached the army that President Polk had overruled General Scott's decision that brevet rank had precedence over line rank, and that Colonel Twiggs was, in fact, the ranking officer of the Army of Occupation after the commanding general. Infuriated, General Worth wrote out his resignation and General Taylor accepted it at once, unhesitatingly deciding it would be better for Worth, in his present frame of mind, to leave immediately. Lieutenant Meade, on the other hand, wrote that "General Taylor used every argument he could to induce General Worth to remain." Of Worth's action, Meade declared: "I considered it most ill-judged, and that it would require all of General Worth's previous reputation for gallantry and good conduct to sustain it."

On April 9, Worth was separated from his command and after a dramatic farewell to his troops he rode out for Point Isabel and from there he traveled to Washington personally to argue his case. Lieutenant Colonel Hitchcock took a dim view of Worth's resignation "while the very atmosphere is animated with rumors of attacks upon us." There was no wasted affection between the self-righteous Hitchcock and the aggrieved Worth, especially as it was the former's "brief" that won the Presidential reversal of General Scott's decision on brevets. Hitchcock concluded:

I cannot help asking myself what would have been thought of the patriotism of a revolutionary officer who had abandoned his post in the presence of the enemy on an alleged grievance which, in the opinion of almost everybody, is without any proper or defensible foundation.

Ten days later, Hitchcock, who had been ill, off and on, for weeks and barely able at rare intervals to sit his horse on the long trek from Corpus Christi, departed on sick leave. Worth, on reaching Washington and learning that hostilities had broken out on the Rio Grande, withdrew his resignation, on which General Scott had written:

. . . the U. States have not had, in my time, an army officer superior, in general merit, according to his respective grades, to Genl. Worth, and certainly but very few who are his equals. His loss to the service now, when in his highest usefulness, would be seriously great—nay irreparable.

Worth gained permission to rejoin Taylor on the Rio Grande, where he would serve with significant distinction at Monterrey, before joining Scott at Vera Cruz. Hitchcock did not return to Taylor's army at all when his extended sick leave terminated. He later joined Scott, after a reconciliation from a long-standing hostility and, from his lofty post as Inspector General of Scott's army, he continued his feud with General William Jenkins Worth, "whose ancient friendship and companionship in battle" with Scott would soon be shattered to bits.

Meanwhile, the first shots had been fired on the Rio Grande and Taylor's sentries fired them, not at Mexicans across the river, but at an American deserter swimming the stream. The quiet was broken on the afternoon of April 4, when a rapid discharge of musketry below the camp caused excitement on both sides of the Rio Grande. "The long roll was beaten and the regiments promptly formed: the 1st Brigade, which was near the river, with a yell rushed to their arms," stated Captain Henry. ". ... The Mexicans scampered from the bank, and thought we had commenced upon them."

Approximately forty-seven percent of Taylor's army was made up of foreigners, mainly Irish (twenty-four percent) and Germans (ten percent). The Mexicans made liberal offers of grants of land —200 acres for privates and 100 acres extra for each year of service, and as much as 500 acres for sergeants with 250 acres extra for each year served—to induce desertions. A strong plea was also made to Catholics among Taylor's troops to abandon their "unholy cause" and become "peaceful Mexican citizens." In a direct appeal to religious prejudice they were repeatedly told that "it was sinful to fight against their Church and religion."

According to Captain Philip Barbour, more than thirty deserters went over to the enemy shortly after the army reached the Rio Grande. Taylor reported that "the evil of desertion . . . increased to an alarming extent" and that the only way effectively to counteract "the insidious arts of the Mexican general," was to order the pickets to shoot any soldier detected swimming the river ". . . These measures seem to have checked and nearly stopped the practice."

Taylor's first significant loss, other than the departure of General Worth and Lieutenant Colonel Hitchcock, came on April 10, when Colonel Truman Cross, Chief Quartermaster of the army, rode out alone beyond the boundaries of the camp. He never returned. Taylor sent out a search party under Lieutenant Theodoric Porter, but the group was ambushed by bandits, and Porter slain in the fight. More than a week later, Colonel Cross's remains were discovered and in a military funeral they were laid to rest at the base of the flagstaff in Fort Texas.

General Mejía had utter scorn for Zachary Taylor and thought him "more contemptible than the lowest of Mexican tailors" and General Ampudia considered the American general "an absolute nullity," but the third Mexican commander at Matamoros in the space of two weeks, General Mariano Arista, showed more judgment than either of his predecessors. Also, infinitely more politeness in dealing with Taylor.

Arista, who reached Matamoros on April 24, had lived in Cincinnati, and was accused by his enemies of being partial to Americans. A strikingly handsome man with large frame, he had a fair, freckled complexion and sandy hair, a combination unusual among his countrymen. An American officer described Arista "as a man of great firmness, of good business habits, an excellent judge of character, and withal of undoubted courage."

Immediately upon arrival, Arista addressed a letter to Taylor in which the arguments of his predecessors were repeated, but the language was dignified, restrained, polite. He asserted that recent events were "clearly hostile to Mexico, and . . . decidedly foreign to the dignity and principles which . . . Americans have heretofore proclaimed . . ." Mexico was "oppressed and forced into a struggle which we cannot refuse, without dereliction of the most sacred duty of men . . . I am resolved to take efficient measures to oblige the forces of the United States to respect us." General Arista then concluded his letter:

> Hostilities have commenced, and I do not hesitate to assure your excellency that arms are hereafter to be used, and that you must not be surprised that the troops under my command should wait for no further signal.
>
> The Mexicans have been calumniated as barbarous, in the most caustic and unjust manner . . . I do not believe that the troops under my command will do anything to confirm such an aspersion; they will exhibit the feelings of humanity and genorsity which are genial to them.

The next day, April 25, General Taylor acknowledged the letter, noting Arista's contention that a state of war existed and that he intended to prosecute it. Taylor referred the Mexican general to his communications with Mejía and Ampudia and expressed the hope "for the interest of humanity, equally dear to both countries . . . that . . . friendly relations would not be interrupted." His advance to the Rio Grande was "the simple occupation of the territory" until diplomatic agents could settle the boundary. For that reason Taylor said he had abstained "from any act that could possibly be interpreted into hostility" and that he had blocked the Rio Grande as a defensive measure only after Ampudia's "peremptory summons . . . to vacate my position within twenty-four hours." Old Zach concluded his letter to Arista with a dignity and firmness that matched the tone of the Mexican's letter:

> From your known high character, both as a public officer and private citizen, I was strengthened in my hope that some arrangement could be made by which friendly relations might be maintained on the frontier, until a final settlement of the question of boundary, or until other definitive action should be had by our respective governments. But, if such is not to be the case—if hostilities are to ensue—the responsibility must rest with them who actually commence them.

Later the same day, Taylor learned that a strong force of Mexican cavalry had crossed the river upstream—Arista had, in fact, sent General Anastasio Torrejón with 1,600 troops across the river—and he sent out Captain Seth B. Thornton, with Captain William H. Hardee as second in command, with a force of sixty-three dragoons to investigate. "Everyone was on the *qui vive* to ascertain the truth . . ." wrote Captain Henry. His journal for April 26 described how the army learned the truth:

> The camp was electrified by the news brought by Chapita, the Mexican guide, who accompanied Captain Thornton. He returned, and stated Captain Thornton had an engagement with a large body of Mexicans, and all had been either cut to pieces or taken prisoners. The excitement which prevailed in camp can hardly be imagined; the report was passed from tent to tent, and an immediate engagement was thought not improbable.

About 11 o'clock, a wounded dragoon arrived in a cart, accompanied by a note from General Torrejón, regretting he had no hospital facilities to take care of the wounded. The officers and men who had been captured would be treated with all the rights of prisoners of war. The wounded dragoon was confused as to what had happened, but he thought that Thornton and several other officers had been killed, along with some soldiers, and that the rest of the force had been captured. Later it was officially learned that

Thornton was alive, but that Lieutenant Mason, two sergeants, and fourteen troopers had fallen in the ambuscade.

"All idea of there being *no fight* has ceased," wrote Captain Henry in his diary. *"War has commenced . . ."*

In his headquarters tent, Zachary Taylor got off hurried calls to the governors of Texas and Louisiana, asking each for four regiments of volunteers, a total of about 5,000 men. Then old Zach wrote his dispatch to the War Department: "Hostilities may now be considered as commenced . . ."

8

The Fight at Palo Alto

The steamer *Galveston,* docking at New Orleans on May 1, brought the news that hostilities had broken out on the Rio Grande and that General Taylor had called upon the governor of Louisiana for four volunteer regiments of infantry.

The *Picayune,* the next morning, headlined the startling information to its readers and the nation:

WAR!!

To Arms!! To Arms!!

The war has begun in earnest! The Enemy

Is upon our soil!! Louisiana Volunteers,

the hour has arrived!!

Even as New Orleanians were reading of the attack on Thornton and the *Picayune's* pony express was hurrying its editions with the news to the north, tension on the Rio Grande had heightened.

Believing that Arista contemplated an attack on his supply base at Point Isabel—and rightly divining the Mexican general's intention—Taylor decided to leave a garrison of about 500 men in Fort Texas and march the rest of his little army to the coast. He knew that General Torrejón was already on the American side of the Rio Grande. Torrejón, in fact, had made a wide loop around Taylor's position to post himself on the river to cover Arista's crossing with the main body of Mexicans, downstream from Matamoros.

At 4 P.M. on May 1, the army started out from Fort Texas and it marched until midnight, when the troops slept on their arms on the open prairie, without benefit of campfires. Chilled that night and suffering from the heat and thirst the next morning, the army reached Point Isabel about midday, fatigued and bedraggled, but without having encountered the enemy. For this, General Taylor could thank faulty staff work by Arista's aides. Only a handful—only two, states a contemporary Mexican history of the war—of the many boats Arista had ordered were provided. The result, according to the Mexicans: "This dispiriting operation, that lasted for twenty-four hours, gave the enemy time to avoid meeting us, by which an excellent opportunity was lost of defeating them . . ."

Thwarted in intercepting Taylor on his march to Point Isabel, General Arista decided on a twofold plan: He would advance to Palo Alto and take a position across Taylor's line of march back to Fort Texas. And, quoting the contemporary Mexican history, Arista "determined to make more critical the position of the Americans abandoned in the fortification . . . and already sufficiently straitened."

Fifty-eight-year-old Jacob Brown, who had enlisted in the War of 1812 as a private and had worked himself up to major in the next thirty years, commanded the little force Taylor had "abandoned" in Fort Texas. He had the Seventh Infantry, four eighteen-pounders and a company of foot artillery to man them, and Lieutenant Braxton Bragg's battery of field artillery—a total complement of about 500 men and eight guns. "Hold out as long as you can," was the tenor of General Taylor's instructions to Brown as he pushed off for Point Isabel. Other instructions were to use the ammunition sparingly and to attempt no offensive operations. Signal shots, fired by the eighteen-pounders at 6:30 A.M., would announce to Taylor at Point Isabel that the fort had been invested.

After the army marched away, Major Brown pitched his tents and divided his command so as to serve the six bastions of the fort, placing them under the six senior officers. With daybreak on May 2, Brown had his men out with shovels to complete the digging of the ditch and the raising of the parapet of a yet unfinished bastion. That afternoon and night, there was much activity in Matamoros. Bells rang and bands played and troops marched back and forth, and vestured priests, with a retinue of accolytes, moved from battery to battery, blessing the troops and their guns. It was evident to Major Brown and his men that an attack on the fort was imminent. The guard was redoubled, and reveille the next morning was set for an earlier hour.

Barely had reveille sounded in the fort on May 3 than it was echoed across the river in the Mexican positions. With the breaking of dawn the Mexican batteries opened up a heavy fire on the American position. Brown replied with his eighteen-pounders and after twenty minutes of firing one Mexican battery was silenced.

The rumbling of the guns reached the tents of Taylor's sleeping army at Point Isabel. "I was awakened at dawn," said Lieutenant French. "I was sleeping on the ground. A dull distant sound broke on my ear. I rested my head on my elbow, and heard nothing; putting my ear again to the earth, I heard the boom! boom! of distant cannon. It was heard by others, and soon the camp was astir." It was five o'clock, Captain Barbour noted, when "a heavy cannonade was heard in the direction of Matamoros." In an instant the army was "in great excitement and eager to go to the relief of our brave commander at the Fort." "Before reveille . . . the heavy, booming sound of cannon came rolling in from the direction of the fort," wrote Captain Henry. "The camp was wild with excitement; we knew our gallant fellows were resisting a bombardment, and all were anxious to fly to their rescue."

Lieutenant Meade wrote his wife of the suspense that prevailed at Point Isabel. "General Taylor, as you may well imagine, was in great anxiety," said Meade. "He could not leave this point without increasing its defenses . . . At the same time, the sound of the enemy's guns, and the consciousness that our force was too small in the fort for any purpose than merely to repel assault, made all anxious to hasten to its relief."

Captain William Walker, whose Texas Rangers had recently joined Taylor's little army, volunteered to attempt to reach Fort Texas and bring back word from Major Brown on the condition of his command. Walker left on the evening of May 3 on his hazardous expedition, escorted to the edge of the chaparral by a party of dragoons under Captain Charles A. May. The latter's instructions were to wait for Walker's return until the following morning and escort him back to Point Isabel. When Walker failed to keep the rendezvous, May, fearing daybreak would reveal his group to Mexican patrols, rode back to the army. The sensitivity of Taylor's troops to a possible surprise attack by Arista's superior numbers was evident in an incident Captain Henry recorded:

Early in the morning [May 4] we had an exciting *scare:* the cry was the "enemy are advancing." The long roll was beaten, troops paraded, and immediately marched out to meet them. The enemy was Captain May and his command.

Throughout May 4, Taylor was still without word on conditions at Fort Texas, his only reassurances coming from the continuing sound of the guns. "What General Taylor's feelings were during this suspense I do not know," wrote Lieutenant Grant, "but for myself, a young second lieutenant who had never heard a hostile gun before, I felt sorry that I had enlisted."

On the morning of May 5, Walker returned from his mission with cheering news from Fort Texas. The fort had received only slight injury despite the 1,500 shots and shells rained into it; only one man, a sergeant, had been killed; Major Brown had expended but little ammunition and was confident he could hold out as long as his provisions lasted. From Major Brown's official report, Taylor learned that Bragg's six-pounders were outranged and had ceased firing and had been re-posted to repel an assault from the rear. "We are constantly on the alert, and I cannot speak too highly of the efficiency of the officers and men of my command," Brown reported. Old Zach breathed a sigh of relief, although the same day he reported to Washington: "Though not at all solicitous in regard to the safety of our fort, I was anxious to hear from Major Brown . . ."

With the arrival of recruits from New Orleans and the 500 sailors and Marines whom Commodore Conner had placed at his disposal ashore, Taylor felt that Point Isabel could defend itself, and he prepared to march to open communications with the fort and throw forward supplies of ordnance and provisions. The General promised the Adjutant General in a dispatch written before setting out: "If the enemy oppose my march, in whatever force, I shall fight him."

Old Zach exuded this same eagerness for battle and confidence in its outcome in Order No. 58, which he issued to his troops on May 7:

The army will march today at 3 o'clock, in the direction of Matamoros. It is known the enemy has recently occupied the route in force. If still in possession, the general will give him battle. The commanding general has every confidence in his officers and men. If his order and instructions are carried out, he has no doubt of the result, let the enemy meet him in what numbers they may. He wishes to enjoin upon the battalions of Infantry that their main dependence must be in the bayonet.

The impact of the General's calm confidence on his little army can be gathered from the comments of several of his young officers. "The order, in advance, announced a victory," declared Captain Henry. "There was no doubt expressed in it. Commanding a much inferior force, composed of troops few of whom have ever 'smelt gunpowder,' our brave general, nevertheless, speaks to them as to old veterans." Lieutenant Grant was impressed by Taylor's composure before battle: "No soldier could face either danger or responsibility more calmly than he. These are qualities more rarely found than genius or physical courage."

Eagerness for action in some of Taylor's officers was motivated by a burning desire to drive the Mexicans across the Rio Grande before the volunteer troops arrived. "This *must* be done before the arrival of volunteers," Captain Barbour told his wife, "or the army is *disgraced*." Lieutenant Meade entertained the same idea: "We are all anxious to give them [the Mexicans] a sound thrashing before volunteers arrive, for the reputation of the army; for should we be unable to meet them before they come, and then gain a victory, it would be said the volunteers had done it, and without them we were useless. For our own existence, therefore, we desire to encounter them."

Meanwhile, at Fort Texas, Major Brown and his men kept busy within the earthwork. Upon completion of the east bastion, Brown turned the troops to building bomb-proofs at the various stations. These shelters "were formed by layers of barrels of pork, with poles laid across, and the whole covered with embankments of earth." During the night of May 4, the Mexicans erected a field battery to bring Fort Texas under crossfire. The following morning, Mexican cavalry and infantry were discovered in position, north of the fort, supported by the new battery. Dawn of May 6 revealed that the American position was surrounded by Mexicans.

Arista had ordered General Ampudia to invest Fort Texas, believing that "the situation of the Americans in the fortification was very soon effectually compromised." On noting the situation, Major Brown, at 6:30 A.M., fired the appointed signal by the eighteen-pounders to alert Taylor that the fort was now under its heaviest attack.

The Mexican artillery, and a mortar which could not be reached by the American guns, poured an "iron shower" upon the fort. About 10 A.M., a bursting shell tore off the right leg of Major Brown, exposing "the muscles and bare and jagged bone." As he was borne to a bomb-proof, the brave old veteran called out: "Men, go to your duties, stand by your posts; I am but one among you."

Until midday, "shot and shells fell in one continual shower" and for four hours thereafter the Mexicans delivered "a dull and sullen fire" on the fort. Once, a movement of cavalry and infantry, advancing on the fort from the north, was dispersed by well-delivered canister from Lieutenant Bragg's field pieces. Close to 5 o'clock, Mexican bugles sounded a parley and two officers with a white flag advanced toward the fort with a summons from General Arista to surrender.

Captain E. S. Hawkins, who had succeeded to the command when Major Brown was wounded, read of Arista's "respect for humanity" which imposed upon him "the duty of mitigating the disasters of war" and then, with the unanimous concurrence of his officers, he rejected the invitation to surrender. Within an hour, Arista had Hawkins's answer:

Your humane communication has just been received and, after the consideration due to its importance, I must respectfully decline to surrender my forces to you.

The exact purport of your dispatch I cannot feel confident that I understand, as my interpreter is not skilled in your language; but if I understood you correctly, you have my reply.

Hawkins's rejection sparked a renewal of the furious bombardment of the fort, to which the Americans did not answer because ammunition was running low and it was necessary to conserve it for the expected Mexican assault, which Arista had, indeed, ordered Ampudia to make. But when he learned that Taylor had begun his return march from Point Isabel on the afternoon of May 7, Arista canceled the attack on the fort and ordered Ampudia to join him. "Triumph would . . . have crowned our arms," asserts a Mexican account, "if the advance of Taylor upon the army of Arista had not obliged Ampudia to reinforce him, by abandoning all the advantages he had obtained."

As Taylor's men plodded across the prairie, they heard the booming of the guns and they marched on with the assurance that the little fort was still holding out. Progress was slowed by the train of more than 200 wagons—Lieutenant Meade thought there were as many as 300—and when the army went into bivouac, it had advanced no more than seven miles.

By sunrise on May 8, Taylor had the army in motion again. Two eighteen-pounders, which the General had picked up at Point

Isabel, were close up, each requiring teams of ten oxen to draw them. Close up, too, was Taylor's precious wagon train, loaded with ammunition, supplies, and provisions.

The army marched almost a dozen miles to the pond of Palo Alto, where advance elements sent word back to Taylor that the enemy was in battle line about two miles away, athwart the American route. It was about noon when Taylor halted his force and formed the command in columns of attack. "With the greatest deliberation," wrote Captain Henry, Taylor permitted the men to fill their canteens and refresh themselves a bit. "Soon the long roll sounded," said Lieutenant French, "hearts beat, pulses kept time, and knees trembled, and would not be still." Lieutenant Grant, as he looked down the long line thought "what a fearful responsibility General Taylor must feel, commanding such a host and so far away from friends."

General Arista, meanwhile, had ridden up and down his cheering line, promising that "glory would ensue from a triumph." As he inspected his force, standing at its arms, "banners floated to the wind . . . the horses pawed the ground, the bands performed inspiring . . . music, and shouts filled the air of 'Viva la República.' "

According to Lieutenant Sam French, Arista missed a real opportunity while indulging in such heroics. "He had been in line of battle all morning awaiting our coming, yet he *permitted us to deploy undisturbed* . . . instead of assuming the offensive as he should have," wrote French.

Arista, perhaps through admiration, made no response even when Lieutenant Jacob Blake, who had volunteered to make a reconnaissance of the Mexican line, rode into easy range. "With a courtesy becoming a knight of the Middle Ages," wrote Lieutenant French, "he permitted Lieut. Blake, in the presence of the armies, to ride down to within musket shot of his line, to dismount and survey his troops through his glass, then to remount and ride along down his front without allowing a shot to be fired at him."

The Mexican right was anchored on a wooded knoll, where General Luis Noriega commanded a force of 150 cavalry. Next in line were a single piece of artillery, a battalion of sappers, the Second Light Infantry, and the Tampico Coast Guard battalion. Arista's center consisted of Ampudia's infantry—the Fourth, under Colonel José López Uraga, the Tenth, under General José María García, and the Sixth and First under General La Vega—a com-

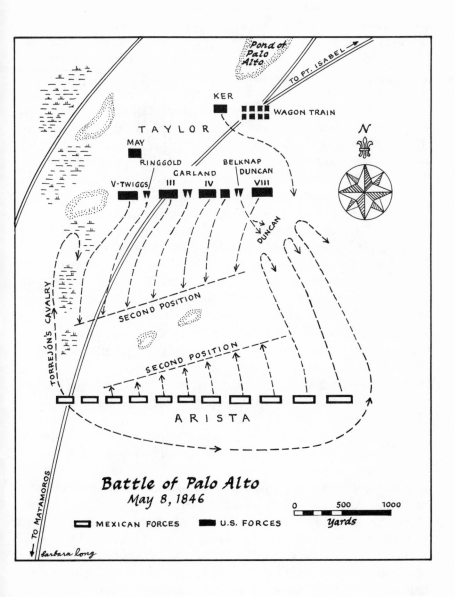

Battle of Palo Alto
May 8, 1846

◻ MEXICAN FORCES ◼ U.S. FORCES

Yards

pany of sappers, and seven pieces of artillery, two eight-pounders and five four-pounders. On the Mexican left was General Torrejón's Lancers, about 1,000 strong, their right protected by two small cannons. Strung out across the plain, Arista blocked Taylor's passage with about 6,000 troops (Arista reported his strength at 3,000 and estimated Taylor's as slightly less) and twelve pieces of artillery.

Taylor's right, under the command of Colonel Twiggs, and consisting of Colonel James S. McIntosh's Fifth Infantry and Twiggs's Dragoons, was thrown across the Point Isabel–Matamoros road. Next in line was Major Samuel Ringgold's battery with the Third and Fourth Infantry to Ringgold's left. Between these two regiments, which Lieutenant Colonel John Garland commanded, were placed the "two great, long, heavy iron eighteen-pounders," which, according to Lieutenant French, "came into line by words of command not laid down in the works of tactics." Taylor's left wing was assigned to the First Brigade, commanded by Brevet Lieutenant Colonel William G. Belknap. It consisted of Captain James Duncan's battery, an artillery battalion serving as infantry, and the Eighth Infantry, which was posted on Taylor's extreme left. Captain May's squadron of cavalry was in reserve behind Twiggs, and the rest of the mounted troops, under Captain Croghan Ker guarded the wagon train in the rear.

With barely 2,200 men in line, Taylor was outnumbered at least two to one by the Mexicans, but he had twenty pieces of artillery to Arista's twelve. Old Zach, accordingly, decided that instead of placing his reliance in the bayonet, he would stake victory in his artillery superiority in number and quality of guns and trained artillerymen to man them.

When the American line came within half a mile of Arista's position, at 2:30 P.M., the Mexican batteries opened fire. Taylor halted his line, advanced the guns of Ringgold and Duncan, and they began firing at once. "The firing of the enemy was incessant," wrote Captain Henry, "although not very accurate." The first Mexican shots did not reach the Americans, but before Taylor halted the troops, the cannonballs began to bounce harmlessly through the ranks. "They hurt no one," said Lieutenant Grant, ". . . because they would strike the ground long before they reached our line, and ricochetted through the tall grass so slowly that the men would see them and open ranks and let them pass."

The batteries of Ringgold and Duncan delivered a withering

fire into the Mexican line. "Every moment we could see the charges from our pieces cut a way through their ranks making a perfect road," Lieutenant Grant wrote his future wife, "but they would close up the interval without showing signs of retreat." In his report, Taylor generously acknowledged that the "constancy with which the Mexican infantry sustained this cannonade was a theme of universal remark and admiration."

As the battle opened, Lieutenant Sam French sat his horse, a bit to the rear of the line, watching after the caissons. A shell struck and killed an artillery driver close to him. "That was the first man I saw killed in battle," he wrote. "It was war, but it was not pleasant, and I thought it was no place for me to sit on my horse idle." Dismounting, French took command of a howitzer and helped work it. "As no one demurred at what I was doing," he said, "I remained in charge of it all day."

And so it was that, when Torrejón's cavalry, supported by two field pieces, made a detour to turn Taylor's right in an attempt to get to the wagon train, Lieutenant French found himself with Lieutenant Randolph Ridgely rushing to the support of the Fifth Infantry, which, formed in a square, challenged Torrejón's advance. ". . . When the Mexican cannon was being loaded to fire on the square, Ridgely and I came up, and so *quickly* did we bring our guns into action that we unlimbered, loaded, and fired before the Mexicans could," declared French.

The result was inevitable. Deadly fire from the front of the square unhorsed about twenty-five Mexicans and blunted the charge. The Third Infantry, rushing to the support of the Fifth, delivered a hot fire. And Ringgold, advancing two other guns to join Ridgely and French, added to "the great execution," as Taylor reported it, in the Mexican cavalry.

A cannonball delivered a mortal wound to the gallant Ringgold, father of the "flying artillery," which not only passed its test at Palo Alto, but won the day for Taylor. Enemy sources confirmed this. "The artillery of the Americans, much superior to ours, made horrid ravages in the ranks of the Mexican army," stated a contemporary Mexican account.

During the first hour of the nearly five-hour-long engagement, a wad from one of Duncan's guns set the dry grass of the prairie afire and the breeze from the Gulf of Mexico blew the smoke into the eyes of the Mexican soldiers. Arista called the fire and the dense smoke screen it created an American "stratagem."

Taylor now pushed his right wing forward and swung his line about thirty-five degrees from his original position, Noting this as the smoke lifted, Arista made a similar adjustment of his force, with the result that the armies faced each other again.

Under cover of the smoke, meanwhile, Duncan swung his guns to the left and posted them to enfilade the Mexican right with destructive fire. At the time, Arista was about to launch an attack on the Eighth Infantry, on Taylor's extreme left. A surgeon noted that Duncan's "grape and canister . . . mowed them down in great numbers," while Captain Henry commented on "the murderous effect of his fire." To Duncan's efficient gunnery, Captain Barbour attributed the Mexican right wing being "thrown into the utmost confusion." General Taylor, in his report on the battle, stated that "Duncan . . . completely repulsed several successive efforts of the enemy to advance in force upon our left flank. Supported in succession by the 8th infantry and by Capt. Ker's squadron of dragoons, he gallantly held the enemy at bay, and finally drove him with immense loss from the field." The disconcerted Mexicans trampled each other as the American batteries "broke them, destroyed them, and obliged them to retire," states a Mexican source.

By now, darkness had fallen and the Battle of Palo Alto had ended. "Fortunately," states a Mexican history of the war, "the Americans did not avail themselves, nor scarcely notice the disorder in our force for at this time night had completely closed in."

The Americans bivouacked on the battlefield, sleeping on their arms, while the Mexicans withdrew into the chaparral, a little to the rear of their original positions. Taylor's troops had every reason to be thrilled by their conduct in this first pitched battle against a regular army that American troops had fought since the Battle of New Orleans in 1815. Lieutenant Sam French put his finger on the reason for Taylor's victory at Palo Alto. "They turned their guns on our batteries," said French. "We fired at their infantry as instructed."

Taylor's casualties were nine killed, forty-four wounded, and two missing. The death toll later reached eleven when Major Ringgold succumbed, and Captain John Page, several months later, died from his wounds. "The wounds of the men were very severe, most of them requiring amputation of some limbs," wrote Captain Henry. "The surgeon's saw was going the livelong night, and the groans of the poor sufferers were heartrending."

9

"By the Army Proper"

An old military axiom states, "A council of war never votes to fight," and General Taylor may have had this in mind when he acceded to the request of Colonel Twiggs and held a council of war in the pre-dawn hours of May 9.

But, as one of his young officers commented, Old Zach had doubtless made up his mind beforehand as to just what he intended to do. The General listened patiently to those who urged caution. Entrench, assume a defensive position, and wait for reinforcements —that was the opinion of a majority of the ten officers present. "It leaked out after the council broke up that 7 out of 10 were in favor of this suggestion of inaction," recorded Captain Philip Barbour. "Col. McIntosh, Captain Morris and Duncan to their praise be it spoken were in favor of fighting again. The General sided with them."

If the story told by Lieutenant John Sedgwick is correct, Duncan was not at the council, but he rode by Taylor's tent as it was breaking up and Taylor asked his opinion.

"We whipped 'em today and we can whip 'em tomorrow!" the confident artillerist replied.

"That is my opinion, Captain Duncan," said Old Zach. Turning to the officers of the council, Taylor added: "Gentlemen, you will prepare your commands to move forward."

Sunrise disclosed to Taylor and his little army that Arista was pulling out of his position, and about 6 A.M., the Mexican troops took up the march on the road to Matamoros. Taylor made no attempt to harass the departing enemy, but concentrated on establishing a defensive cordon about the wagon train, with which he left the two eighteen-pounders and two twelve-pounders, and sufficient artillery men to man the four pieces. The wounded officers and men were sent back to Point Isabel, after which Taylor was

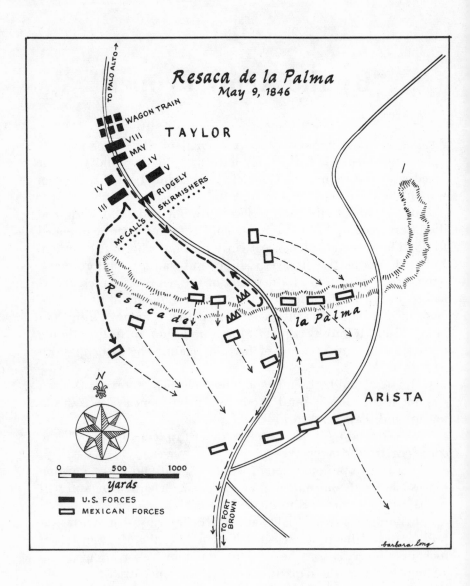

Resaca de la Palma
May 9, 1846

ready to push on after the Mexicans, who had disappeared into the thick chaparral.

Taylor had no way of knowing the state of morale in Arista's army, which, according to Mexican sources, had "passed the night sad and dispirited" and had, as it started its retreat from Palo Alto, "a fatal presentiment of a rout." Continuing, this Mexican history of the war stated:

> There commenced to be credence given to rumors of treason which had circulated before. The battle of the next day was dreaded in advance . . . It was the rumor instigated by rivalry and hatred, which soon ran through the army that the General-in-chief [Arista] was a traitor . . . that he had formally agreed to sell the army, and to deliver it up to the rage of the enemy. These destroyed at the roots the morale and discipline.

After a reconnaissance had satisfied Taylor that the Mexicans were indeed retreating, he sent an advance party of about 250 under Captain George A. McCall into the chaparral "to feel out the enemy and ascertain his position." The main force followed on the road, on either side of which was the almost impenetrable chaparral. "It is almost impossible to understand with what our little army had to contend unless the ground is seen," wrote Captain Philip Barbour. "On each side extending for miles was a dense thorny thicket or chaparral cut by deep ravines and narrow ponds through which passes the road to Matamoros."

At one of these ravines, the Resaca de la Palma (called by the Mexicans Resaca de Guerrero), Arista halted his retreat at 10 A.M., and established a defense line to await Taylor's coming. But as time passed without the appearance of the Americans, Arista became convinced that Taylor would not attack him that day, and he ordered the wagons to be unloaded, the mules of the artillery to be unhitched, and the pack animals to be unharnessed. Even when McCall's skirmishers made contact with his defenses at about 2:30 P.M., Arista, "being governed the whole time by a fatal infatuation, could not believe that they intended a regular battle."

But that was exactly Old Zach's intention. Word from McCall reached Taylor at 3 P.M. and he hurried the army forward to join his skirmishers about four o'clock. "The enemy [was] in force in our front," reported Taylor, "occupying a ravine which intersects the road, and is skirted by thickets of dense chaparral." The bow-shaped Resaca de la Palma, once the bed of the meandering Rio Grande, was about a mile in length, fifty feet wide, and eight to ten feet deep.

Taylor advanced Ridgely's battery on the road and deployed McCall's skirmishers into the chaparral on either side of the road. The Fifth Infantry and half of the Fourth Infantry were thrown into the heavy woods on the left while the Third Infantry and the other half of the Fourth plunged into the chaparral on the right of the road. Captain May's squadron of Dragoons and the Eighth Infantry were held in reserve.

Almost at once units lost their identity in the thick, thorny growth, and companies were broken up into small parties. "When I came up to the skirmishers under McCall," wrote Captain Ephraim Kirby Smith, "I had not more than twenty of my men with me and not another of the Fifth in sight." Captain Barbour reported a similar experience: "After wandering through the thicket in the hottest fire for some time, I succeeded in finding my way out and gained the road where I met Col. Garland who told me the 3rd was deployed to the right. I pushed on with 12 men of my company, all I could keep together in the thicket . . ."

All this while, Mexican batteries were spraying the chaparral with grape and canister, "whipping the bushes about our ears," as an officer put it. Lieutenant Grant led his company through the thicket "whenever a penetrable place could be found." When the bullets commenced "to whistle very thick overhead," Grant ordered his men to lie down, "an order that did not have to be enforced." After the battle, Grant admitted to Julia Dent, his future wife: "There is no great sport in having bullets flying about one in every direction. But I find I have less horror when among them than when in anticipation."

Meanwhile Ridgely's battery had gone into action. "We could not see their guns, nor they see ours, owing to the undergrowth," said Lieutenant Sam French, "but the guns were discharged at the smoke that each other made."

To his unequal duel with the Mexican guns, Ridgely had another annoyance—Mexican skirmishers—with which he could not cope. Finally, he sent French off to the General.

"Go to General Taylor and ask him to send some infantry supports," Ridgely ordered.

French galloped up the road at full speed, reining his horse before Taylor and his staff, and delivered Ridgely's message.

"The infantry has been deployed and will soon be there," was the answer. Lieutenant French wheeled his horse and returned at a run.

For more than half an hour, Ridgely had been fighting the Mexican guns alone. "[We] had driven them from off the plain into the ravine or dry bed of the river, and had obtained possession of an open camping ground directly in front of their pieces and not over a hundred yards distant," said French. Still no support was to be seen anywhere. Ridgely called again to French.

"Go to General Taylor as quickly as possible, and tell him to *send me* assistance to capture the Mexican batteries in front of us." As he spurred his mount, French now noted that the road and the woods on both sides of it were swarming with infantry, edging its way through the thick and discomforting growth.

"General, their guns are just in our front and can be taken," French reported to Taylor.

"My God, where is May?" exclaimed Old Zach. "I can't get him up!"

A few moments later, Captain May rode up to Taylor and asked if he should charge the battery across the ravine.

"Charge, Captain, nolens volens!" ordered Old Zach, a note of impatience in his voice. May took off, in a column of fours, and raced down the road to Ridgely's battery, his long black beard flying in the wind.

"Hello, Ridgely! Where is that battery?" shouted May. "I am ordered to charge it."

"Hold on, Charley, till I draw their fire, and you'll soon see where they are," Ridgely shouted back.

He blasted away with his guns and the Mexicans answered immediately. "Away went May toward the Mexican guns, and our guns after him at a run," said Lieutenant French. "We came up to them muzzle to muzzle."

May's Dragoons overran the Mexican position, but saddles were emptied by the sizzling fire of the Mexican infantry, and although the gallant General La Vega was captured, May was compelled to ride back with the guns remaining in Mexican hands.

Taylor now ordered Lieutenant Colonel Belknap's Eighth Infantry into the fray, supported by part of the Fifth Infantry. "Take those guns, and by God keep them," commanded Old Zach.

Belknap's command swept forward and swarmed over the Mexican position. Gunners abandoned their pieces and took to flight.

Ridgely quickly manned the captured guns and turned Mexican ammunition on the fleeing enemy.

Taylor sat his horse in characteristic fashion, one leg crooked around the pommel of his saddle, as the battle raged. Once, when it was suggested to him during the height of the Mexican firing that he was exposing himself too much, Old Zach replied: "Let us ride a little nearer, the balls will fall behind us."

From close range, Taylor saw the Mexican line crumble. What had been, in the struggle through the chaparral almost each man for himself, now became a full-scale infantry advance as the Third Infantry and part of the Fourth crossed the ravine, turned Arista's left and stood off valiantly an assault by Torrejón's Lancers. Under the persistent fire of Taylor's foot soldiers, the Lancers recoiled and broke.

All this while, Arista, confident that his position was impregnable, remained in his tent reporting on his "victory" of the previous day at Palo Alto. Almost too late did he realize the magnitude of the battle and the imminence of his capture as Taylor's victorious troops drove into his camp. A Mexican history of the war described the chaos:

> The disorder which defeat had produced on the left of our line soon extended to the corps on our right. This last had not been under fire, but dispersed shamefully . . . The most horrible confusion reigned on the field, and everything announced a grievous disaster to our arms.
>
> The General-in-chief, who, although he remained in his tent writing, was convinced at last, unfortunately very late, however, from the rapidity of the defeat, that his impression had been a mistake. Full then of regret, and burning with rage, he burst out into complaints against the cowards, and sought to be killed; or hoping even yet to check the enemy, he placed himself at the head of the cavalry, which being stationed in the rear, was preserved untouched. He made the last effort. He charged boldly on the victors and penetrated to our first position. But the enemy . . . opened a terrible fire, and shot down our lancers with safety. There was now nothing left, except to retreat . . .

Taylor's men pursued the Mexicans relentlessly. "On, on we

went, keeping up a run, and yelling like mad!" wrote Captain Henry. "The enemy now and then gave symptoms of a stand, but were driven on, scattering themselves in the chaparral, and availing themselves of every trail that led to the river . . . Many were drowned in their attempts to swim the river." Captain Ephraim Kirby Smith reported that "three hundred were drowned in crossing," while Lieutenant Sam French described the routed Mexicans "returning, not with captured flags and the spoils of war, not with waving banners and triumphant shouts of victory, but fleeing when no one pursued, and madly plunging into the river to gain the shore . . ." As the Mexicans fell back before the gathering momentum of the Americans, "a deafening shout of triumph went up from the whole of our men," wrote Captain Philip Barbour. "[This] struck such terror into the Mexican ranks that they fled in all directions. The pursuit now commenced and on we went, Dragoons, Artillery, Infantry in one mass at full run, yelling at every step, which was kept up for three miles, and found that the enemy had crossed to the other side, some in boats, some in swimming, while the greater part kept up the river . . . and crossed some miles above."

The spoils of battle were impressive in prisoners and materiel of war. Fourteen officers, including a general, a colonel and a lieutenant colonel, were among the many dozens captured. Also taken: eight field pieces, with ammunition, priming tubes, and slow match for them; 393 stands of small arms with 155,600 rounds of musket ball-cartridges; 500 mules and 450 pack-saddles; 20 horses, six oxen and six wagons or carts; 50 entrenching tools; 40 sacks of subsistence and many miscellaneous items. Of particular interest, among the officers' baggage taken in the victory, were the portfolios, writing desk, canopy, and other baggage of the Mexican General-in-Chief, Mariano Arista.

Although Taylor had an aggregate of 2,222 officers and men for the struggle at Resaca de la Palma, he reported that the actual number engaged with the enemy "did not excess 1,700." Three of his young officers fell bravely. Lieutenant Z. Inge of the Dragoons was shot from his saddle in May's charge of the Mexican battery; Lieutenant T. L. Chadbourn of the Eighth Infantry and Lieutenant R. E. Cochrane of the Fourth Infantry, to quote Taylor, "met their death in the thick of the fight." With them fell in action thirty-six troopers. Twelve officers were wounded, some severely, and seventy-one men, while five Americans were reported missing.

Perhaps the most amazing wounds of the battle were suffered by
Colonel McIntosh, who, said Lieutenant French, "was pinned to
the earth with bayonets, one entering his mouth and passing
through his neck." "Old Tosh" miraculously survived to fight on
other days.

Taylor estimated the two-day Mexican losses "moderately" at
1,000 men. "Our victory had been decisive," Old Zach reported to
the War Department. "A small force has overcome immense odds
of the best troops that Mexico can furnish—veteran regiments, perfectly equipped and appointed . . . The causes of the victory are
doubtless to be found in the superior quality of our officers and
men." To his daughter, Taylor wrote: "Bayonet to bayonet & sword
to sword, we completely routed them." Describing the fight to his
son-in-law Dr. R. C. Wood, Taylor said: "We succeeded in gaining
a complete victory, dispersing them in every direction, taking their
artillery, baggage or means of transportation, a number of standards
& with a great loss of killed, wounded & prisoners . . . the war I have
no doubt is completely brought to a close on this side the Rio
Grande . . ."

While Taylor was fighting at Palo Alto and Resaca de la Palma,
Fort Texas was still under fire from Mexican guns and mortars. On
May 8, four mortars from the north, south, and west played on
Captain Hawkins's position, but although more than 150 shells and
nearly 100 round shot fell upon the fort, there were no casualties.
The sound of the guns at Palo Alto captured the command's atten-
tion. "The excitement . . . during this distant cannonading was
intense," Hawkins reported.

The night of the 8th was very quiet, but the troops were alerted
by their guns. With day, Fort Texas found itself still under bombardment. At 2 P.M. Major Brown died, and later in the afternoon
the sounds of the re-engagement of the armies at Resaca de la
Palma reached the embattled garrison. Shortly before six o'clock,
fleeing Mexican cavalry and some infantry passed within view of the
men in the fort, and soon pursuing Americans burst into sight.

The ordeal that the defenders of the fort lived through—the casualties, however, were only two dead, and thirteen wounded in more
than 160 hours of siege and bombardment—showed on their faces,
"haggard from want of sleep" having been "harassed night and
day . . . from the morning of May 3 to the afternoon of May 9."
Captain William Henry, who had come through two hot fights,

looked at the gallant defenders of Fort Texas, renamed Fort Brown
for its dead commander, and exclaimed: "I would have rather
fought twenty battles than have passed through the bombardment
of Fort Brown." Henry said that the fort had received 2,700 shot
and shell.

Taylor paid his tribute to the heroes in the fort in his praise of
"its heroic and indomitable commander," whose loss Old Zach
characterized as "irreparable."

Curiosity naturally led many back to the battlefields in their first
leisure moments. Others were detailed to bury the dead. It was a
sickening sight. Captain Ephraim Kirby Smith found the "scent of
carnage . . . almost insupportable," and he noted that "the vultures
were already at their widespread feast, the wolves howling and fighting over their dreadful meal."

The young West Pointers exulted in Taylor's twin victories.
They were delighted by Old Zach's Order No. 59, which lauded
the "coolness and readiness of the troops on the 8th and the brilliant impetuosity with which the enemy's position and artillery
were carried on the 9th," and that officers and men "displayed the
best qualities of the American soldier" in "the noble manner in
which they have sustained the honor of service and of the country."

Lieutenant Meade expressed his pride: "We all congratulate ourselves heartily in having done everything without any assistance
whatever, and we now trust the country will look upon the army in
a more favorable light, and be disposed to award them some little
efficiency." So, too, did Captain Ephraim Kirby Smith: "It is a
glorious fact for the army that there were no volunteers with us."
And Captain Henry was no less proud: ". . . These conquests have
been effected by the *army proper* . . . We only asked for *an opportunity*, few as we were, to *prove* to our country she had a safe
anchor in our *small* but gallant force."

On May 11, General Taylor left his headquarters at Resaca de
la Palma for Point Isabel, leaving Colonel Twiggs in command of
the army, with instructions to "hold himself strictly on the defensive
until the return of the commanding general."

That night, "a solemn silence" hung over Matamoros. "We see
no military displays, no music," observed Captain Henry. "Even
the dogs have ceased barking."

10

Meanwhile—In Washington

Nine days after his victory at Resaca de la Palma—and five days after President Polk had signed the war bill in faraway Washington —Zachary Taylor occupied Matamoros without firing a shot.

Detractors of Taylor as a military man have criticized Old Zach's failure to follow up his twin victories with an assault on the Mexican town. They have said that Taylor could have crossed the river, captured Matamoros and most of Arista's demoralized army if he had acted immediately.

Even Taylor's sympathetic biographers seem to accept this criticism. Holman Hamilton wrote:

> It does not seem to have occurred to Taylor to cross the Rio Grande at once. Had he followed this course directly after the Mexican rout, at the probable cost of a few more lives and regardless of the risks involved, Arista's entire army might have surrendered on the spot and an even prouder laurel might have been added to Taylor's brow. Not only had American morale been heightened by the success of American arms at Palo Alto and Resaca de la Palma, but the gallant defenders of Fort Texas had also won a signal victory. For nearly a week they had steadfastly resisted their assailants with little loss, and albeit fatigued, they were in good enough condition to continue fighting.

Brainerd Dyer, another Taylor biographer, qualified his criticism of the General:

> Had the government supplied Taylor with the pontoon bridge which he had requested months before but which no bureau chief in Washington could find funds for, he could

have crossed the river and taken possession of Matamoros on the next day. Even without this equipment he could have crossed in a day or two by bringing up the river the scows and flats of the Quartermaster's Department at Point Isabel; but Taylor saw no need for haste.

Criticism of Taylor, it seems, is based upon future events. At the time he elected delay, he not only did not have the means to cross the river, but his adversary still had a numerical advantage in fighting men, and Taylor's troops were fatigued. Moreover, the defenders of Fort Brown could not be asked to take the offensive after undergoing 160 hours of siege and bombardment. Although Lieutenant George Meade later was mildly critical of Taylor for not knowing "how to use his engineers," immediately after Resaca de la Palma Meade wrote his wife, "we would do wrong to cross, were it not certain they would offer no resistance." But could Taylor be certain Arista would offer no resistance?

Taylor, himself, was confident that if he had the means to cross the river, he would have won another victory. "A ponton bridge, the necessity of which I exhibited to the department last year, would have enabled the army to cross on the evening of the battle, take the city, with all the artillery and stores of the enemy, and a great number of prisoners; in short, to destroy entirely the Mexican army," he reported.

But Old Zach didn't have the bridge and he bided his time. He returned from Point Isabel on May 14 and the next day, a bold party under Lieutenant Richard Graham swam the Rio Grande and cut out some boats on the Mexican side. Taylor meanwhile had received some heavy mortars with which he menaced the town, and his force was augmented by the arrival of Lieutenant Colonel Henry Wilson with four companies of the First Infantry.

Taylor made his plans to cross the river on May 17 above Matamoros, while Wilson's new arrivals created a diversion below the city. The troops, alerted to march at 1 P.M., were anxious to move, but there was a delay. The Mexicans had sounded a parley, and General Tomás Requeña crossed from Matamoros with a proposal from General Arista for an armistice. Taylor bluntly refused. He reminded the Mexican that a month earlier he had suggested an armistice to General Ampudia, while the governments could negotiate their differences, and Ampudia had rejected it. "I replied . . .

that circumstances were now changed," reported Taylor. ". . . I was receiving large reinforcements, and could not now suspend operations which I had not initiated or provoked."

Taylor told Requeña that he intended to occupy Matamoros at once, but that Arista, if he left the public property behind, could withdraw his force. The Mexican departed, promising an answer in the afternoon, but when no answer came, Taylor resumed his operation. The next day, the 18th, Taylor marched unopposed into Matamoros. The night before, Arista had taken flight and Old Zach's campaign on the Rio Grande was over.

Meanwhile, back in Washington, events had rushed one upon another after Taylor's dispatch of April 26 had reached President Polk on May 9, with the news that, as Polk later stated in his message, "Mexico has passed the boundary of the United States, has invaded our territory, and shed American blood upon the American soil."

On May 11, the President sent his message to Congress and on May 12, the House of Representatives voted for war. The Senate, the next day, concurred, and Polk immediately signed the bill. Congress appropriated $10,000,000 for the prosecution of the war and the President was authorized to call for 50,000 volunteers, of whom 20,000 were to be raised immediately.

May 13 had been a day of "incessant application, anxiety, and labor," for Polk and when a cabinet meeting adjourned about 11 P.M., he confessed himself "much exhausted." But much had been accomplished. For one thing, the President had appointed General Winfield Scott, Commander-in-Chief of the United States Army, as commander of the army to be raised. His diary reveals Polk's reservations, if not, indeed, his reluctance, to name Scott:

> Though I did not consider him in all respects suited to such an important command, yet being commander-in-chief of the army, his position entitled him to it if he desired it . . . General Scott did not impress me favorably as a military man. He has had experience in his profession, but I thought was rather scientific and visionary in his views.

Undoubtedly one of Scott's "scientific and visionary" views was to raise at once the 20,000 men Congress had authorized for immediate induction, for Polk added in his diary: "I did not think that so many as 20,000 volunteers besides the regular army was necessary, but I did not express this opinion, not being willing to take the responsibility of the campaign by refusing to grant to General Scott all he asked."

This same day, May 13, orders went out from Washington to the commanders of two widely separated naval forces.

To Commodore David Conner, Commanding Home Squadron: "You will declare and enforce a blockade of as many of the ports of Mexico as your force will enable you to do effectually . . . Your blockade must be strict and absolute; and only public armed vessels of neutral powers should be permitted to enter the Mexican ports . . . You will approach Tampico, and take, and, if practicable, will hold possession of that town . . . You will keep up a constant communication with our army on the Del Norte [Rio Grande], and adopt prompt and energetic measures to render it all assistance that may be in your power . . ."

To Commodore John D. Sloat, Commanding U.S. Squadron, Pacific: "The state of things alluded to [on] . . . June 24, 1845, has occurred." (On that date, Secretary of Navy Bancroft had written Sloat that should war with Mexico come, he was to employ his forces "to the best advantage . . . to possess . . . the port of San Francisco, and blockade or occupy . . . other ports . . . to preserve, if possible, the most friendly relations with the inhabitants and . . . encourage them to adopt a course of neutrality.") "You will therefore now be governed by the instructions therein contained, and carry into effect the orders then communicated, with energy and promptitude, and adopt such other measures for the protection of the persons and interests, the right and the commerce of the citizens of the United States, as your sound judgment may deem to be required."

At the same time that the Navy Department sent these instructions to Commodores Conner and Sloat, the War Department sent orders to Colonel Stephen Watts Kearny, commander at Fort Leavenworth, Kansas, to move his regiment, the First Dragoons, to Santa Fé to protect American traders. The President called upon the governor of Missouri to supply 1,000 mounted volunteers to reinforce Kearny's command.

Kearny's orders were extended on June 3, 1846, "to take the earliest possible possession of Upper California." Kearny was given "a large discretionary power" for his mission and the choice of routes to California was left to his "better knowledge and ampler means of getting accurate information." Naval forces, Kearny was told, will probably be in possession of all the coastal towns and "will cooperate . . . in the conquest of California." Once New Mexico and Upper California were secured, Kearny was to "establish temporary civil governments therein—abolishing all arbitrary restrictions that may exist." He was to assure the inhabitants that it was the intention of the United States "to provide them a free government," and Kearny's conduct was to be such as "to conciliate the inhabitants and render them friendly to the United States." To ease the burden of this difficult task, the rank of brevet brigadier general was conferred upon Kearny.

By the early summer of 1846, American operational plans were thus to prosecute the war on four fronts:

1. General Taylor, at Matamoros with an army that grew almost daily by the arrival of volunteers, to invade northern Mexico, with Monterrey as his major objective.

2. Commodore Conner to blockade the Mexican ports on the Gulf of Mexico.

3. Commodore Sloat to seize San Francisco and blockade other California ports.

4. General Kearny to occupy Santa Fé, and then to march west to take possession of California.

And then, of course, there was the fifth front—Washington, where war and politics made controversial bedfellows.

11

"A Hasty Plate of Soup"

Winfield Scott, a tried and true soldier, fancied himself a writer. Thomas Hart Benton, a seasoned politician, fancied himself a soldier. And President James K. Polk, a strong political partisan, fancied himself as impartial. All three were wrong.

For all his education, and it was a broad one; for all his general knowledge, and it was acquired in a lifetime of wide and varied reading; for all his command of language, and it was considerable, Scott had a positive genius for writing long and inept letters. These, when publicized, frequently presented the General in an unfavorable light, and often held him up to ridicule, and several times placed him on the verge of, as one of his biographers states, "committing suicide with a goose quill."

As for Senator Benton's high appraisal of his capacity to lead an army, suffice to say that his vaulting military ambition was in inverse ratio to his actual qualifications. Polk recorded an interview with Benton in his diary:

> He said there ought to be a lieutenant-general of the army who should be general-in-chief. He said it required a man of talents and resources as well as a military man for such command, and that with a view to obtain peace more depended upon the talents and energies of the officer than upon mere bravery. He then said if such an office was created by Congress, he would be willing to accept the command himself. I remarked generally that I would have confidence in him and would be pleased to see him at the head of the army in such an expedition.

Polk's obstinate partisanship is reflected in his readiness to accept so unqualified a commander as Senator Benton, which would be a certain means of preventing Scott or another Whig general from gaining any glory in victory over Mexico. To his diary, Polk once protested: "I had never suffered politics to mingle with the conduct of the war." But this was not the way Senator Benton recalled matters. The President, Benton wrote in his memoirs "wanted a small war, just large enough to require a treaty of peace and not large enough to make military reputations dangerous for the Presidency."

Polk was, indeed, not happy that the only generals in the army—Scott, Edmund Pendleton Gaines, and John Ellis Wool—were Whigs, and as such were politically anathema to his rugged Democratic principles. "These officers are all Whigs and violent partisans," Polk wrote, "and not having the success of my administration at heart seem disposed to throw every obstacle in the way of my prosecuting the Mexican War successfully."

What provoked this indictment was this: The President had sponsored a bill in the Senate, shortly after the declaration of war, creating two additional major generals and four new brigadier generals. Indignant that he had not been consulted, Scott berated Secretary of War Marcy, as he wrote a friend, about the administration's plans for the new generals:

> One of each grade was designed to supersede me and Wool —in the command of the troops against Mexico. It was avowed that all these generals were to be Democrats. Seeing the bill in print the morning of [May] 20th, and knowing already of the Democratic clamors against me, 'I smelt the rat' and immediately told the Secretary that I saw the double trick, first to supersede me, and, at the *end* of the war, say in six or eight months, disband every general who would not place Democracy above God's country.

Scott didn't stop there. He, Wool, and Adjutant General Roger Jones sought out friends in Congress to prevent passage of the bill, and it was this activity which angered Polk. There was no doubt of Winfield Scott's political ambitions. He had long had his eyes on the White House. And the sixty-year-old General had substantial military credentials which made him a man always to be considered by the Whigs.

Born in Virginia in 1786, Scott won military honors in the War of 1812, attaining the rank of brigadier general before he was twenty-eight, and thereafter he served in the army with distinction.

His six feet, four inches, decked in the military finery which he so loved and which won for him the title, "Old Fuss and Feathers," made him an impressive figure. Twice Scott had sought in vain, in 1840 and again in 1844, the Whig nomination for the Presidency; now, two years before the election, the General loomed as the logical Whig choice in 1848. But although Scott had political aspirations, they did not dilute his patriotism, devotion to duty, and tireless capacity for hard work.

The thousand details of preparing for war, Scott tackled immediately after his verbal appointment by Polk on May 13. But the civilian commander-in-chief in the White House quickly grew impatient. When it came to Polk's attention on May 19 that the General did not plan to leave for the Rio Grande before September 1, his pique overflowed into his diary:

> I told the Secretary of War that any such delay was not to be permitted, and that General Scott must proceed very soon to his post, or that I would supersede him in the command. The Secretary of War informed me that General Scott was embarrassing him by his schemes, that he was constantly talking and not acting. I told the Secretary to take the matter into his own hands; to issue his orders and cause them to be obeyed.

Up to this point, General Scott had received no written orders assigning him to the command of the army to be raised, and in a long and particularly ill-advised and indiscreet letter to Secretary of War Marcy on May 21, he pointed this out. It would have been better had Scott stopped there, but he rambled on with his "suicidal" pen:

> In the midst of these multitudinous and indispensable occupations, I have learned from you that much impatience is already felt, perhaps in high quarters, that I have not already put myself in route for the Rio Grande and now, with fourteen hours a day of preliminary work remaining on my hands for many days, I find myself compelled to stop that necessary work to guard myself against, perhaps, utter condemnation, in the quarters alluded to.
>
> I am too old a soldier, and have had too much *special* experience not to feel the infinite importance of securing myself against danger (ill-will or pre-condemnation) in my rear before

advancing on the public enemy. Not an advantageous step can
be taken in a forward march without the confidence that all is
well behind . . .

My explicit meaning is—that I do not desire to place myself
in the most perilous of all positions—*a fire upon my rear from
Washington, and the fire, in front, from the Mexicans* . . .

The President's reaction to Scott's "foolish and vindictive" letter,
which Marcy immediately delivered to him, was recorded in his
diary:

Without the slightest reason for it, General Scott makes base
and false insinuations in reference to the administration, as
connected with the command of the army on the Mexican
frontier, which I had on the commencement of hostilities requested him to assume. He uses language not only exception-
able but unbecoming an officer. . . . I repeat this insinuation is
wholly false and proves, as I think, two things: 1st, that General Scott seeks a pretext to avoid going to the Del Norte to
take command of our army, and 2d, that his partisan feelings
are such that he is unfit to be entrusted with the command . . .

After discussing the matter with his cabinet, the President instructed Marcy to inform General Scott that he was being "excused"
from command of the army in Mexico and he was to remain at his
duties in Washington. This document, dated and delivered to Scott
on May 25, was a much-revised missive. After Marcy had composed
it, Attorney General John Y. Mason revised it. This revision was
delivered shortly after noon in person by the Secretary of War to the
President by whom it was again "carefully examined and revised."
The Cabinet met at 2 P.M., the text was submitted to it for approval. Secretary Buchanan "suggested and prepared a modification
of one of the paragraphs" after which the letter finally went on its
way.

The messenger from the War Department found Scott in a nearby
restaurant preparing to eat his supper. When the General's eye
reached the final paragraph of Marcy's letter a time-bomb went off:

. . . The President would be wanting in his duty to the country
if he were to persist in his determination of imposing upon you
the command of the army in the war against Mexico. He would

probably misunderstand the object you had in view in writing your letter, and disappoint your expectations, if he did not believe it was intended to effect a change of his purpose in this respect. I am therefore directed by him to say that you will be continued in your present position here, and will devote your efforts to making arrangements and preparations for the early and vigorous prosecution of hostilities against Mexico.

The rhetorical subtleties with which Scott's removal from the Mexican assignment were clothed could not hide the seething anger of the President. Marcy's much-worked prose had an immediate effect, and, as the waiter placed supper before him, the General pushed from the table and rushed back to his office to do, unhappily, what he was perversely equipped to do with a skill bordering on genius. Scott wrote another letter, a letter even more inept and ill-advised than the earlier one and which was, to quote a biographer, "destined to work greater devastation on his reputation."

Infelicitous was the beginning of Scott's reply to the Secretary of War: "Your letter of this date, received at about 6 P.M., as I sat down to take a hasty plate of soup, demands a prompt reply." That "hasty plate of soup" tickled the nation's funny bone and Scott was held up to laughter, if not ridicule, when, after rumors had circulated in the press, the exchange of letters was published. Newspaper gibes about "Marshal Tureen," did not soothe Scott's irritation, for he realized that irreparable damage had been done to his Presidential ambitions. Such, too, was the opinion of some of his friends. "I am apprehensive that General Scott has committed political suicide," wrote Anthony Butler to John J. Crittenden.

In the reply to Marcy, Scott piled indiscretion upon indiscretion, and sarcasm crept in at several places. He pointed out that he had used "high quarters" not "highest quarters," and disclaimed any intention of offending the President. He declared he had received "an intimation—not an order" that he would be commander of the army. He charged Marcy, despite "many personal courtesies," of allowing himself "to be influenced against me," and complained of "the want of that confidence and support necessary to my official position."

Although noting "the subdued tone" of Scott's second letter and "a high compliment" the General passed on him, Polk found nothing in Scott's answer to alter his decision to keep him in Washington instead of sending him to the Rio Grande to take command.

During the time of this bitter exchange of letters, word of Taylor's two victories on the Rio Grande reached Washington. Two days after press reports had arrived in the capital, there came Old Zach's official dispatches on May 25. On that day, "a number of leading Whigs . . . in a panic about the soup," called upon Scott "to inquire whether Taylor was a Whig or not, and whether he might not advantageously be Scott's substitute as their next Presidential candidate?" Scott, who related this in his *Autobiography*, professed that he was amused at the "cowardice and candor . . . of his backsliding Whig friends," and he described Taylor, "omitting (it is believed) any allusion to his lack of general information."

It isn't likely that Winfield Scott held forth on Zachary Taylor as he later did in his *Autobiography*, otherwise he would not have concluded at the end of the visit, that, then and there, Old Zach was "fixed as the next Whig candidate for the Presidency."

Taylor, Scott wrote in 1864, was "slow of thought, of hesitancy in speech, and unused to the pen," but he was endowed with "a good store of common sense." As his "mind had not been enlarged and enriched by reading," Taylor was "quite ignorant, for his rank, and quite bigoted in his ignorance." Scott thought that "few men have ever had a more comfortable, labor-saving contempt for learning of every kind," than Taylor. Yet Old Zach, Scott agreed, "had the true basis of a great character: pure, uncorrupted morals, combined with indomitable courage. Kindhearted, sincere, and hospitable in a plain way, he had no vice but prejudice . . ."

President Polk followed up the good news from the Rio Grande by sending the next day Taylor's name to the Senate for promotion to the rank of brevet major general, "for his gallant victories obtained over the Mexican forces . . ."

To General Scott's credit, he did not permit Polk's reprimand nor a change of heart by leading Whigs to distract him from fulfilling efficiently the duties of his office as commanding general of the army. And, obviously, the news of the outbreak of hostilities and Taylor's occupation of Matamoros multiplied the problems. Fourteen hours a day at his desk was not an unusual custom of General Scott.

From Matamoros, Taylor began to clamor for shallow-draft steamboats to navigate the Rio Grande and the demand for wagons for Taylor, and for the volunteer troops who were streaming into

New Orleans, became insistent. The volunteers themselves soon became an embarrassment, thanks to the unauthorized exuberance of General Edmund Pendleton Gaines.

After the Mexican attack on Thornton's patrol, General Taylor had called upon the governors of Louisiana and Texas for a total of 5,000 volunteers to serve for three months. General Gaines, without consulting the War Department or informing Taylor, had issued a call to the governors of the Mississippi Valley states for an unspecified number of troops, and thousands responded to this call for six months service. Later, after "Gaines's Army" had been sent home—few of the men volunteered for longer service—and Gaines had been found guilty by a court of inquiry of illegal and unauthorized action, Polk noted in his diary that Gaines's "conduct at New Orleans greatly embarrassed the government and will cost the Treasury many hundreds of thousands of dollars." Gaines was relieved of his command of the Western Division of the army, and, wrote Polk, "cannot repeat the mischief."

To procure the much-needed wagons, Quartermaster General Thomas S. Jesup dispatched officers all over the country, urging them to "do the best you can, and in the shortest possible time." Orders for thousands of wagons were placed in Cincinnati, Philadelphia, Pittsburgh, Troy, Buffalo, Columbus (Georgia), Savannah, and anywhere else that a wagon manufacturer was prepared to accept army contracts.

Jesup's agents also scoured the country for such military items as iron camp kettles and mess pans; horse and mule shoes with appropriate quantities of nails; horse and mule collars; mules and draft horses; harnesses and spare wagon parts; smith and wheelwright tools; oxen and ox wagons, with necessary chains, yokes, and bows; pack-saddles; pontoon equipment; scows and barges; and other necessary articles.

Down at Matamoros, Zachary Taylor, fretting because his swelling army was "paralyzed," thought and wrote unkind things about the Quartermaster Department and his old friend, Jesup, in Washington. But the truth of the matter, not apparent to Taylor because of the long communications lag, was that Commissary General Jesup and his officers were doing a fantastic job, considering that no war appropriations were made until May 13, 1846, four days after Taylor routed Arista at Resaca de la Palma.

12

"The Disgraceful Volunteers"

A single sentence, embodied in a letter to his son-in-law Dr. R. C. Wood, on May 19, the day after Matamoros was occupied, neatly summed up the twin problem Zachary Taylor would face during the summer of 1846: "I have much fear so many volunteers will come we will hardly find anything for them to do; the enemies principal posissions [sic] are so far off, with deserts intervening that it will be I fear impossible to reach them for want of transportations."

Volunteers and transportation—the presence of the first and the absence of the second—were Old Zach's headaches. As early as May 20, Taylor had disclaimed to the War Department any desire for more volunteers than the eight regiments he had called upon the governors of Louisiana and Texas to provide. "I well knew that if the Mexicans fought us at all, it would be before the arrival of the volunteers," wrote Taylor.

The first volunteers to reach Taylor were 700 Louisiana troops under General Persifor F. Smith. A civilian, the forty-eight-year-old Smith had fought in the Indian War in Florida, and his military ability was well known to Taylor. Old Zach expressed his pleasure at General Smith's arrival. "He will afford me efficient aid, should we have anything to do," he said.

During the next two weeks, the volunteers continued to arrive. By June 3, Taylor reported to the War Department, his entire force amounted to nearly 8,000 troops and more volunteers were on the way.

The problem of what to do with the three-months and six-months volunteers was a pressing one. Taylor reported on that date that some volunteers had expressed "alarm and dissatisfaction" because rumors from home stated that the units would be disbanded unless they volunteered for twelve months. Taylor extolled the "promptness and enthusiasm seldom exhibited in any country," with which these volunteers had rushed to arms. They were "willing and anxious" to complete their term, Taylor said, and he added his belief that if they were engaged in active operations against the enemy, a vast majority would gladly continue their service until the close of the campaign. Under date of August 3, the Secretary of War authorized Taylor to retain the six-month volunteers, but to discharge them "at or before the end" of the period for which they volunteered. Marcy agreed with Taylor's "expectation" that during a campaign, the six-month volunteers would reenlist.

Meanwhile the Secretary of War had written Taylor on June 8 that he, in his new grade of brevet major general, would conduct the ensuing campaign and that soon he would have 20,000 twelve-months volunteers, some of whom were allocated to an invasion of Chihuahua under General John E. Wool. "It is desirable," wrote Marcy, "that you should find yourself in sufficient strength to capture and hold Monterrey with your present force." The Secretary told Taylor that President Polk was eager for and hoped soon to receive the General's views and suggestions for the fall campaign. He posed several questions, the import of which were:

Should Taylor strike for Mexico City or confine his operations to the northern provinces of Mexico?

If the former, how would supplies be obtained?

Could they be drawn from the country or need they be sent from the United States?

If they were to be sent from the United States, what were the facilities and difficulties of transportation?

"These are very important questions, and the answers to them will have an essential bearing in settling the plan and objects of the campaign," wrote Marcy.

The Secretary concluded with a request for Taylor's opinion of the type of troops best suited to operate in the interior of Mexico and what proportion should be infantry, artillery, and cavalry. Then Marcy asked for yet one more opinion: "A peace must be conquered in the shortest space of time practicable. Your views of the manner of doing it are requested."

Marcy's letter crossed in the post a request Taylor had made to the War Department on May 21 for instructions. He stated then that his future movements would depend to a great degree upon the extent to which the Rio Grande proved navigable for steamboats. If a depot could be established at Camargo, and it could be supplied by the river, then operation against Monterrey were possible. "A direct movement from this point [Matamoros] to Monterrey would require vast transportation, chiefly by pack-mule and would, moreover, be hazardous in summer on account of the scarcity of water . . . ," Taylor reported.

Four days after Marcy's letter, General Scott wrote Taylor more specifically as to what troops to expect in the near future. He said that the twelve-months volunteers to be sent to the Rio Grande would total 16,280 and if Taylor "deemed an augmentation necessary" his request would be favorably considered. These with regulars to fill out the regiments already with Taylor, or soon to join him, would in a short time create a total force of 23,070 men. Scott told Taylor it was the President's wish "that, with your accustomed energy, you take up lines of march beyond the Rio Grande, and press your operations toward the heart of the enemy's country . . ."

On July 2, in a letter to the Adjutant General, Taylor replied to Marcy and Scott. He stressed how difficult it was to get exact intelligence on the interior of Mexico either because of "ignorance or interested motives" of those from whom information was sought. Taylor said that beef and occasional issues of mutton could be had off the country, but for bread, dependence would have to be upon the depot. He pointed out that from Camargo to Mexico City was little less than 1,000 miles, and the resources for subsistence never superabundant, were, for long distance actually deficient. "I consider it impracticable to keep open so long a line of communications," stated Taylor. "It is therefore my opinion that our operations from this frontier should not look to the city of Mexico, but should be confined to cutting off northern provinces—an undertaking of comparative facility and assurance of success."

Most of the new troops, barely arrived in camp, set about "playing the devil and disgracing the country," according to Captain Philip Barbour. Trigger-happy volunteers, with a total disregard for positive orders to the contrary, fired their arms at will in and about camp with an enthusiastic recklessness. "Bullets come whizzing by us as thick as in action," wrote Lieutenant George Meade, "and I really consider spending a day in my tent, uninjured, equivalent to passing through a well-contested action." By the time young Lieutenant George B. McClellan reached the Rio Grande several months later, the reputation of the volunteers for lawlessness had spread among the Mexicans. "The people are very polite to the regulars," wrote McClellan, ". . . but they hate the volunteers as they do old scratch himself . . . The volunteers carry on in a most shameful and disgraceful manner; they think nothing of robbing and killing Mexicans." Captain Henry noted in his journal that in "several disgraceful riots" in Matamoros, "volunteers were conspicuous." General Worth, who had rejoined Taylor late in May and had been given back his old command, had nothing but scorn for the volunteers. To him, they didn't even add up to 100 percent. "Every regiment of volunteers costs equal to three of regulars, plus loss of arms, accoutrements, and equipage," declared Worth. "Thirty-three percent are sick, and the remaining 66 not worth a straw."

Although the volunteers' conduct was a source of anxiety to Taylor, he didn't lose his patience. "I will try & get through in the best way I can & with at least all the good feelings & temper I can command even should they drive me out of my tent," said Old Zach.

With the multiple problems of command on his mind, Taylor had little time to think of his personal affairs beyond hoping for a speedy end to the war and his retirement to the peace and quiet of his plantation, near Baton Rouge, Louisiana. Old Zach had "a great horor [sic] of being made a lion of," but that did not deter enthusiasts from New Orleans. A delegation brought him the sash that General Braddock had given George Washington and with it a handsome presentation sword. Nor could the unassuming old man on the Rio Grande prevent citizens of Trenton, New Jersey, from drawing up on June 11 a resolution nominating "the hero of Palo Alto and Resaca de La Palma" for President of the United States, and calling "all true republicans" to disregard party lines and party questions to "elevate a brave soldier, a successful general, and a true republican to that high office." Nor was Taylor prepared for the prediction of Thurlow Weed, Whig leader and editor of the Albany *Journal,* that he would be elected to the Presidency in 1848.

To his brother, Lieutenant Colonel Joseph P. Taylor, who had conferred with Weed, Old Zach wrote:

Memoranda of the conversation you had with an Albany editor, and to which you request a reply, seems to me too visionary to require a serious answer. Such an idea never entered my head, nor is it likely to enter the head of any sane person. I shall be well satisfied to get creditably through this campaign. For your friend's confidence in me, however, you will make my acknowledgments.

To his son-in-law Dr. Wood, Taylor wrote on June 21 that Polk and Scott had no reasons to worry about his political ambitions. "They need have no apprehensions of being interfered with by me for that high office, which I would decline if proffered & I could reach it without opposition." One may accept Old Zach's disclaimers at this time at face value, but the idea was not an unattractive one. He did, indeed, have a "horor" of all the fanfare and adulation that Palo Alto and Resaca de La Palma had brought. Official honors began to pour in on him. Barely a month after he had been named a brevet major general, this rank as a line officer was conferred upon him. And on July 18, Congress bestowed its thanks upon Taylor "for the fortitude, skill, enterprise and courage which have distinguished the recent operations on the Rio Grande . . ." and medals were ordered struck in Old Rough and Ready's honor. He was annoyed by the artists who flocked to Matamoros to draw or paint his portraits and the writers who hurried to the Rio Grande to write glowing biographies.

Old Zach, under the pressure of his army's business, first grew to tolerate these annoyances and then to accept them patiently. The tiniest seed of ambition had been planted unsolicited in an untilled mind. Watered and nourished by time, more victories on the battlefield, and Taylor's growing conviction that "Scott, Marcy & Co. have been more anxious to break me down, than they have to break down . . . the Mexicans," the seed would one day break into bloom and mature.

With the coming of the rainy season along the Rio Grande in June, Taylor became impatient for the steamboats, which had been procured at New Orleans and other Gulf ports, to arrive. The river was at its best for navigation, and Old Rough and Ready was eager to push upstream to Camargo. Actually, early in June Taylor had sent his first troops marching up the river, a battalion of Lieutenant Colonel Wilson's First Infantry with Braxton Bragg's battery of artillery, to occupy Reynosa.

It wasn't until the first week in July that Taylor began the movement of his army to Camargo. Those troops that moved by steamboat had ample time to study the scenery as the heavily laden little vessels poked along at "a snail's gallop," seldom making more than two miles an hour due to their inherent lack of power, the strong current, and innumerable bends in the river, and the green mesquite, which was the only wood available to burn. Captain Philip Barbour's boat had to run into shore frequently and "stop long enough to get a sufficient head of steam on to make the slightest progress."

Those troops which, for lack of space aboard the steamboats, had to march the more than 100 miles to Camargo—by river it was about 400 miles—underwent terrific hardships from heat and thirst. "I am free to confess, had not my pride come to my rescue, I should have given out," recorded Captain William S. Henry. "The greatest cause of suffering was want of water. No men in the world drink more water than soldiers, and . . . in their improvidence, they soon exhaust their canteens, and then commences their suffering . . . The men actually dropped down from thirst; the ground was so hot it burned your feet, and the dense chaparral prevented our feeling the influence of the sea-breeze."

On August 4, General Taylor and his staff left Matamoros for Camargo and the campaign, almost three months after Palo Alto and Resaca de la Palma, was at last under way.

Camargo was a "dilapidated town," the 3,000 inhabitants of which had been routed out by a recent flood. The heat was stifling, sometimes registering up to 112 degrees, and a plague of insects added to the discomfort of the troops. Bad water brought on widespread dysentery and diarrhea, and death was often the companion of disease. "I never saw so sad a looking place," noted Captain Barbour. In expressing his horror, one of Taylor's generals called Camargo a "Yawning Grave Yard." An officer of the First Ohio Regiment, Major Luther Giddings, was appalled at the mortality among the unacclimated volunteers. "The dead march," he wrote, "was ever wailing in our ears."

To the minor discomforts of gnats, mosquitoes, and other flying annoyances there were added such ground-bound pests as scorpions, tarantulas, centipedes, and frogs. "Last night ants tried to carry me off in my sleep," wrote one trooper. Despite everything, Taylor made progress in reorganizing his army for the invasion of northern Mexico.

The First Division, commanded by David E. Twiggs, now a

brigadier general, was composed of Captain Charles May's four companies of the Second Dragoons; the batteries of Ridgely and Webster; the First, Third and Fourth Infantry Regiments, with Bragg's battery attached; and the Baltimore Battalion—an aggregate of 2,080 men.

General Worth commanded the Second Division which was made up of the batteries of Duncan and Taylor; the Fifth, Seventh, and Eighth Infantry Regiments; Blanchard's "Phoenix Company" of Louisiana volunteers; and two companies of Texas Rangers—a total of 1,780 troops.

Commanding the Third Division, made up of the pick of the volunteer regiments, was newly appointed Major General W. O. Butler, who had fought as a young officer under Andrew Jackson against the British at New Orleans. Butler's division was comprised of the First Ohio, First Kentucky, First Tennessee; a Texas regiment; and a Mississippi regiment, commanded by Zachary Taylor's one-time son-in-law, Colonel Jefferson Davis.

One West Point graduate, on the eve of the army's march to Monterrey, suddenly found himself without a command. Colonel Albert Sidney Johnston was chagrined when his Texas troops decided to take their discharge. In vain did he plead with them to stay. A delegation of the Texans went to Taylor's tent, before which Old Zach was shaving. Sensing what was on their minds, Taylor beat the Texans to the draw: "I suppose you want to go home. Well, I don't want anybody about me who don't want to stay. I wouldn't give one willing man for a dozen that wanted to go home."

On August 17, Taylor had a grand review of the regulars, which Captain Henry considered "one of the most magnificent military displays we have had since the last war." On August 20, General Worth took up the route to Monterrey.

Four days earlier, at Vera Cruz, Antonio López de Santa Anna, "the enigma that was Mexico," returned from exile.

13

"Napoleon of the West"

In a village on the outskirts of Havana, the self-styled "Napoleon of the West," Antonio López de Santa Anna, devoted himself to his child-bride, groomed his fighting cocks, frequently played cards for heavy stakes, and dreamed of returning to power in Mexico.

Living quietly in exile in Cuba at the invitation of Don Leopoldo O'Donell, Captain General of the Island, how could Santa Anna fulfill his destiny? "Providence wished that my history be the history of Mexico since 1821," he once said. But in the fall of 1845, history was passing him by, and Santa Anna schemed and plotted to return to its mainstream in his native land.

A distinguished Mexican historian, Lucas Alamán, has characterized Santa Anna brilliantly:

> A combination of good and bad qualities; with very real natural ability but without either moral or intellectual training; a spirit with initiative, but without a fixed purpose or definite objective; with both energy and a disposition to rule but handicapped by grave defects; skillful in making general plans for a revolution or a campaign, but most unfortunate in directing a single battle . . .

Although a number of biographies of Santa Anna have appeared in English, there is little about him that the average American knows beyond his extermination of the gallant defenders of the Alamo and his defeat and capture in the Battle of San Jacinto when Texas won its independence in 1836.

A contemporary pamphleteer's hostile biography of Santa Anna painted him as an arch traitor, a specialist in betrayal:

> . . . first he had been a traitor to Spain; second, a traitor to

Iturbide; third, a traitor to the triumvirate; fourth, a traitor to the federation in 1828; fifth, a traitor to the legitimate government in 1832; sixth, a traitor to the federal system in 1835; seventh, a traitor in 1842 to the second constitution, and finally a traitor to Congress and the constitution in 1844.

On December 17, 1844, the Chamber of Deputies deposed Santa Anna and out of the revolution against the dictator emerged José Joaquín Herrera as President of Mexico. Santa Anna, still at the head of an army of about 8,000, made a show of resistance, but his support evaporated as city after city pronounced against him and for Herrera.

Finally, Santa Anna gave up the game, tried to escape, was arrested, imprisoned, and then exiled. Before he sailed with his family from Vera Cruz for Cuba, on June 3, 1845, Santa Anna, master of the extravagant phrase, the high-sounding proclamation, addressed himself to the Mexican people, who had but recently torn down his statues, spat upon his pictures, and exhumed his amputated leg and dragged it through the streets. Calling upon his countrymen to examine his political behavior, he declared: "When I had all power, I did not raise scaffolds for political offenses; I banished no citizens to foreign lands, to eat bitter bread and to weep in exile. No one was despoiled of his property nor oppressed by arbitrary imprisonment. Generosity and clemency were my program."

Then the departing dictator paved the way for some future emotional revolution among his countrymen that would cause him to be summoned back to lead a real revolution:

> Mexicans! in my old age and mutilated, surrounded by a wife and innocent children, I am going into exile to seek a resting place among strangers. Mercifully forgive the mistakes I made unintentionally; and believe me, in God's name, that I have labored sincerely that you should be independent, free and happy. If I have not succeeded in fulfilling your desires blame only my lack of ability . . .

Santa Anna settled in a village called the Cerro, about three miles from Havana. Lieutenant Raphael Semmes of the United States Navy, who visited the Cerro, said the ex-President of Mexico was "celebrated for heavy games of *monte,* which he played,

and for the excellent rules and arrangement of his cock-pit . . .
the excellence of the . . . cocks, and . . . the skillful manner in
which he heeled and handled them."

A regular visitor to Santa Anna was the American Consul at
Havana, General R. B. Campbell, but the language barrier between them made an exchange of ideas somewhat difficult. Yet
Lieutenant Semmes, who wrote within five years of the event,
states that Santa Anna expressed himself as opposed to war between the United States and Mexico. "He seemed desirous," wrote
Semmes, "to impress General Campbell with the belief that, if he
were again at the head of affairs, he would speedily reestablish
friendly relations between the two countries."

Another visitor to the exiled ex-president was Colonel A. J.
Atocha, by birth a Spaniard and by naturalization an American
citizen. He had been engaged in the banking business in Mexico
and when Santa Anna was exiled, Atocha had been expelled for
alleged connections with the dictator. Early in 1846, Atocha appeared in Washington and on February 13 he was received by
President Polk. It was not their first meeting, for in June Atocha
had called at the White House concerning claims he had against
the Mexican Government. This time his mission was more important, more confidential. Atocha told the President that he had
recently visited Santa Anna in Havana, where, despite his exile the
ex-President "was in constant communication with his friends in
Mexico, and received by every vessel that left Vera Cruz hundreds
of letters."

Polk listened with great interest as his visitor hinted that Santa
Anna supported the Paredes revolution against Herrera and that
Santa Anna might soon return to power in Mexico. Then Atocha
got down to specifics, as President Polk recorded in his diary: "He
said that Santa Anna was in favor of a treaty with the United
States, and that in adjusting a boundary line between the two
countries the Del Norte [Rio Grande] should be the western
Texas line, and the Colorado of the West down through the Bay
of San Francisco to the sea should be the line on the north, and
that Mexico should cede all east and north of these natural boundaries to the United States for a pecuniary consideration and men-
tioned thirty millions of dollars as the sum."

Atocha told Polk that Santa Anna felt that such an amount
would place the government on a stable basis, support the army
until the country's finances improved, and meet Mexico's most

pressing debts. Polk's visitor then expressed Santa Anna's surprise that the United States had lifted its naval blockade of Vera Cruz, and that General Taylor remained at Corpus Christi instead of moving to the Rio Grande. He led Polk to believe that it was Santa Anna's opinion "that the United States would never be able to treat with Mexico, without the presence of an imposing force by land and sea." Polk recorded that in this opinion Atocha concurred. "Col. Atocha did not say that he was sent by Santa Anna to hold this conversation with me," Polk wrote, "but I think it probable he was so . . ."

Three days later, on February 16, Colonel Atocha returned to the White House, and he and Polk conversed again for more than an hour. After general conversation on conditions in Mexico and American relations with that country, Atocha repeated his "proposition" of the previous visit. Polk commented that Mexico must satisfy American claims against it, and he said "that if the government of Mexico had any proposition to make, such as was suggested, it would be considered when made."

Colonel Atocha pointed out to the President that "no government or administration in Mexico dared to make such a proposition, for if they did so there would be another revolution by which they would be overthrown. He said they must appear to be forced to agree to such a proposition." Speaking for Santa Anna, and himself, too, Atocha recommended that Taylor march at once to the Rio Grande, that a strong naval force gather off Vera Cruz, and that the United States should demand payment for the claims of its citizens. Atocha stressed that since Mexico had no money to meet the claims, it would, under threat of attack, agree to the boundaries suggested.

Santa Anna's last words, when he left him, Atocha declared, were: "When you see the President, tell him to take measures, and such a treaty can be made and I will sustain it."

Polk was not impressed with his visitor. To his diary, the President confided: "Col. Atocha is a person to whom I would not give my confidence . . ." Accordingly, the President heard him out but "communicated nothing to him."

But Santa Anna's scheme—for Polk was satisfied that the Mexican ex-President had sent Atocha to him—intrigued the President and he was not unwilling to connive with the "Napoleon of the West" to establish the boundaries he desired. Accordingly, Polk sent Commander Alexander Slidell Mackenzie, USN,—he was a brother of John Slidell, but had taken an uncle's name for his own—to Cuba to negotiate with Santa Anna. The President gave Mackenzie verbal instruction, which the latter, without authority, committed to paper and presented to Santa Anna, during a three-hour conference on July 7, 1846. This purported message from the President of the United States to the ex-President of Mexico stated that Polk would be pleased to see him return to power and had already given instructions to the blockading force off Mexican ports "to allow General Santa Anna freely to return to his country." (On May 13, Secretary of the Navy George Bancroft had addressed Commodore David Conner: "Commodore: If Santa Anna endeavors to enter the Mexican ports, you will allow him to pass freely.")

As to negotiations with Santa Anna, Polk's "note" indicated the United States' willingness to make "an ample consideration in ready money" for territory ceded to it. Mackenzie reported Santa Anna's favorable response and quoted him to the effect that if the United States would "promote his patriotic desires, he offers to respond with such a peace as has been described." Santa Anna then gave Mackenzie advice on how increased United States military and naval pressure would serve to make easier the negotiation of a treaty.

Mackenzie reported at length on his interviews with Santa Anna, attempted to evaluate the General's motives, and expressed a belief in "the entire sincerity of his views." He urged that articles be published in the American press playing up Santa Anna's administrative skill, his understanding of his country's needs, and his devotion to its best interests.

Meanwhile Santa Anna had been mending his political fences in Mexico from long range. He convinced the liberal leader, Gómez Farías, that if he returned to power he would establish federalism in the republic. On July 31, as Zachary Taylor gathered his army at Camargo for the march on Monterrey, the revolution that unseated General Paredes broke out. General José Mariano Salas assumed the Presidency, but it was generally understood that he was merely a stand-in for Santa Anna.

On August 16, the British ship *Arab* steamed into Vera Cruz, unchallenged by Commodore Conner's blockading warships—Conner had been informed who was aboard the vessel—and General Antonio López de Santa Anna, with his seventeen-year-old wife and other members of his family and his staff, stepped ashore. That very day, Commodore Conner reported the arrival to Washington:

> I have allowed him to enter without molestation . . . I
> could have easily boarded the *Arab,* but I deemed it most
> proper not to do so, allowing it to appear as if he had entered
> without my concurrence.
>   It is now quite certain the whole country—that is, the gar-
> risons of every town and fortress—have declared in his favor.

Vera Cruz's reception was not an enthusiastic one. An eyewitness said, "a most discordant band screamed national airs" while
small boys set off firecrackers. Between two files of troops, the
party moved and Santa Anna's child-wife "pouted at the cool reception, for not one 'viva' was heard." As for the General in full
dress, he "looked anything but pleased" at the perfunctory greet-
ing. But Santa Anna doubtless brushed aside this indifferent welcome. "A superb egotist," wrote one of his biographers, "[Santa
Anna] was so confident of his own ability that he was thoroughly
convinced his nation's best interests demanded that he dictate
its policies."

Immediately upon landing, Santa Anna issued a long proclamation. He had returned to Mexico, he asserted, for the sole object
of "saving our country from its enemies, internal and external."
Then followed more than 4,000 words of justification of his past
actions, and future promises. He concluded with heroics:

> Mexicans! There was once a day, and my heart dilates with
> the remembrance, when leading on the popular masses and
> the army, to demand the rights of the nation, you saluted me
> with the enviable title of soldier of the people. Allow me again
> to take it, never more to be given up, and to devote myself,
> until death, to the defense of the liberty and independence
> of the republic.

President Polk's intrigue with Santa Anna soon became public
property as the nation's press discussed Mackenzie's visit to Cuba,
some unfavorably. In England, the press generally concluded that
Washington and Santa Anna had come to an agreement, that the
dictator's return was "connived at" by "American intrigue." The
Manchester *Guardian* summed up British press sentiment on Santa
Anna's return:

The probability seems to be, that there is an understanding between him and the American government; and we should not be surprised to hear that he has been furnished from Washington with the funds which have doubtless been used to corrupt the Mexican troops. In that case, most probably, the price of his restoration to power will be a treaty of peace, advantageous to the United States . . .

The people of Mexico, somehow, seemed to suspect that Santa Anna's return meant a sellout to the United States. The British Minister Bankhead believed "some secret agreement" had been made and he reported to the Foreign Office Santa Anna's return was "most unpopular in the Country." Noting the lack of enthusiasm and even strong dislike, Bankhead said: "Each party suspects him of Treachery . . ."

On August 8, the day Santa Anna sailed from Havana for Vera Cruz, President Polk sent a message to both Houses of Congress asking for $2,000,000 "to facilitate negotiations with Mexico." It was to the bill appropriating this money in the House that David Wilmot of Pennsylvania tacked on the amendment, known thereafter as the Wilmot Proviso, prohibiting slavery in any lands acquired from Mexico. Although it never passed in the Senate this became one of the wedges of separation, driven between the two sections of the nation, which set the stage for the Civil War a decade and a half later.

Santa Anna reached Mexico City in mid-September as Zachary Taylor approached Monterrey. Less than two weeks later, the "Napoleon of the West" was off to San Luis Potosí to raise and train an army to oppose Taylor in the north.

What had happened to Santa Anna's proposal of a treaty with the United States? Had he ever entertained, seriously, such an idea, or had he only pretended so to dupe President Polk to abet his return to Mexican soil?

One of Santa Anna's biographers, Wilfred H. Callcott, provides the answer:

Whatever may have been the intentions of Santa Anna when he landed at Vera Cruz, he soon realized that the temper of the Mexican people demanded war with the United States, and that to open immediate negotiations would be to throw away all support.

14

The Road to Monterrey

As Zachary Taylor's little army moved along toward Monterrey, the pens of the chroniclers among his officers grew rhapsodic.

Captain Philip Barbour—no, Brevet Major Barbour, for his promotion arrived on the march—thought the army's route from Cerralvo traversed "the most lovely country on earth" and although he confessed that a "description of the scenery . . . is beyond my powers," he felt that "it exceeds in picturesque beauty my most romantic dreams of nature's loveliest and grandest charms." Captain William S. Henry, captivated by the "mountain scenery never surpassed in beauty" attempted to describe the kaleidoscopic effects wrought by every change of light and exclaimed: "Nothing like this, in grandeur or loveliness, have I ever seen!" Although Lieutenant George Meade's letters to his wife mainly described his activities in the pioneer company that preceded the head of the column, he saved one paragraph for the beauty of the country: ". . . It is magnificent, the air balmy and pure, all the tropical fruits growing . . . the mountains twenty-five miles away, but so high we can see them towering away above the clouds, a most magnificent sight."

Major Luther Giddings of the First Ohio Regiment was yet another whose ecstatic pen welcomed the mountains, first seen "floating like clouds in the distance," and which, as the army drew closer, "reared their bold and rugged peaks far into the sky." It is no wonder that Major Giddings lost his baggage on the march, for he could not keep his eye on so prosaic a necessity when it was filled with the grandeur of the mountain scenery "either when night melts into morn, and the growing light disrobes it of [its] cloudy garment . . . when glowing at midday in the soft light of serenest skies; when twilight lingers o'er its craggy sides . . . or when the silvery moon, at evening bright, walks o'er its dewy crest."

Even Old Zach, not given to poetic flights on the beauties of nature, took note of the inspiring vistas on the march: "The country we are now in . . . is decidedly of more interest than any we have heretofore passed over," he wrote his son-in-law. "We are now in sight of high mountains, amidst large brooks of clear cool water running in torrents from them, as well as among springs of running water as pure as it can well be . . ." That the bracing air, the pure drinking water, and the exciting scenery—a relief from the heat, dust, and dullness of Camargo—had a salutary effect on the army there can be no doubt. Taylor so reported to Washington on September 12: "The health of the army is much improved since approaching the mountains, and it is generally in excellent condition for service."

At Marín, within twenty-five miles of Monterrey—"one day's forced march, and two easy ones," said Lieutenant Meade—Taylor concentrated his three divisions for the final stage of the march. Here, too, Taylor was joined by two regiments of Texas mounted troops under Major General James Pinkney Henderson, first governor of the state of Texas. Henderson's arrival added about 1,100 men to Taylor's force. "They are a fine body of men," noted Captain Henry.

Speculation was general as to whether there would be a fight at Monterrey. Lieutenant Meade after hearing "a thousand contradictory stories," made up his mind the Mexicans would not fight. Taylor himself had doubts. "Whether the enemy will fight for Monterrey is quite uncertain, it can only be ascertained by going there," Old Zach wrote. "My impressions are we shall meet with no resistance out of the city, they may attempt to defend it, which I hope will be the case . . ."

Taylor was right, the Mexicans offered no resistance outside Monterrey, although the advance had brief brushes with Mexican patrols, and for some days a mounted force had observed the army's march from a safe distance. However, when Taylor reached Monterrey, he soon found out what General Ampudia's intentions were.

About 9 o'clock on the morning of September 19, General Taylor, riding with the advance, edged to within a mile of the Ciudadela or Citadel of Monterrey—to the Americans it was known as the Black Fort—while some eager troopers, pushing even father ahead, exchanged a few shots with a force of Mexican cavalry on the outskirts of the town.

"The mists still clung around the turrets of its churches, and enveloped its commanding heights," wrote Thomas Bangs Thorpe of the New Orleans *Tropic.* "But the . . . sun . . . dissipated the veil until palace and hill, barricade and fort, with long lines of tents and pendent flags, presented themselves."

General Taylor and his staff gazed at the now distinct outlines of the city against the mountain background. "Suddenly," wrote Thorpe, "a hot sulphurous smoke rose quickly from one of the bastions . . ." Lieutenant Meade, who was with Taylor, had a first-hand view of the Mexican battery's fire. "One ball, I assure you," Meade told his wife, "came closer to me than I desire it to do again, just passing about two feet on one side of my knee." Major Barbour, who rode up as Taylor and his party were withdrawing out of range, got the details: "The first shot passed within 10 feet of the General and subsequently two balls passed through both the Texas regiments without touching a hair of man or horse."

Taylor picked an ideal place for his camp, about three miles from Monterrey in a lovely grove of pecan and oak trees in which there were many springs of cold, clear, pure water. The grove, the actual name of which was El Bosque de San Domingo, was called variously (and erroneously) by the Americans Walnut Grove and Walnut Springs. Captain Henry thought "a more charming spot for a picnic could not possibly be desired." But in addition to its comforts, the grove could be readily defended.

Monterrey, situated on the left bank of the San Juan River (the stream was also known as the Santa Catarina), ran generally east and west. Its defense to the north, outside the city and nearest to Taylor's main avenue of approach, was the Black Fort, a formidable stone mass, holding 400 defenders and mounting a dozen guns, some of them eighteen-pounders. On the eastern end of the city, just outside its north-eastern corner was a redoubt with four guns. Because this work stood in front of a tannery, it was known as Fort Tenería. The stone tannery itself was fortified, the parapet of its flat roof having been reinforced with sandbags, and it was strongly garrisoned. Several hundred yards—Lieutenant Sam French said "about two hundred yards"—south of La Tenería was an earthwork known as El Diablo, the Devil. Other smaller works were nearby and a very strong bridgehead, La Presa, guarded the Purísima Bridge over the Ojo de Agua Canal on the edge of the city. The Cathedral, fronting on the Grand Plaza, had been turned into an arsenal.

On the west, Monterrey's defenses were two heavily fortified hills, one on each side of the river. The Loma de Independencia, north of the stream, was between 700 and 800 feet high and very precipitous on its western slope. On the western crest of Independencia stood a sandbag redoubt, facing the Sierra Madre Mountains and down the slope, at the eastern end of the hill, overlooking the city, was the Obispado, or Bishop's Palace, which was a formidable fortress, albeit in a partially ruined state. Across the San Juan River from Independencia was the Loma de Federación or Federation Hill, about 500 feet high, and equally as steep as Independencia. On Federación were two works, a single-gun redoubt at the western end and the more formidable Fort Soldado at the eastern end.

At the base of Independencia, and between it and the river, ran the road from Monterrey to Saltillo. Within Monterrey, the parapeted, flat-roofed houses, with loopholes for small-arms fire, and the easily barricaded narrow streets completed the impressive position which Ampudia and his approximately 10,000 troops defended.

Taylor immediately sent out reconnaissance parties under Major Joseph K. F. Mansfield to study the Mexican defenses. Lieutenant Meade, who was on the mission, reported it "sufficiently hazardous." Sharp volleys of grapeshot were delivered upon Mansfield's group when it penetrated to within 500 yards of Independencia, but no damage was inflicted upon the scouting parties. Mansfield reported to Taylor late the night of the 19th that although the position on Independencia was strong, he felt it could be carried.

From the reconnaissance reports, it was evident to Taylor and most of his officers that the army had not the artillery with which to invest and bombard Monterrey, and that an assault on the town was necessary. "The city *has to be carried*," declared Major Barbour, "and as there are no guns in our train of sufficient caliber to batter, the bayonet will probably have to do the work. It is a perilous undertaking and we must anticipate immense slaughter, but . . . the General is in high spirits . . . and has unshaken confidence in the little army."

Taylor's plan of attack evolved from Mansfield's report. The weakest link in Ampudia's defensive chain was at the western end of the city. There, Taylor decided, he would make his major effort. To General Worth, with a force of nearly 2,000, he assigned the task of cutting the Saltillo road to sever Ampudia's communications and "if practicable," to carry the Mexican positions on the two hills, Independencia and Federación. With the rest of the army, Taylor would create diversions at the eastern end of the city.

Apparently, Taylor had had a change of heart concerning Worth. In June, after Worth's return to the army, Old Zach had written his son-in-law: ". . . He has been pampered and bloated for things he never done, or acts he never performed, but from assumption, & getting others to state occurences the truth of which may be very well called in question, if stronger language could not be properly applied, and his flourish among the wounded was in keeping with many other of his acts, all for effect."

Taylor, when he wrote this, was undoubtedly still irked by Worth's departure in a huff in the face of a potential enemy. But nearly two months later, after the promotion to brigadier general of Twiggs and Stephen Watts Kearny, Taylor softened considerably. "I can truly say since the promotions of T. & K. I feel very much for Worth; he looks completely broken down," he wrote his son-in-law.

Moreover, Taylor probably recognized that for all Worth's vanity, wounded pride, and an occasional tendency to drink, he was a man who would fight, and Old Zach had an instinctive fondness for fighters.

At 2 P.M. on September 20, Worth began his wide detour to the right, moving through fields of corn, sugar cane, and peas. His command consisted of his First Division of Regulars, Captain A. G. Blanchard's Phoenix Company of Louisiana Volunteers, and Colonel Jack Hays' mounted regiment of Texans, units of which were commanded by Captain Ben McCulloch and Captain Acklen. George Wilkins Kendall of the New Orleans *Picayune*, the first modern war correspondent, who rode with General Worth and served as an aide, said the troops carried "scanty provisions in their haversacks for four days."

The terrain was difficult and progress was slow, primarily because the engineers, operating ahead of the column, had to prepare a way for the movement of the artillery. But, although the march of his column "early attracted the attention of the enemy," Worth's advance of six miles was unopposed. About 6 P.M. Worth pitched his camp near the Saltillo road, just out of range of the battery on the western crest of Independencia. Accompanied by his staff and Lieutenant Meade, General Worth personally reconnoitered the ground.

"Our advance was covered by about fifty Texans," Meade wrote his wife, "and we proceeded along the road for two miles, till we came into the gorge through which the Saltillo road runs, where the enemy were reported in large force on our front. Having seen all we wanted, we were about retiring, when they opened fire upon us from a fence alongside the road . . . but it was promptly returned by the Texans, and we came quickly back to camp."

A misty rain that had set in as the troops went into camp grew into a storm, and Worth in a progress report to Taylor, written at 9:30 p.m., said that he "had infinite difficulty in getting the troops into a tolerably defensive position for the night."

Worth's estimate of the situation, made in this same hurried note, confirmed the reconnaissance reports: ". . . To the Saltillo road . . . it is manifest their attention is intensely directed . . . I am strongly persuaded this is regarded as their weak point."

15

"The Town is Ours"

William Jenkins Worth was determined that Monterrey would provide him a "grade or grave." During a miserable night in the open, with his men sleeping on their arms, without benefit of camp-fires, General Worth made his plans for the next day. His first objective was to secure the Saltillo road to cut off reinforcements and supplies from Ampudia.

Early on September 21, the marching order was given, and Hays's mounted Texans, acompanied by skirmishers under Charles F. Smith, moved out in the advance. As they marched, both groups spread or contracted as the valley widened or narrowed. Suddenly, as the head of the march turned a blind bend in the road, they came upon the enemy, a strong force of Lancers, supported by infantry, with another mounted force in reserve. Their green and red pennons, seen above the corn, "gave them a daring and dashing appearance," wrote George Wilkins Kendall.

Immediately the Lancers charged—"most gallantly," noted Lieutenant Meade—into a withering musket-fire from Smith's skirmishers and some of the Texans, who had dismounted and had taken cover behind a fence to the left of the road. There was a furious mêlée for a few brief moments among the opposing horsemen, but Worth hurried forward two companies of the Eighth Infantry and Captain Sam Walker's Texas Rangers, who engaged the Mexicans in bitter hand-to-hand fighting.

The reserve Lancers rushed forward to support their embattled comrades. The batteries of Duncan and Mackall, always close up, now unlimbered and delivered a deadly fire over the heads of the American troops into the galloping Mexicans. As the Lancers moved toward the fight, the muskets of Smith and the Texans blazed away on their flank and rear. Under fire on three sides, the Mexican situation now became unendurable. "They were received with so warm a fire as to throw them into confusion," noted Lieutenant Meade. "The Lancers," wrote George Wilkins Kendall, "tumbled from their saddles by the dozens." (Kendall later recalled this charge as "one of the most brilliant made by the Mexicans during the war.")

The enemy, Worth later reported, "retired in disorder . . . upon the Saltillo road, and was closely pursued, until we got possession of the gorge, where all the *debouches* from Monterrey unite, whereby the force just defeated, as also reinforcements and supplies from that direction, were excluded from city."

The beaten Mexicans, leaving 100 dead and wounded on the field, among them the gallant leader of the charge, Lieutenant Colonel Juan Nájera, dispersed. The infantry and some of the cavalry retired into Monterrey, while, according to Lieutenant Meade, "twelve hundred of the cavalry went in the direction of Saltillo, and have not been heard from since."

Worth scribbled a brief note at 8:15 A.M. and dispatched it to Major Bliss:

Be pleased to inform the Commanding General that I have met the enemy in force, and defeated him with considerable loss. The resisting force has retired on the hill, near the Bishop's palace & the town. Their positions are completely severed, and I occupy a strong point on the Saltillo road, my right resting in the direction of the San Juan. With the main force here, the town is ours. My loss is small.

Worth did not permit his men to rest on their laurels, but he set out at once to make his premature, but prophetic, claim a reality. First, however, to get his men from under the plunging fire directed upon them from Federación, he pushed down the Saltillo road about half a mile. Then the General prepared to storm Federación, and seize the two forts on its summit.

By noon, the storming party of about 300 men, composed half of regulars and and half of Texans, under the command of Captain Charles F. Smith, was ready. General Worth, riding along the line, addressed the the troops: "Men, you are to take that hill—and I know you will do it." "We will," they shouted, and moved out. The entire division, wrote Kendall, watched "the movements of the little band . . . with breathless anxiety." Smith passed unob-

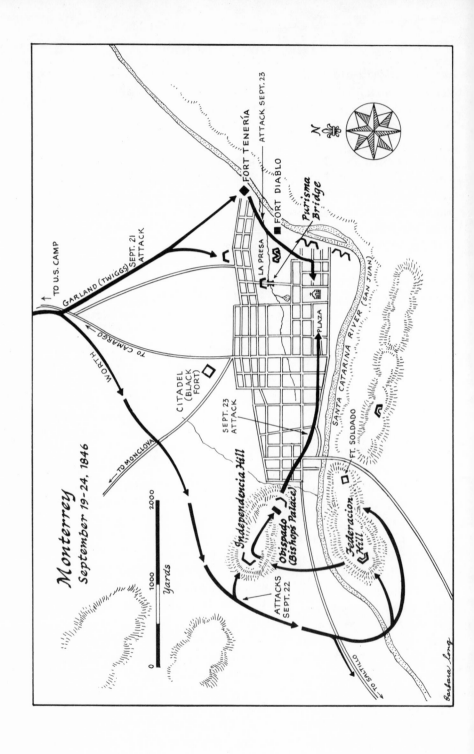

Monterrey
September 19–24, 1846

Yards
0   1000   2000

TO U.S. CAMP

GARLAND (TWIGGS) SEPT. 21 ATTACK

WORTH

TO CAMARGO

TO MONCLOVA

CITADEL (BLACK FORT)

FORT TENERÍA

ATTACK SEPT. 23

FORT DIABLO

Purísma Bridge

LA PRESA

PLAZA

SEPT. 23 ATTACK

SANTA CATARINA RIVER (SAN JUAN)

FT. SOLDADO

Independencia Hill

Obispado (Bishops Palace)

ATTACKS SEPT. 22

Federación Hill

TO SALTILLO

Barbara Long

served through a dense cornfield toward the San Juan, but when the command reached the river, it was greeted by a shower of grape and canister from the batteries on the crest, where troops could also be seen massing.

Smith's men plunged into the ford in waist-deep water under the heavy attack, but in less than five minutes they reached the safety of the chaparral at the base of Federación, unscathed by the rain of balls. Worth immediately detached Captain D. S. Miles's company from the Seventh Infantry and sent him forward to support the first party.

Captain Miles found an easier crossing of the San Juan, downstream from where Smith crossed, and he pressed on toward the base of Federación. The Mexican batteries could not depress their guns to harass the Americans effectively, but swarms of sharpshooters quickly scattered among the undergrowth along the rocky hillside and poured a constant fire into Smith's and Miles's men, who determinedly commenced the difficult ascent.

Worth now called upon General Persifor F. Smith to lead the Fifth Infantry, under Major Martin Scott, and Blanchard's company of Louisiana Volunteers into action, and to assume command of the entire operation when he reached the battle area. General Smith forded the San Juan in front of Worth's position and struck off for the hill in the face of galling fire.

Meanwhile, the first two attacking groups had held their fire as they doggedly climbed in a rain of bullets the steep and ragged cliff. They advanced slowly to the crest by holding on to jagged projections, cracks in the rock, and the thick growth along the hillside. With an exultant shout, C. F. Smith's men scrambled over the top, swarmed into the Federación battery and routed its gunners. As the Mexicans fled, their own guns were turned upon them. When the American flag was run up, the roar from the troops in the valley soared upward to the weary but still eager victors.

General Smith, noting the progress of the others, moved obliquely up Federación in the direction of El Soldado. He was determined that both Mexican works should be carried simultaneously. Eagerly his men pressed up the cliff—so steep, noted Kendall, that the last twenty yards were "almost perpendicular"—and with wild cry, they burst upon the summit, to be greeted by a terrific grape and small-arms fire. Shouting at the top of his voice, General Smith ordered: "Take that other fort!" His troops rushed forward as the Mexicans, abandoning Soldado, fled down the northern slopes toward Independencia.

At twenty minutes to four in the afternoon, Worth jotted a note to Taylor: ". . . I have the satisfaction to report that both heights are in our possession . . . by daylight tomorrow morning I expect to be in possession of the works in rear of the Palace."

This was cheerful news for General Taylor, for on the eastern edge of Monterrey his own force had been pretty well mauled in what had been planned as a diversion but which developed into a full-scale attack. In the midmorning Taylor gave Lieutenant Colonel John Garland orders to move forward. "Colonel, lead the head of your column off to the left, keeping well out of reach of the enemy's Shot," ordered Old Zach, "and if you think . . . you can take any of them little Forts down there with the bay'net you better do it—but consult with Major Mansfield, you'll find him down there."

Mansfield, from early morning, had been "down there" reconnoitering the Mexican installations. When Taylor received word from him that it was propitious to move, he ordered Garland forward with Twiggs's division, minus the Fourth Infantry which was left to guard a battery established in a depression in front of the Black Fort. Twiggs remained in camp, indisposed (he had taken medicine, following his established custom before battle, to clear his bowels).

There was more eagerness than judgment in Garland's advance, for the line of march brought the troops under the direct fire of the Black Fort and their right flank and rear were raked by its guns. At the same time, the guns of Fort Tenería opened up frontally on Garland, and when he swung to the right, his left flank came under Tenería direct fire, too. Captain Henry, who was in the charge, described what happened:

> For five hundred yards we advanced across a plain under fire of the two batteries. We rushed into the streets. Unfortunately, we did not turn soon enough to the left, and had advanced but a short distance when we came suddenly upon an unknown battery, which opened its deadly fire upon us. From all its embrasures, from every house, from every yard, showers of balls were hurled at us. Being in utter ignorance of our locality, we had to stand and take it: our men, covering them-

selves as well as they could, dealt death and destruction on every side; there was no resisting the deadly, concealed fire, which appeared to come from every direction . . . We retired into the next street, under cover of some walls and houses.

The first officer to fall was Major Philip Barbour, who died, a ball piercing his heart, as he rallied his men. (The night before, in his journal, Major Barbour had written: "I feel as calm and collected as if I were in the Astor House, having long since made up my mind that, during a time of war, my life is the rightful property of my country, and cannot be taken from me, or preserved, except by the fiat of the great God who gave it. And to His will, whatever it be, I am perfectly resigned.")

Under terrific fire were the Baltimore-Washington Volunteers, whose gallant commander, Lieutenant Colonel William H. Watson, brushed aside any suggestion of retreat. "Never, boys! Never will I yield an inch!" he cried. "I have too much Irish blood in me to give up." A moment later, a Mexican bullet snuffed out his valor. By now, Captain Braxton Bragg's battery had penetrated into the town, but there was little it could do. Lieutenant Sam French said that the Mexican shot and shells exploding about them and passing through adobe buildings covered "the men, horses and guns with lime and dust, blinding us so that we could see nothing."

Bragg's battery was ordered out of the fight to return to camp. In the withdrawal, a shot killed two wheel horses to one of the caissons, and French and Lieutenant John Reynolds joined the men in pushing the horses and harnesses into the ditches on either side of the road. Another shot passed through two horses of one of the guns. When the battery cleared the town, Captain Bragg ordered Lieutenant French to return to the ditches and salvage the harnesses on the dead horses. On the way, French met General Taylor.

"Where are you going?" demanded Old Zach.

French told him his mission.

"That is nonsense," exclaimed Taylor, and he ordered French to rejoin the battery in camp.

Orders came, at last, for the infantry to retire, but they didn't reach a handful of troops under a captain of the First Infantry with the unlikely name of Electus Backus. Fortunately, Captain Backus and his men had turned left, instead of right, on entering the town

and they had worked their way into a building in the rear of Fort
Tenería. From the flat roof of a shed, which had a two-foot parapet,
Captain Backus's fifty men poured damaging musket fire into the
Mexican batteries.

It was not for long that Electus Backus and his men fought alone,
for the Fourth Infantry, relieved of its support of the ineffectual
battery, launched the next attack. But, like the first, it was repulsed
with considerable loss. About the same time, the Ohio Regiment
attacked to the west, near the Purísima Bridge strongpoint, and it,
too, was badly cut up. "We moved rapidly through a labyrinth of
lanes and gardens, without knowing or seeing upon what point of
the enemy's line we were about to strike," wrote Major Luther
Giddings. "At every step the discharges from the batteries in front
became more deadly, while we had no opportunity for burning a
cartridge." From this helpless condition, the Ohio Regiment was
forced to retire. General Taylor, who was nearby "animating, directing, and watching every shock and charge in the fight," learned
at that time that Fort Tenería had been carried by General Quitman's Mississippi and Tennessee regiments. Old Zach ordered the
Ohio troops back into the fray.

Quitman's command had, indeed, routed the defenders of Tenería. The Tennesseans, under Colonel William Bowen Campbell,
and the Mississippians, under Colonel Jefferson Davis, deployed
into a line and fired into the breastworks as they advanced. "The
combat began to be terrible," a Mexican defender wrote. "The
Americans kneeling, concealing themselves in every sort of posture;
in possession of the ground close to the fort, within pistol shot, and
even on the counterscarp . . . maintained a lively fire upon our
parapets." Jefferson Davis described the scene from the attacking
side: "In the redoubt musketeers lined the breastworks between
the pieces of artillery, and on the flat roof of the Tenería, musketeers in large numbers fired over the heads of men in the redoubt.
After firing a few minutes, it was perceptibly our best policy to
storm the covering work, and I ordered my men to advance . . .
The whole regiment moved forward . . . The Mexicans ran hastily
out of the redoubt."

Lieutenant Colonel A. K. McClung of the Tennesseans meanwhile had shouted to his men: "Tombigbee boys, follow me!" And
in the rush forward, McClung was the first to leap upon the
Mexican breastworks. So closely did Quitman's troops pursue the

Mexicans, who fled to a stone house in the rear of the works, that Colonel Davis reached the gate just a stride behind. "I reached the gate as they were closing it," Davis recalled, "and, jumping against it, forced it open. The cry immediately went up of surrender, and the officer supposed to be in command advanced and delivered his sword."

Throughout the attack of Quitman's volunteers—who took pride that they had accomplished what the regulars had failed to do—Captain Electus Backus's First Infantrymen, from the shed roof, had constantly sprayed the redoubt with a sizzling musket fire, a point which the regulars raised in rebutting the volunteers' claims. There can be no doubt that the isolation of Electus Backus and his half hundred men in the town during the withdrawal proved the key to the hard-won, bloodily-bought foothold Taylor got at last in the eastern end of Monterrey. Efforts to carry El Diablo proved fruitless and Taylor finally called off the attack, garrisoned Fort Tenería, and returned with his haggard troops to Walnut Springs.

It was a tragic day, in contrast to Worth's sweeping success at the other end of town. As a diversion, the attack was poorly planned, if planned at all. And when it developed into a full-scale assault, Taylor committed his troops in piecemeal fashion. Old Zach was his usual brave, resolute self, disregarding personal safety and maintaining complete confidence in his troops. But he was deficient both strategically and tactically on September 21, 1846, at Monterrey. The American losses in dead and wounded reached almost 400, and throughout the chilly, rain-swept night, the wagons made their way, picking up the dead and wounded.

It was another dreary night for Worth's troops on the western edge of Monterrey, pelted by the cold, driving rain in their fireless bivouac. But it was a short night for the assault party, commanded by Lieutenant Colonel Thomas Childs, for at 3 A.M. on September 22, it was scheduled to begin the ascent of the precipitous Independencia, which rose more than 700 feet above the floor of the valley. Childs had a strong force of about 500 men, consisting of three companies of the Eighth Infantry, three companies from the Third and Fourth Artillery, and 200 dismounted Texans from the commands of Hays and Walker. It moved out on schedule to the point at the base of the hill chosen by Captain Sanders and Lieutenant Meade of the Engineers. "Without a whisper," wrote George Wilkins Kendall, "the men set out on their perilous undertaking." A heavy fog, added to the pitch-blackness of the overcast night, created, said Kendall, "a gloom so impenetrable that no man could see his fellow."

Child's men edged their way up the rough face of the hill, clinging to the bushes and jagged rocks, in their tortuous advance. A Louisiana volunteer wrote a friend that it was "so steep that a slip of the foot would often have thrown us hundreds of feet below." As dawn broke, the assault party was within a hundred yards of the summit, when the clanking of their tin canteens announced their approach to the Mexicans. A number of sharp-shooters, who had been stationed the previous evening in clefts in the rocks, in anticipation of an attack, fired ineffectually at the Americans and then abandoned their positions in haste. Childs held his fire until his men were within a few yards of the crest. Then he gave the order. "A well-directed and destructive fire, followed by the bayonet of the regulars and rush of the Texans, placed us in possession of the work," reported General Worth.

A mile across the town, lying on his back in the mud of Fort Tenería to protect himself from "the spiteful fire" from El Diablo, Captain William S. Henry's attention was suddenly riveted on the west. He recorded the moment:

Just at the gray dawn of day . . . I witnessed the storming of the height which commanded the Bishop's Palace. The first intimation we had of it was the discharge of musketry near the top of the hill. Each flash looked like an electric spark. The flashes and the white smoke ascended the hill side steadily, as if worked by machinery. The dark space between the apex of the height and the curling smoke of the musketry became less and less, until the whole became enveloped in smoke, and we knew it was gallantly carried. It was a glorious sight, and quite warmed up our cold and chilled bodies.

Meanwhile, an assault on the Bishop's Palace, 400 yards down the slope, was out of the question without artillery. The Mexican guns had been rushed to the security of the Bishop's Palace, before the Americans had captured the redoubt. Worth reported to Taylor at 8:30 A.M. that "The height in rear of the palace was gallantly carried" and that he was "making arrangements to get a gun upon the eminence, but it will be with infinite difficulty." Lieutenant

Rowland and a twelve-pound howitzer were detached from Duncan's battery, and, according to Lieutenant Meade, the gun "was taken to pieces and carried up by hand to the summit." The operation required the services of the engineer, Captain Sanders, and fifty men from the line, but within two hours, Lieutenant Rowland was firing his piece at the Bishop's Palace, with damaging effect. Shrapnel shells exploded in the Palace and burst about its openwork in front. After several hours of preparation by Rowland's well-directed gunnery, Childs advanced under the howitzer's covering fire. He had received reinforcements, for Major Scott with elements of the Fifth Infantry, and Captain Blanchard's Louisiana Volunteers, had descended Federación and scaled Independencia to join in the attack.

In preparation for a possible counterattack, Childs pushed ahead some infantry under Captain John R. Vinton, the movement being concealed from the Mexicans. Hardly had the main force started forward than bugles sounded within the Bishop's Palace and out surged cavalry and infantry in a bold charge. The sortie was met with furious concentrated fire from Child's entire front, while the Mexican flank was swept by Vinton's men, pouring in deadly volleys from cover.

First halted and then repulsed by the searing blasts of musketry, the Mexicans broke and fled, with the Americans in hot pursuit. Fugitives and pursuers dashed into the Bishop's Palace almost together, with the Mexicans continuing their flight, under brisk fire, down the slope and into the town. Lieutenant George W. Ayres was the first into the Palace and he seized the Mexican colors. "In a few moments," reported Worth, "the unpretending flag of our union had replaced the gaudy standard of Mexico."

By now the captured Mexican pieces—a six-inch howitzer, a twelve-inch howitzer, and two nine-pounder brass guns—were turned on the scrambling enemy masses fleeing into the town and the fire was increased when the batteries of Duncan and Mackall galloped up and unlimbered. Worth's tremendous victory on the western edge of the town was now complete, but neither he nor his weary men seemed willing to let up until Monterrey was captured. In a field dispatch to the *Picayune*, George Wilkins Kendall said of Worth's troops: "From the time the Mexican Lancers commenced the attack upon our advance, late on the afternoon of the 20th up to the final capitulation on the afternoon of the 24th, there was literally no rest to the soles of the feet of any man in Worth's command."

Throughout the day-long battle on Independencia, the eastern sector of the town remained quiet. That is, except for the cheers "that reached every part of the city" from Twiggs's and Butler's men when the American flag broke out into the wind above the Obispado. There was no fighting, only the periodic bombardment of Fort Tenería by the guns of El Diablo and the Black Fort.

At 7 A.M., on September 23, from the Bishop's Palace, Worth began shelling the town. "It was cheering," wrote Captain Henry, "to see Worth pouring it into them, and that, too, with their own pieces and ammunition." Soon, the rattle of small arms in the direction of Tenería announced the resumption of action after a day's lull. General Quitman's troops, advancing to assault El Diablo, found it deserted.

Taylor now launched a major assault on the eastern end of Monterrey and when the sound of heavy firing reached Worth, at 10 A.M., he assumed that "orders for my cooperation (having to travel a circuit of some six miles) had miscarried, or failed to reach me." Accordingly, Worth ordered two attack columns to move along the two principal streets leading from Independencia. But instead of presenting targets for sweeping artillery fire and snipers on the rooftops, Worth's men borrowed a technique that the Texans had employed against the Mexicans at San Antonio in 1836. Armed with pickaxes and crowbars and improvised battering rams, they burrowed their way through the walls of the houses, working their way from house to house, and square to square. "At dark, we had worked our way through the walls and squares, and reached to within one block of the great plaza," reported Worth, "leaving a covered way in our rear—carried a large building which towered over the principal defenses, and during the night and ensuing morning, crowned its roof with two howitzers and a six-pounder."

Meanwhile, during the previous night "in the midst of frightful disorder," Ampudia had abandoned all exterior defenses on the eastern end of the town, except the Black Fort, and had concentrated his force around the Cathedral. Nevertheless, Taylor advanced cautiously, if determinedly, into the city. "At ten in the morning," states a Mexican account, "the enemy occupied the posts deserted the night before, and at eleven invested with firmness, generalizing their fire which grew warm to the very houses on the principal plaza."

This time, the American artillery swept the streets, as Taylor closed on the Mexicans, driving them, as Old Zach told his son-in-law, "from house to house into the principal open square near the Cathedral, where they had collected the greater portion of their forces with the intention of making their last stand."

The fighting was severe, but only in one instance, noted Captain Henry, could it be compared to that of the 21st. This was in a street running directly from the Cathedral. "To cross the street you had to pass through a *shower of bullets*," he said.

Unperturbed as usual, Old Zach moved about on foot with his staff. He sauntered across the street of the "shower of bullets," and, said Henry, "by every chance should have been shot." The captain ran across to Taylor to urge him to take cover. "Take that ax and knock in that door," was Old Zach's reply.

During the day's fighting, the governor of the province sent a white flag to Taylor requesting permission to withdraw the women and children. Taylor declined. "The flag is a good symptom," observed Captain Henry, "their time is drawing near. I hardly think they will hold out another day." Captain Henry did not miss it by much, for before daybreak on September 24, Ampudia sent Taylor a proposal to surrender provided he be permitted to withdraw his army and its arms and baggage of every description. This Taylor refused, but later in a personal interview with Ampudia, he agreed to a commission of three officers from each army to work out terms of capitulation.

General Worth, General James Pinkney Henderson, and Colonel Jefferson Davis represented General Taylor, while General J. M. Ortega, General Tomás Requeña, and Manuel M. Llano, governor of Nuevo León, acted for Ampudia.

Hour after hour, the negotiations dragged on, with repeated threats by the American commissioners countering repeated objections by the Mexicans. Late on the night of September 24, agreement was finally reached on terms, which Taylor reported to Washington, were "less rigorous than those first imposed" but to which he had agreed because of "the gallant defense of the town, and the fact of a recent change of government in Mexico, believed to be favorable to the interests of peace."

The Mexicans were to surrender the city, fortifications, cannon and munitions and all public property, except that all units of Ampudia's army would retain their arms and accouterments, the artillery being permitted one field battery of six pieces, with twenty-one rounds of ammunition. Within a week, the Mexican army would evacuate the city and withdraw to a line through the pass of Rinconada and Linares, about forty miles from Monterrey. Beyond this line, Taylor agreed his forces would not move for eight weeks, "or until the orders of the respective governments can be received."

To his son-in-law Dr. R. C. Wood, Taylor explained his leniency to the Mexicans at Monterrey:

> These terms were liberal but not considered too much so by all reflecting men belonging to the army here especially considering our situation; besides it was thought it would be judicious to act with magniminity [sic] towards a prostrate foe, particularly as the president of the U. States had offered to settle all differences between the two countries by negotiation, & the Mexican commander stating that said propositions he had no doubt would be favorably met by his got [government] as their [sic] was a genl wish for peace on the part of the nation.

With the armistice there was time for stock-taking. Taylor's army of 425 officers and 6,220 men had suffered about seven and a half percent casualties, virtually all at the eastern end of town. Twelve officers and 108 men were killed, and 26 officers and 307 men were wounded for a casualty total of 453. The Mexican casualties, among Ampudia's more than 10,000 defenders, were probably considerably higher than Taylor's. Forty-two Mexican artillery pieces fell with Monterrey into the American hands.

As the Mexican flag came down at noon on September 25, in the capitulation ceremonies, the Mexicans fired an eight-gun salute. A twenty-eight gun salute—one for each state in the Union—fired from Independencia greeted the American flag as it ran up the pole and whipped in the breeze. With the bands playing "Yankee Doodle," Old Zach's army marched into Monterrey as the Mexicans marched out.

George Wilkins Kendall, who rode with the American Dragoon escort of General Pedro de Ampudia through the American lines, noted in an article to the *Picayune:* "The base and lying wretch— for every page in his black history proves him such—looked crestfallen, nervous, and timid to a degree."

16

The War in the West

If modern communications had existed in 1846, a succession of thrilling reports would have reached the White House during the third week of August.

From Vera Cruz, President Polk would have learned that Santa Anna had landed on the 16th and, hopefully, he would have expected that the machinery for peace negotiations, which he had secretly oiled, would soon be put into motion by the returned exile.

From Los Angeles on the 17th, Mr. Polk would have had word from Commodore Robert F. Stockton that "the flag of the United States is now flying from every commanding position in the Territory, and California is entirely free from Mexican domination."

And from New Mexico, the President would have heard from General Stephen Watts Kearny on the 18th that, after a march of nearly 900 miles from Fort Leavenworth, he had occupied Santa Fé that day, without firing a shot or shedding a drop of blood.

Thus it was that more than five weeks before Zachary Taylor captured Monterrey, American naval forces had seized California and the newly organized Army of the West had established United States rule in New Mexico.

Colonel Kearny—his commission as brigadier general overtook him on the march three days before he occupied Santa Fé—was another veteran of the War of 1812, after which he had spent more than twenty-five years on the frontier. In 1846, at fifty-two, he was not only commander of the First Dragoons, but he was also the commanding officer of the frontier post of Fort Leavenworth. He was a man of action, possessing tremendous energy. He was also a strict disciplinarian. The story was told that when Kearny heard a young officer address some troops as "gentlemen" he turned scornfully on him and said: "There are colonels, captains, lieutenants and soldiers in this command, but no such persons as 'gentlemen.'"

At the same time that Colonel Kearny received his marching orders, President Polk called upon Governor Edwards of Missouri for 1,000 mounted volunteers to reinforce the First Dragoons. Moreover, Kearny was authorized to raise a force among the Mormons, then encamped near Council Bluffs. The response of the Missouri Volunteers was immediate, and three of the eight companies mustered in reported to Kearny by June 6, within two weeks after the call for troops had reached the Governor. By June 18, the First Missouri Mounted Volunteers were organized with a Kentucky-born frontier lawyer, Alexander W. Doniphan, a private in the ranks, elected by the men as colonel of the regiment. It was a happy choice, as time would tell.

Meanwhile, eager to get his command on the march, Kearny sent two companies of Dragoons out on June 5 and about 100 loaded wagons and 800 head of cattle were on the route, ahead of the main body, a few days thereafter. Kearny's force consisted of the First Dragoons, 300 strong; Doniphan's 860 Mounted Volunteers; the Laclede Rangers, a mounted company from St. Louis; two companies of infantry; two companies of light artillery; a party of topographical engineers, commanded by Lieutenant William H. Emory; about fifty Indian scouts; and an interpreter. When two previously detached companies of the First Dragoons joined the regiment, Colonel Kearny's total force to conquer New Mexico was slightly under 1,700 men. To transport men, materiel, and supplies, and to provide rations "on the hoof," for the little Army of the West, 1,556 wagons, 459 horses, 3,658 mules, and 14,904 oxen were employed in the movement.

Supplementary orders to Kearny, sent from the War Department on June 3, extended his mission. After subduing and occupying New Mexico, Kearny was to continue to the Pacific Coast to join the Navy in the conquest of California. Accordingly, the governor of Missouri was asked for another thousand mounted volunteers, and these under Sterling Price were to join Kearny at Santa Fé.

After moving his troops out in detachments, throughout the last two weeks of June, Colonel Kearny and his staff rode out from Fort Leavenworth on the last day of the month.

"There are many obstacles which impede the progress of an army," wrote one of Colonel Doniphan's men. "There was no road, not even a path leading from Fort Leavenworth into the regular Santa Fé Trail." To reach the well-rutted Santa Fé road, which the

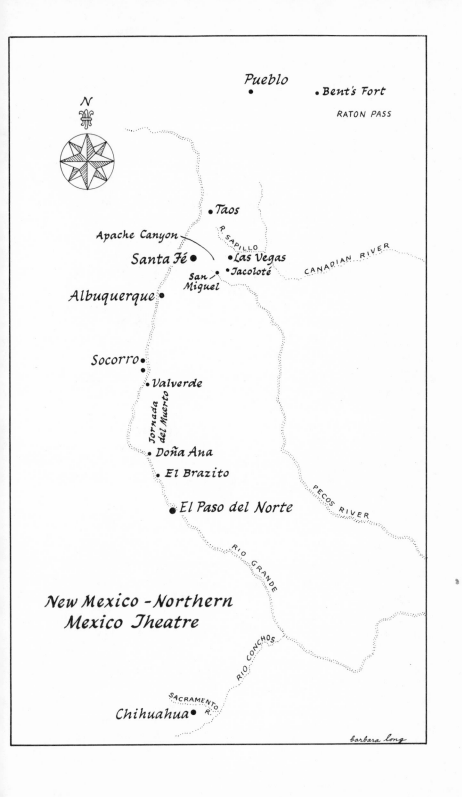

N

Pueblo

Bent's Fort

RATON PASS

Taos

Apache Canyon

R. SAPILLO

Santa Fé

Las Vegas

Jacoloté

San Miguel

CANADIAN RIVER

Albuquerque

Socorro

Valverde

Jornada del Muerto

Doña Ana

El Brazito

El Paso del Norte

PECOS RIVER

RIO GRANDE

New Mexico - Northern
Mexico Theatre

RIO CONCHOS

SACRAMENTO R.

Chihuahua

barbara long

caravans of merchants from Independence to Mexico had traced for years, was an arduous and backbreaking operation. Deep ravines and creeks with steep banks had to be crossed and often wagons bogged down up to the axles in the soft prairie soil, and the men had to dismount and lift or drag them from the mire by hand.

During the march, noted Lieutenant Emory, "an excellent understanding . . . prevailed between regulars and volunteers" and he approved "the cheerfulness with which they came to each other's assistance." The troops celebrated the Fourth of July by covering twenty-seven miles in "the heated rays of an almost vertical sun," but, thanks to the Dragoons' sutler, liquid refreshments for the occasion were provided. "It seems we have as much of the spirit of '76 as the spirit of John Barleycorn," wrote a soldier-diarist, "for marching across these plains is not what it is cracked up to be."

The advance party of the First Dragoons reached the rendezvous below Bent's Fort on the Arkansas River on July 22 and by July 28, the two infantry companies of volunteers, having covered 600 miles in twenty-nine days, marched in ahead of the mounted men who had preceded them. "The long-legged infantry," a cavalryman admiringly dubbed them. By July 31, Kearny's entire force was concentrated across the river from Bent's Fort, which stood near the present town of Las Animas, Colorado. Built in the early 1830's by the three Bent and two St. Vrain brothers, it stood at the crossing of many trails and was not only a trading post but a clearing house for news and rumors from New Mexico and Missouri. Within its adobe walls, fifteen feet high and four feet thick, the American flag flew over an area 180 feet by 135 feet.

During the brief halt at Bent's Fort, Kearny wrote a letter to the rascally governor of New Mexico, Manuel Armijo, who held both the civil authority and the military office of commandante-general as well. Bloated in body and in self-esteem, Armijo was a blustering bully, more robber than administrator. He was clever, venal, licentious, and cowardly. He made a brave front, but generally lived up to his avowed philosophy: "It is better to be thought brave than to be so."

The letter which Kearny dispatched to Santa Fé by Captain Philip St. George Cooke and twelve Dragoons informed Armijo that he came "as a friend & with the disposition and intention to consider all Mexicans & others as friends who will remain quietly & peaceably at their homes & attend to their own affairs." He announced his determination to take possession of the country, but pledged that the inhabitants would be secure "in their Persons, their Property, their Religion." At the same time, Kearny embodied the same ideas in a proclamation to the people of New Mexico.

Accompanying Captain Cooke was a picturesque figure well known for two decades in the Chihuahua and New Mexico trade, the wealthy James W. Magoffin. The Kentucky-born Magoffin had married into a Mexican family. Now living in Independence, Missouri, Magoffin had recently been in Washington where, at the insistence of Senator Thomas Hart Benton, he had talked at length with President Polk and Secretary of War Marcy. Impressed by Magoffin's knowledge of New Mexico, the President had hurried him west with letters for Kearny. Sixteen days after leaving Independence in a buggy, he reached Kearny. Recognizing at once Magoffin's usefulness, Kearny enlisted his services.

On August 2, Kearny resumed the march, and soon the army was trudging over ground so parched that it appeared to one soldier not to have been refreshed by rainfall "since the days of Noah's flood." This was the Great American Desert, "sterile, sandy, parched, and destitute of water . . . dreary, sultry, desolate, boundless solitude . . ." By the time the Army of the West reached Raton Pass—7,500 feet above sea level on Lieutenant Emory's barometer —it was on half rations and these later were further reduced. The horses were exhausted, and wolves and buzzards lurked behind the column waiting to gorge themselves on the dying animals. Ammunition, too, was running low, so wasteful had the men been in impromptu buffalo hunts on the march.

As he pushed on, Kearny received word that Armijo was assembling a large force to challenge the American passage. On August 14, a Mexican lieutenant and a small party of Lancers approached with an answer from Armijo to Kearny. The note's meaning, Lieutenant Emory recorded, was this: "You have notified me that you intend to take possession of the country I govern. The people of the country have risen, en masse, in my defense. If you take the country, it will be because you prove the strongest in battle. I suggest to you to stop at the Sapillo and I will march to the Vegas. We will meet and negotiate in the plains between them."

As he approached Las Vegas, Colonel Kearny called a halt, summoned the Mexican Lieutenant, and said: "The road to Santa Fé is now as free to you as to myself. Say to General Armijo, I shall soon meet him, and I hope it will be as friends." To Kearny's surprise, perhaps to his amusement, the Mexican lieutenant embraced him and rode away toward Santa Fé.

That night the troops camped in sight of the town and the next morning Kearny entered Las Vegas to address a peaceful gathering of the alcalde and the people. To the edge of town, three travel-stained horsemen galloped up—Major Swords, Captain Richard Weightman, and Lieutenant Jeremy Gilmer—who, having heard that a fight was imminent, had ridden all night not to miss it. They brought with them Kearny's commission as a brigadier general, dated June 30. The trio had to settle for oratory, as General Kearny announced from the roof of a low building, that New Mexico now belonged to the United States. The people, he said, were absolved of their Mexican allegiance, he pledged respect for their property and religious freedom, and he promised protection against raids by the Apaches and Navajos, and finished by a mass administration of the oath of allegiance to the United States.

The ceremony concluded, General Kearny hurried forward with the column toward a gorge, two miles away, where a large force of Mexicans reportedly awaited the American advance. For the first time in the march, the guidons and colors were unfurled. "The drooping horses seemed to take courage from the gay array," noted Lieutenant Emory. "The trumpeters sounded 'to horse,' with spirit and the hills multiplied and re-echoed the call." As the head of the column approached the gorge it broke into a brisk trot, and then into a full gallop as it rushed gallantly to meet an enemy that wasn't there. "The men looked disappointed," recorded Lieutenant Emory, but probably many agreed with Private Jim Hughes's philosophical approach: "It is perhaps better thus to have gained a bloodless victory by the terror of our arms than to have purchased it with blood and loss of life."

Kearny pushed on through Tecolote and San Miguel, where, at both places, the ceremony of Las Vegas was repeated. He learned as he advanced toward Santa Fé that in Apache Canyon, a narrow defile about seven or eight miles long, about fifteen miles from the town, Armijo with a strong force, presumably about 7,000, supported by artillery, lay in wait.

However, Lieutenant Emory noted a rumor that General Kearny received on the march on August 17, that the Mexican leaders in El Cañón had quarreled. This gave the cowardly Armijo a pretext for quitting the scene, which he seems to have done hurriedly. "He has long been suspected of wishing an excuse to fly," observed

Emory. The rumor was soon confirmed when the fat and jovial alcalde of a nearby little settlement, a comic figure on his mule, cantered up to General Kearny. The alcalde extended his hand in welcome to the army and with a roar of laughter exclaimed: "Armijo and his troops have gone to hell and the canyon is all clear."

Assured by the alcalde's information and by subsequent intelligence that reached him that "not a hostile rifle or arrow was now between the army and Santa Fé," Kearny determined to cover the last twenty-nine miles to the New Mexican capital and raise the United States flag over the palace before sundown on the eighteenth. By 6 A.M., the army was under way, and shortly after noon the troops reached El Cañón from which the faint-hearted Armijo had fled so ingloriously. With the critical estimate of an expert, Lieutenant Emory flatly declared: "It is a gateway, which, in the hands of a skilled engineer and one hundred resolute men, would have been perfectly impregnable."

As the army approached Santa Fé, two Mexican officials brought a letter of welcome from Juan Bautista Vigil, Lieutenant Governor of New Mexico, announcing Armijo's flight and extending to General Kearny the hospitality of the town. Seemingly, James Magoffin's diplomatic mission had been highly successful in paving the way for the peaceful advent of the Army of the West. Magoffin was aided, no doubt, by Armijo's "real disinclination to actual resistance."

The head of the column reached Santa Fé after 3 P.M., and by 6 P.M., Kearny's entire force had arrived. Vigil and the leading citizens welcomed the General and his staff and wined and dined them. As the sun went down, the United States flag was hoisted over the palace, while from a height commanding the town, a salute of thirteen guns roared. The next day, August 19, General Kearny addressed the people in the plaza, repeating what he had previously said at Las Vegas and San Miguel, and the response was one of friendly warmth. Once again he administered the oath of allegiance. The next day a delegation of Pueblo chiefs called on General Kearny, promising submission.

On August 22, General Kearny issued a proclamation claiming the whole of New Mexico and declaring that temporarily he would serve as governor. He called upon the New Mexicans "to exert themselves in preserving order, in promoting concord, and maintaining the authority and efficiency of the laws," and pledged to provide "a free government with the least possible delay, similar to those in the United States." When that time came, the General said, "the people of New Mexico will then be called on to exercise the rights of freemen in electing their own representatives to the territorial legislature."

"The people of the territory are now perfectly tranquil, and can easily be kept so," Kearny wrote Adjutant General Jones on August 24. "The intelligent portion know the advantages they are to derive from the change of government, and express their satisfaction at it."

Meanwhile, Lieutenant Emory had begun work on Fort Marcy, on a site 600 yards from the center of Santa Fe on the only spot "which commands the whole town and is itself commanded by no other." It was designed to garrison 208 men.

Kearny had not heard from Colonel Sterling Price and the 1,000 Missouri Volunteers of his command, nor from the Mormon battalion that Captain James Smith had recruited. Nevertheless, he wrote General John E. Wool, who commanded the Army of the Center and who had been ordered from San Antonio into Chihuahua, that he soon would have more troops than he needed and that he would send the surplus to Wool.

Kearny recruited two lawyers, Colonel Doniphan and Private Willard Hall, from the Missouri Volunteers and set them to work drafting a new constitution for the government of New Mexico. Hearing that Mexican reinforcements from El Paso had started north and that the people south of Santa Fé had rallied around Armijo and were preparing to resist United States rule, Kearny led an expedition from Santa Fé on September 2. It consisted of about 715 mounted troops, including 100 artillerymen with eight pieces. It was a fruitless adventure, for neither Mexicans nor rebels were found after a march of 100 miles, and Kearny returned to Santa Fé on September 11.

For the next two weeks General Kearny was busy preparing to push on to the Pacific. On September 16, he wrote the Adjutant General that "as the territory is now so perfectly quiet," he had set September 25 as the day of departure. On September 22, he installed Charles Bent as governor of New Mexico. Then, having issued orders to Colonel Doniphan to march his command to Chihuahua to join General Wool immediately upon Colonel Price's arrival, and for the Mormon battalion to follow him to California, General Stephen Watts Kearny, at the head of 300 men of the First Dragoons, rode out of Santa Fé for the Pacific.

17

The Navy Takes California

In 1842, Commodore Thomas Ap Catesby Jones had incorrectly guessed that the United States and Mexico were at war, and he had landed sailors from the Pacific Squadron on October 20, and had occupied the California port of Monterey.

When the truth dawned upon Commodore Jones—he was the same who gallantly commanded five gunboats on Lake Borgne that the British overwhelmed at the beginning of the campaign against New Orleans in 1814–1815—he hauled down the American flag, saluted the Mexican flag, and sailed away. But in consequence of his patriotic rashness, Commodore Jones endangered sensitive diplomatic relations between the two countries and at the same time jeopardized his own rank in the Navy.

The thought of Jones's premature zeal four years earlier was very much on the mind of Commodore John D. Sloat, as word of the outbreak of hostilities on the Rio Grande reached him aboard the USS *Savannah*, riding at anchor off the Mexican port of Mazatlán.

Sloat had received orders, dated June 24, 1845, alerting him to the strained relations between the United States and Mexico. While instructing him to be "assiduously careful to avoid any act which could be construed as an act of aggression," he was ordered to possess the port of San Francisco and blockade or occupy other ports "if you ascertain with certainty that Mexico has declared war against the United States."

On April 17, 1846, Commodore Sloat had received orders from Washington, delivered by Marine Lieutenant Archibald Gillespie, instructing him to act according to his June, 1845, orders, "in the event of actual hostilities between the Mexican Government and our own."

On May 17, just three weeks after the ambuscade of Captain Thornton on the Rio Grande, Commodore Sloat learned of the incident. Mindful of Commodore Jones's impetuosity in 1842, Sloat hesitated. Did he know "with certainty" that Mexico had declared war? Could he be sure "actual hostilities" had broken out? He decided to wait, before acting.

Two weeks later, early in June, unconfirmed reports of Taylor's victories at Palo Alto and Resaca de La Palma reached Sloat. Once again the Commodore pondered over his course of action and he hesitated a second time.

Finally, on June 7, Sloat got more information on the Rio Grande fighting and also learned that the Home Squadron was blockading Mexican ports on the Gulf of Mexico. That was the clincher for Sloat, so he raised anchor and sailed off in the *Savannah* to execute his orders.

Putting in at Monterey on July 2, he found the *Cyane* and *Levant* in the harbor and learned that the *Portsmouth* was at San Francisco. On arrival, Sloat paid a courtesy call on the Mexican officials—was he vacillating because of lingering uncertainty as to the outbreak of war?—and he conferred with United States Consul Thomas O. Larkin. The latter was not convinced the two countries were yet at war, but Sloat, stiffening his back, decided to act. On the morning of July 7, Captain William Mervine landed at ten o'clock with 250 sailors and Marines and ran the United States flag above the custom house. A proclamation by Commodore Sloat announced that "henceforth California will be a portion of the United States," and he promised all "peaceable inhabitants" would be secure in all their rights, their property, their freedom of religion.

Acting on orders from Sloat, which reached him on the evening of June 8, Commander John B. Montgomery put ashore from the *Portsmouth* a landing party which raised the American flag over San Francisco, posted Sloat's proclamation, and took possession of the area for the United States.

In the vast area of Upper California, as it was then called, there was a population of barely 25,000. Of the 10,000 whites, it was estimated that 800 were Americans. There were, in addition, about 15,000 Indians, of which perhaps 5,000 were semicivilized. Power was generally vested in three men—Governor Pío Pico, who was pro-British; Commandante General José Castro, who posed as a Mexican patriot, but preferred independence for the province, with himself as its ruler; and M. G. Vallejo, one of the big landowners, who was pro-American.

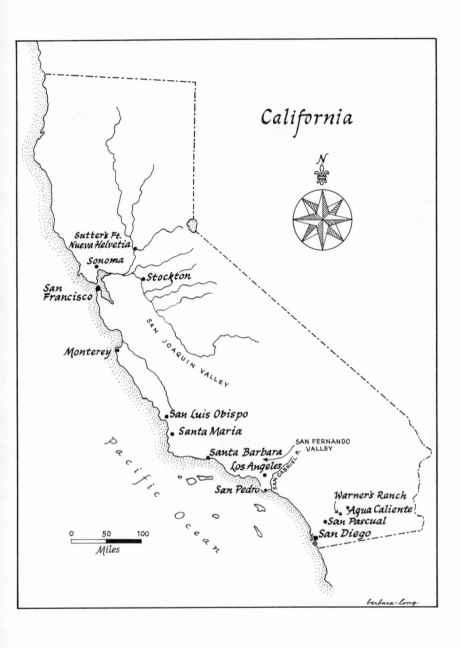

California

N

Sutter's Ft.
Nueva Helvetia
Sonoma
Stockton
San
Francisco
SAN JOAQUIN VALLEY
Monterey
San Luis Obispo
Santa Maria
Santa Barbara
SAN FERNANDO
VALLEY
Los Angeles
Pacific
SAN GABRIEL R.
San Pedro
Warner's Ranch
Agua Caliente
San Pascual
Ocean
San Diego

0   50   100
Miles

barbara long

Neglected, if not forgotten by the central government of Mexico, California was in 1845, to quote a British consul, "at the mercy of whoever may choose to take possession of it." President Polk was one who chose to possess it. He had written Consul Larkin: "The interests of our commerce and our whale fisheries on the Pacific Ocean demand that you should exert the greatest vigilance in discovering and defeating any attempt which may be made by foreign governments to acquire a control of that country." To John Slidell, on his futile mission to Mexico, was given authority "to purchase for a pecuniary consideration Upper California and New Mexico."

So, irrespective of war, and war aims, Polk contemplated early in 1846 the acquisition of California, either by direct purchase from Mexico or, after Californians had established their independence, the annexation by mutual agreement with the young republic. Accordingly, there was no place in Polk's California policy for British possession of the province.

Such was the setting for the drama that unfolded when the intrepid "pathfinder," Brevet Captain John Charles Frémont, son-in-law of Senator Thomas Hart Benton, arrived in December, 1845, at Nueva Helvetia, site of the present city of Sacramento. To this settlement, established by the German Swiss Captain John A. Sutter, and generally known as Sutter's Fort, Captain Frémont led his weary men and horses in the dead of winter. In May, Frémont and his party of sixty-three men—armed, but for diplomatic reasons not soldiers—had left Fort Leavenworth on a junket of exploration. Captain Sutter, whom Frémont had visited the previous year, again received him with cordiality and provided the young army officer with fresh horses and supplies. Frémont moved south into the San Joaquín Valley, where he went into camp and then he himself proceeded to Monterey to seek General José Castro's permission to winter in California. Castro granted the request, but limited Frémont's party to the unsettled areas. Whether deliberately, or by a broad interpretation of Castro's permission, Frémont moved his men into the settled coastal area and, by a series of further encroachments, Frémont's party was established within twenty-five miles of Monterey itself.

This was too much for General Castro, and on March 3, 1846, he ordered Frémont out of California. Frémont defied the order, threw up a breastwork, raised the American flag, and hurried off a grandiloquent message to Consul Thomas O. Larkin in Monterey that if attacked, he would "fight to extremity and refuse quarter, trusting to our country to avenge us." Discretion tempered Frémont's valor when he observed, four miles from his fort on Pico Gavilán—Hawk's Peak—the military preparations of Castro, assembling men and artillery. Frémont later testified that "not to compromise the government of the United States, or the American settlers, who were ready to join me at all hazards," he withdrew from his position. "Slowly and growlingly" he described to his wife his retirement, first to Sutter's Fort and then in unhurried stages out of California.

It was about five weeks after this incident that Lieutenant Archibald Gillespie of the Marines arrived in California with instructions for Commodore Sloat and Consul Larkin. He also had letters for Captain Frémont, one of introduction from Secretary of State Buchanan and others from Frémont's father-in-law, Senator Benton. Having completed his official mission, Gillespie set out on the trail of Frémont. After a hazardous journey of more than 600 miles, Gillespie caught up with Frémont in Oregon, on the shores of Klamath Lake, on May 9, the day of Taylor's victory at Resaca de la Palma. From "passages enigmatical and obscure" in one of Senator Benton's letters which Frémont "studied out," he concluded he was "required by the government to find out any foreign schemes in relation to the Californians, and to counteract them."

An Indian attack on Frémont's camp that night resulted in three of his men being killed. After pausing to punish the marauders, Frémont started the return trip to California, satisfied, as he later wrote that "I had my warrant [for] taking possession of California." By the end of May, Frémont and Gillespie were at Sutter's Fort.

Meanwhile, word of Paredes's revolt in Mexico and the unseating of President Herrera, had reached California and sparked the beginning of a civil war. In Monterey, Commandante General Castro declared for Paredes and prepared to move against Governor Pío Pico at Los Angeles. The latter called for a convention to meet at Santa Bárbara on June 15 to proclaim independence, but Castro's refusal to permit delegates from the north to attend resulted in its cancellation. British naval forces in the Pacific, commanded by Sir George Seymour, hovered nearby.

The situation regarding California, therefore, at the beginning of June, 1846, was this: The United States and British fleets were off the coast; Frémont, determined on independent action, was at Sutter's Fort; Castro and Pico were preparing for civil war, the chief bone of contention between them being the division of the custom house revenues; Kearny was about to march for California, via Santa Fé.

To Frémont were assigned the opening lines in the *opéra bouffe* which was the conquest of California. In this entire operation with momentous consequences, it is doubtful if all the forces on all sides ever, cumulatively, reached 2,000. On June 10, Frémont "opened the show." Ezekiel Merritt, called by Frémont his "field lieutenant among the settlers," with a dozen of Frémont's men intercepted and seized 170 horses being driven from Sonoma to Castro's camp. The pretext for this "large-scale horsestealing" was Frémont's professed belief that Castro was mounting an aggressive movement against the American settlers and that the seizure was a preventive measure.

On June 14, another "preventive step" was taken when Merritt and thirty-four men seized the Mexican post at Sonoma, taking over the property and cattle, and seizing eighteen prisoners, among them the pro-American Mariano Vallejo, founder of Sonoma, and his brother, Salvador, a pioneer winemaker in California. Also included was one of Consul Larkin's agents, Jacob Leese, who was engaged in conciliating Californians toward the United States. Although Senator Benton later claimed, with pride, that his son-in-law "acted entirely on his own responsibility" without instructions from the government to begin hostilities, Frémont remained in the background.

While Merritt, with about ten men, conveyed the prisoners to Frémont's camp, William Ide and the remaining men proclaimed the Bear Flag Republic, hoisting a new standard with the words "California Republic" and the device of a grizzly bear. An appeal to commander Montgomery of the *Portsmouth* for arms and supplies was politely refused with that officer making it clear that he would not "in any manner . . . take sides with any political party . . . or even indirectly to identify myself, or official name, with any popular movement (whether of foreign or native residents) of that country."

Frémont later asserted that he had made common cause with the American settlers not only for their mutual safety and to defeat Castro, "but in the total overthrow of Mexican authority in California, and the establishment of an independent government in that extensive province." Frémont was near Sutter's Fort on July 10 when he received "the joyful intelligence" that Commodore Sloat had seized Monterey and that war existed between Mexico and the United States. "Instantly, we pulled down the flag of independence," he declared, "and ran up that of the United States."

Meanwhile, on June 16, Frémont had asked Commander Montgomery for supplies and money for his return trip to the United States. This, undoubtedly, was a subterfuge to acquire for the Bear State Republic what the commander had already refused to give. For, having had his request granted and having received official letters for delivery in Washington, Frémont immediately marched, not on the homeward trail, but for Sonoma where he was pushing his plans for the conquest of California under the Bear State Republic banner, when he learned of Sloat's occupation of Monterey.

After seizing Monterey, Commodore Sloat had written to both Castro and Pico, seeking their cooperation. He called upon the former to surrender all troops, arms, munitions, and public property, and urged "immediate compliance" to preclude "the sacrifice of human life and the horrors of war." To the latter, Sloat said that he came "as the best friend of California" and he invited Pico to Monterey to satisfy himself of this fact.

The outcome of Sloat's overtures was to throw the two rivals into each other's arms. They joined forces against the common foe. With 800 men and ten cannon they took up position at Los Angeles with the avowed intention of defending the capital and the honor and integrity of Mexico.

Independent action for Frémont was now over, and on July 19, with 160 mounted riflemen he rode to Monterey and placed his command at Commodore Sloat's disposal. But, about this time, Commodore Robert F. Stockton, on the frigate *Congress*, arrived at Monterey, and on July 23, he relieved Sloat as naval commander in the Pacific. The next day, he received Frémont's command into the service of the United States, named Frémont major of the "California Battalion of Mounted Riflemen" and appointed Gillespie as captain.

Stockton then shipped Frémont's force by the *Cyane* to San Diego, and several days later he sailed on the *Congress* to San Pedro. On August 7, Stockton landed his "gallant sailor army," 360 strong, and the two commands converged on the Castro-Pico force of about

500 in the fortified Camp of the Mesa, three miles from Los
Angeles. But the embattled Mexicans didn't wait for a fight. Stockton reported that as the Americans approached, "General Castro
broke ground and run for the city of Mexico," while Pico and
the other officers fled in different parties in different directions.

On August 13, Commodore Stockton, accompanied by Major Frémont, with eighty horsemen, and Consul Larkin, entered Los
Angeles and, unmolested, took possession of the city, To Secretary
of the Navy George Bancroft, Stockton, with a marked lack of
modesty, reported:

> . . . The flag of the United States is flying from every com-
> manding position in the Territory of California, and . . . this
> rich and beautiful country belongs to the United States, and
> is forever free from Mexican dominion . . .
>
> Thus, in less than a month after I assumed the command of
> the United States force in California, we have chased the
> Mexican army more than three hundred miles along the coast;
> pursued them thirty miles in the interior of their own country;
> routed and dispersed them, and secured the Territory to the
> United States; ended the war; restored peace and harmony
> among the people; and put a civil government into successful
> operation.

On August 22—the day General Kearny claimed all of New
Mexico and General Taylor's army was on the road to Monterrey—
Commodore Stockton organized a civil government for California,
with himself as temporary governor. He announced he would appoint Frémont as permanent governor later.

A month later, despite Stockton's fulsome forecast, Los Angeles
revolted, and on September 25, Gillespie was under siege in the
City of the Angels. On that same day, General Zachary Taylor
marched into Monterrey and General Stephen Watts Kearny
marched out of Santa Fé for California.

18

Revolt and Reconquest

General Kearny, with his 300 Dragoons, followed the course of the Rio Grande for twelve days. On October 6, 1846, as he still pushed southward on the riverbank, he came upon the famous scout Kit Carson and a party of sixteen men, bound from California to Washington with dispatches from Commodore Stockton and Major Frémont.

Lieutenant Carson told Kearny that California was in the quiet possession of the United States, and he detailed the steps whereby the Navy had seized the province. General Kearny was assured by Carson's report that "the American flag was playing from every important position in the territory, and that the country was ever free from Mexican control, the war ended, and peace and harmony established among the people."

Believing now that his full force was no longer needed in California, Kearny ordered 200 Dragoons, under Major E. V. Sumner, to remain in New Mexico. With the other hundred men and two mountain howitzers, commanded by Captain B. D. Moore, he continued his march to the Pacific. Kearny persuaded Kit Carson to turn back and guide his column to California although at first the scout demurred. Carson said that he had pledged to deliver the dispatches in Washington and would not think of not fulfilling his promise. The General countered by saying he would place the dispatches in responsible hands for their delivery in Washington. Carson "finally consented and turned his face to the west again," wrote Captain Abraham R. Johnston. ". . . He was on the eve of . . . seeing his family again. It requires a brave man to give up his private feelings thus for the common good; but Carson is one such!"

Progress was very slow, and after several days, Carson remarked that at the rate the column was moving, it wouldn't reach Los

Angeles for four months. When the scout told Kearny that the trail ahead was worse than the ground they had already traversed, the General decided to send his wagons back to Major Sumner in exchange for pack-mules. There was a wait of several days, during the mornings of which ice and frost appeared for the first time. Finally, on October 14, the march was resumed. "All were busy to the hour of starting, from the General down," noted Captain Johnston, "but our pack-saddles were bad and our lash ropes worse; with a few cases of kicking and no accidents, we made our march down the river." Everybody in the command, except Lieutenant William H. Emory, seemed happy over the switch to mules. "With me it was otherwise," he noted. "My chronometers and barometers, which before rode so safely, were now in constant danger."

The next day the party left the stream and turned toward the west, heading for the Gila River. The command passed copper mines abandoned by the Indians, and ruined villages, as it made its tortuous journey over a succession of hills and valleys, steadily climbing toward the Continental Divide. On the way, they encountered the friendly Pima and Maricopa Indians from whom they traded for food and pack-animals. Following the Gila to where it empties into the Colorado, Kearny pushed on for more than a month. One night, not quite two months after he had left Santa Fé, Kearny received surprising news. When a distant campfire was spotted on the night of November 22, Lieutenant Emory led a reconnaissance party to investigate. He found a group of Californians, who were driving about 400 horses to Sonora. But what is more important he found that they were carrying letters which revealed that the peaceful American occupation of California had ended and that the province was in revolt. Kearny must have regretted, as he marched on, that he had sent two-thirds of his force back.

What had happened in California after Carson had started east? Commodore Stockton issued a "paper blockade" of all Mexican west coast ports and laid plans to turn the government over to Major Frémont. The latter was to increase his California battalion to 300 men and to place token garrisons at Los Angeles, San Diego, Santa Bárbara, Monterey, and San Francisco. When all this was accomplished, Stockton would turn the civil authority over to Frémont, as governor, with Captain Gillespie as secretary of the territory, and himself "leave the desk and the camp, and take to the ship and the sea." Stockton had an extravagant scheme to sail his squadron to Acapulco and, after securing the town, to march inland with his bluejackets "to shake hands with general Taylor at the gates of Mexico."

But the California revolt broke out within five weeks of Stockton's raising the American flag, and he had to forgo dreams of a rendezvous with Old Zach in the halls of the Montezumas. The Commodore had reported, on September 18, that affairs were "going as well as we ought to desire" and that the Californians were "getting over their first alarm." The Californians must have concealed their true feelings admirably, so effectively to fool Stockton, for five days later the revolt broke out.

Early in the morning of September 23, a group of Californians under Captain Cerulvo Varela attacked Captain Gillespie's little garrison at Los Angeles and was repulsed. The next day, however, Captain José María Flores of the Mexican regular army rallied about him nearly 500 men at his camp, barely a mile from Gillespie's headquarters. Having produced from hiding arms and munition, Flores proclaimed the independence of California. On September 25, when Kearny had set forth on his long journey for California, Gillespie was under heavy siege. Five days later, Gillespie surrendered, the terms permitting him to take arms and ammunition to San Pedro, where, according to the Mexican understanding of the surrender, he was to sail for Monterey. By his own interpretation, Gillespie was required to retire only to San Pedro, and this he felt he had fulfilled when he boarded the United States merchantman *Vandalia,* which remained at anchor in the harbor.

Early in October, word of the revolt reached Stockton in San Francisco, and he dispatched Captain William Mervine in the *Savannah* to San Pedro to regain Los Angeles. Mervine anchored on October 6, and the next day put ashore sailors and Marines. Gillespie joined him with his little force, and the march on Los Angeles began. It was an inauspicious expedition, for Mervine, after facing opposition from foot soldiers and undergoing repeated harassment from Mexican cavalry, called off the venture after he had lost twelve men.

By now, almost all of southern California was in revolt, and when the legislative body met on October 29, Captain Flores was elected to the combined post of governor and *commandante general.* About this time, Stockton arrived to reinforce Mervine at San Pedro, but he dropped a plan to attack Los Angeles and sailed

instead to San Diego, where Captain Ezekiel Merritt, having occupied the town with a detachment of Frémont's California battalion, was under siege by Flores. The Commodore was obliged to
supply San Diego from the sea. In the north, Frémont was building
up his forces, preparatory to joining Stockton in the south. And
across the rough trails of the present state of Arizona, General
Kearny and his little command plodded on. His mules were nearly
spent, suffering from long, waterless stretches and lack of grass.

On November 25, Kearny's party forded the Colorado River in
a four-feet depth at its 500-yard crossing. It was a narrow and meandering ford, Lieutenant Emory noted, "and a few feet to the
right or left sets a horse afloat." By now, the party was in California.
But the men, as famished as their poor animals, drew little comfort
from this geographical fact. "We are still looking for the glowing
pictures drawn of California," wrote Lieutenant Emory in his
journal on December 1. "As yet, barrenness and desolation hold
their reign. We longed to stumble upon the *rancherías,* with their
flocks of fat sheep and cattle. Meat of horses may be very palatable
when fat, but ours are poor and tough, and it is hard to satisfy the
cravings of hunger with such indifferent food. Two Indians, passed
during the day, showed only indifference for the bedraggled band,
exhibiting no sign of fear or astonishment of this sudden apparition
of ragged bluecoats."

The next day, as the command ascended another "divide," "we
saw in the distance the beautiful valley of Agua Caliente, waving
with yellow grass." Journey's end was near, but there was a still
"slow and painful" marching before the *rancheria* of an American
named Warner came into sight. The starved men set about remedy-
ing their hunger. "Seven of my men ate, at one single meal, a fat
full-grown sheep," said Lieutenant Emory.

The owner, detained in San Diego, had left the ranch in charge
of a young American named Marshall, who filled in General
Kearny on the present situation in California. The Mexicans had
repossessed all the country except San Diego, San Francisco, and
Monterey. He said that Kearny was approaching the Mexican
stronghold, whence they recruited men, horses, and cattle. By an
English settler, E. Stokes, Kearny sent word to Stockton at San Diego
of his approach and, after a day's rest, he pushed on to Stokes's
ranch. Moving to the next *rancheria,* Santa María, on December 5,
the column met up, happily, with the party sent out by Commodore

Stockton, thirty-five strong, commanded by Captain Archibald Gillespie.

Learning from Gillespie that a Mexican force was nine miles distant, at San Pascual, on the road to San Diego, General Kearny sent out Lieutenant Thomas C. Hammond of the First Dragoons and a small party to reconnoiter the enemy. Hammond returned to camp about 2 A.M., having found the Mexicans, about 160 strong, who, unfortunately, discovered his party and thus were alerted. Kearny decided to attack at once, and the call to horse was sounded.

Excitement prevailed among the men, for in the long trek from Fort Leavenworth to within fifty miles of the Pacific, the command had not fired a hostile shot. Now action awaited them, nine miles up the trail, at daybreak on December 6.

The command moved out with Captain Abraham Johnston, the general's aide, leading an advance party of twelve Dragoons, all mounted on the best horses in the party. Then followed fifty Dragoons, under Captain Benjamin D. Moore, most of them mounted on the tired, all but spent mules. The rest of the force followed, with the two mountain howitzers to the rear of the attack column.

Upon contact with the enemy, Captain Johnston bravely charged, but he was shot from his saddle in the very first volley. The Mexican cavalry maintained a steady fire, before seemingly retiring in haste. Commanded by Andreas Pico, brother of the former governor, they had in reality cunningly feigned retreat to entrap the Americans. Into the trap dashed Captain Moore in hot pursuit, with the Dragoons mounted on horses right behind him. The mule-mounted troops were soon distanced, and it was then, noting the gap between the nearer and more distant Dragoons, Pico's men, "well mounted and among the best horsemen in the world," charged with lances. "On account of their greatly superior numbers," reported Kearny, "but few of us in front remained untouched." Kearny believed—or, at least, claimed—that he had won a victory at San Pascual, because "for five minutes they held the ground from us, when, our men coming up, we again drove them and they fled from the field not to return to it, which we occupied and encamped upon."

Kearny's nonexistent victory was a costly one. Captains Moore and Johnston and Lieutenant Hammond were killed and four non-commissioned officers and twelve privates were slain. General

Kearny, who was in the thick of the entire fight, was wounded in two places, Captain Gillespie and Lieutenant William H. Warner were wounded three times each, and Captain Gibson, a volunteer officer, once. Eleven Dragoons were also wounded, Kearny reported, "many of them receiving from two to ten lance wounds, most of them when unhorsed, and incapable of resistance."

Melancholy enveloped the command as the dead were buried that night to "no other accompaniment than the howling of myriads of wolves attracted by the smell." Lieutenant Emory wrote in his journal with a heavy heart: "Community of hardships, dangers, and privations had produced relations of mutual regard which caused their loss to sink deeply in our memories." Kearny's wounds were so painful that he turned over the command the rest of the day to Captain Henry S. Turner.

Day dawned on December 7 "on the most tattered and ill-fed detachment of men that ever the United States mustered under her colors." Lieutenant Emory further described the complement: "Our provisions were exhausted, our horses dead, our mules on their last legs, and our men . . . were ragged, worn down by fatigue and emaciated." The wounded, suffering excruciatingly from the rough ride on the improvised litters of poles that were dragged along the ground by the mules, added to the state of depression in which the command moved forward. Kit Carson, Lieutenant Beale of the navy, and an Indian volunteered to seek aid, twenty-nine miles away at San Diego.

Harassment by Pico's men, who stayed on Kearny's front—once they drove wild horses into the American camp, hoping to start a stampede—continued for several days. On the night of December 10, a sentinel heard voices in English and challenged. Soon the whole force heard the tramp of a marching column, and into Kearny's camp came a detachment of a hundred sailors and eighty Marines, under Lieutenant Andrew Gray, sent in relief by Commodore Stockton when Carson and Beale brought in the word of Kearny's critical position.

On December 12, seventy-nine days after leaving Santa Fé, General Kearny marched into San Diego, in whose harbor the authority of the United States in California, the warships, *Congress* and *Portsmouth,* rode at anchor. Only at San Diego did the American flag fly in southern California.

At Kearny's urging, Commodore Stockton decided to launch an

attack on Los Angeles, but it was not until December 29 that arrangements—including the question of command—were completed. Kearny finally accepted command of the attack column which consisted of fifty-seven of his Dragoons, forty-five sailors in charge of six small pieces of artillery, 397 sailors and Marines acting as infantry, sixty volunteers, and an oxcart wagon train. But Stockton insisted on the overall command of the expedition. The struggle for command power, based on conflicting orders, an accomplished fact, and a clash of personalities, would come later.

By easy stages, the force advanced on the City of the Angels. On January 4, a proposition was sent forward under a flag of truce by Captain José María Flores that an armistice be reached until the outcome of the war settled the fate of California. Stockton refused to parley with Flores on the grounds that he had violated his oath of allegiance to the United States. On January 8, there was a brush at the San Gabriel River, but with "New Orleans!" as the battle cry, the Americans swept aside Flores's opposition and continued the march. When the party had covered half the distance from the San Gabriel to Los Angeles, Flores made another attempt to halt the column. But long-range artillery proved ineffective, and cavalry sorties on the American flanks and rear were easily repulsed.

Captain Flores now gave up the fight for Los Angeles, which the Americans entered the next day, January 10, 1847, and raised again the flag which Captain Gillespie had lowered in surrender three months earlier.

All this while, what had Frémont been doing in the north? Early in December, having recruited his battalion of mounted riflemen to a total of 400, Frémont had started south to join Stockton. He now held the rank of lieutenant colonel in the United States Army, word of his promotion having reached him late in October.

Swooping down without warning, after a march of 150 miles, Frémont captured San Luis Obispo without firing a shot. Don Jesús Pico, cousin of Pío and Andreas, and commandant of the place, was captured and brought immediately before a court-martial for breaking his parole. Found guilty and sentenced to be shot, Don Jesús was pardoned by Frémont, to whom he became greatly attached. "That pardon had its influence on all the subsequent events," declared Frémont. ". . . Many hearts were conquered the day he was pardoned, and his own above all."

Although Mexican horsemen were seen regularly during the

march, there was no fighting. At the San Fernando Valley, Frémont encountered the Mexicans in force on January 13. Under a flag, Frémont sent a summons to the enemy to submit at once or prepare to be attacked. The Mexicans sent back word that they wished to speak with Frémont in person. Here is his account of what happened:

> I went alone to see them, (Don Jesús Pico only being with me). They were willing to capitulate to me; the terms were agreed upon . . . It received the sanction of the governor and commander-in-chief, Commodore Stockton . . . It put an end to the war and to the feelings of war. It tranquilized the country, and gave safety to every American from the day of its conclusion.

The next day, very much pleased with himself—and certainly with justification—for marching 400 miles "through an insurgent country, without spilling a drop of blood—conquering by clemency and justice," Lieutenant Colonel John Charles Frémont entered Los Angeles with the Treaty of Cahuenga, which indeed ended hostilities in California, in his hand. It was a liberal treaty. The California insurgents were guaranteed the same rights as American citizens and were not called upon to take an oath until the war ended. Moreover, they were free to stay or leave the territory. Commodore Stockton, overcoming some initial reluctance, accepted the treaty.

The rivalry between the Californians and the Americans was now over, but the rivalry between the U.S. Army and Navy on the Pacific was just beginning. General Kearny claimed that War Department orders authorized him to establish a government for California. Commodore Stockton countered by declaring that he had that authority from Navy Department orders sent to his predecessor, Commodore Sloat. Moreover, Stockton held that he had already conquered California and had established a government before Kearny had arrived. What Kearny had been sent out to do was an accomplished fact, which he apparently had recognized when, on learning of events in California from Lieutenant Kit Carson, he sent two-thirds of his force back to Santa Fé.

Commodore Stockton then suspended General Kearny from any military command beyond that of his own Dragoons, and on Janu-

ary 16, he named Frémont governor of California, an appointment he had planned in October. Frémont, in accepting it, placed himself in the peculiar position of receiving the governorship from a naval officer, in the face of opposition from an army officer who ranked him by two grades. He later stated his justification:

> Governor Stockton gave me an order to reorganize [the government of California]; General Kearny sent me an order not to reorganize it . . . I informed General Kearny, by letter, that I thought he and Governor Stockton ought to adjust the question of rank between themselves; and, until that was done, I should have to obey Commodore Stockton as theretofore . . .

Kearny swallowed his pride rather than precipitate an open break during the critical period, and he left for San Diego to await the Mormon battalion, which had followed him west.

The Mormons, 350 strong, arrived on January 29 under the able command of Lieutenant Colonel Philip St. George Cooke. The battalion, which had set out from Santa Fé on October 19, toiled over the arduous trail for 102 days, traveling 1,125 miles, to bring the first wagon train over the Rocky Mountains. "I encountered extraordinary obstacles to a wagon road, and actually hewed a passage, with axes, through a chasm of solid rock, which lacked a foot of being as wide as the wagons," Cooke reported to Kearny. ". . . The constant tenor of your letters of instruction made it almost a point of honor to bring the wagons through to the Pacific; and so I was retarded in making and finding a road for them." Cooke was generous in praise of his men, who despite extreme privations and exposures, accomplished in a "cheerful and faithful manner . . . the great labors of this march."

Installing Lieutenant Colonel Cooke in command at San Diego, Kearny sailed for Monterey. There he found that Stockton had been replaced by Commodore W. Branford Shubrick, who had just arrived aboard the *Independence* from the United States. Commodore Shubrick at once recognized Kearny's authority as military commander ashore, but he exhibited instructions from the Navy Department giving him authority to set up the civil government.

Such was the situation until February 13, when Colonel Richard B. Mason arrived from Washington, via Panama, with specific instructions from the Secretary of War and the Secretary of the

Navy (a post now held by John Y. Mason), which solved the difficulty:

> The President had deemed it best for the public interests to invest the military officer commanding with the direction of the operations on land, and with the administrative functions of government over the people and territory occupied by us . . . The establishment of port regulations is a subject over which it is deemed, by the President, most appropriate that the naval commander shall exercise jurisdiction.

Complete harmony prevailed as Shubrick and Kearny published a circular defining their respective responsibilities, and the General issued a proclamation establishing a new government with Monterey as its capital. Somehow, the latest order did not reach Frémont in Los Angeles, and he refused to accede to an order from General Kearny that he turn over command of the military district to Lieutenant Colonel Cooke and discharge those members of his California battalion who refused to be mustered into service under the existing law.

Frémont, leaving instructions not to honor any order from Cooke, rode 400 miles in three and a half days to see Kearny at Monterey. Learning of the changed situation, Frémont immediately returned to Los Angeles, he and his now faithful friend, Don Jesús Pico, and a servant making the 800-mile round trip in eight days. Relations were not smooth between Frémont and Colonel Mason, and at one time they were close to a duel with double-barreled shotguns. When the regiment of New York Volunteers, under Colonel J. D. Stevenson, arrived in March, after a long voyage around Cape Horn, General Kearny appointed Colonel Mason as governor and prepared to return to Fort Leavenworth.

Kearny left the Pacific Coast on May 31, having ordered Frémont to accompany him and remain under his orders on the homeward march to Fort Leavenworth. There, on August 22, General Kearny ordered his arrest on charges of mutiny, disobedience of orders, and conduct prejudicial to good order and military discipline. The court-martial, set in Washington, lasted from November 2, 1847, to January 31, 1848, with Senator Thomas Hart Benton, Frémont's father-in-law, as his chief counsel. Frémont was found guilty of all three charges and was sentenced to dismissal from the service. President Polk approved the sentence but remitted the penalty. But Frémont refused reinstatement and resigned. Thirteen years later, after serving as Senator from California and being the first Republican candidate for the Presidency, John Charles Frémont returned to the army, where as a Union major general, he proved a controversial and unfortunate figure.

19

Meanwhile—Again
in Washington

"The administration and the country are already tired of the Mexican War," wrote John C. Calhoun to a friend on August 8, 1846, "and are in as great haste to get out of it, as they were to get into it."

What prompted the South Carolina Senator's comment was President Polk's efforts that very day to have Congress appropriate $2,000,000 "to facilitate negotiations with Mexico." Although it was a Saturday, and Congress had agreed to adjourn at noon, Monday, the President sent a message to both Houses. The House, after some exciting debate, passed an appropriations bill, but with, as Polk recorded in his diary, "a mischievous and foolish amendment" prohibiting slavery from any territory acquired from Mexico. This, of course, was Representative David Wilmot's famous proviso. "What connection slavery had with making peace in Mexico it is difficult to conceive," the President wrote disgustedly.

On Monday, when the House-passed appropriations measure, with the Wilmot Proviso tacked on, reached the Senate it did not come up until about thirty or forty minutes before adjournment. "Senator [John] Davis of Massachusetts took the floor and spoke until the time had expired, so as to defeat action on it," Polk disappointedly confided to his diary. ". . . Had there been time, there is but little doubt the Senate would have struck out the slavery proviso and that the House would have concurred."

Among the petty annoyances the President experienced that first summer of the Mexican War was the "passion" that members of Congress had to be appointed to the newly created brigadier and major general posts. "They created offices by their own votes and then seek to fill them themselves," noted Polk. Among these was Representative Stephen A. Douglas of Illinois, whom the President advised "in a long and friendly conversation . . . to abandon his application for a place in the army and remain in his seat in Congress."

On September 1, through the British Legation, which had received dispatches from Mexico City, President Polk learned that Commodore Sloat had hoisted the American flag over Monterey and had proclaimed California a possession of the United States. It was this news, doubtless, which prompted Polk to complain to his diary about Zachary Taylor's "want of energy and promptness." Nearly four months had passed since Taylor had crossed the Rio Grande, and nothing, the President thought, had been achieved since then. Polk questioned Taylor's judgment in calling for baggage wagons and posed the question to Quartermaster General Thomas S. Jesup whether pack-mules were not better. Jesup obligingly "gave it as his decided opinion that baggage wagons should be dispensed with and mules employed." General Jesup further stated that were he in General Taylor's place he would prefer mules to cumbersome wagons and that he would not take a single tent with him.

The President took his office as Commander-in-Chief of the nation's armed forces quite seriously, and he lamented that the pressures of the Presidency made it "impossible to give much attention to the details in conducting the war." Always, however, Zachary Taylor's inadequacy remained uppermost in Polk's mind. One may ask, a century and a quarter later, that if Old Zach had been a Democrat—and not already boomed as the Whig candidate for the Presidency in 1848—would President Polk have detected any qualifications for leadership? On September 7, Polk recorded his concern:

General Taylor, I fear, is not the man for the command of the army. He is brave, but he does not seem to have resources or grasp of mind enough to conduct a campaign . . . He is, I have no doubt, a good subordinate officer, but from all the evidence before me I think him unfit for the chief command. Though this is so, I know of no one whom I can substitute in his place.

What evidence did Polk have regarding Taylor's unfitness? His two victories against a vastly superior force, at Palo Alto and Resaca de La Palma? His bloodless occupation of Matamoros? The successful move, beset by transportation problems, of the army to Camargo, the line of departure for the march on Monterrey?

Barely a week later, on September 15, the President was again writing about Taylor. Again he questioned Old Zach's "resources and grasp of mind" for the responsibilities of command, and he criticized the General for providing but "little information" on the topography, roads, available supplies, and so on. "He seems to act as a regular soldier, whose only duty it is to obey orders," complained the President. ". . . He seems disposed to avoid all responsibility of making any suggestions or giving any opinion."

At a cabinet meeting on September 22—at the very time the three-day battle for Monterrey was raging—it was decided that an expedition of about 4,000 men would be sent against Tampico under Major General Robert Patterson, accompanied by Brigadier Generals James Shields and Gideon Pillow. General Pillow's sole claim to military command was that he was once James K. Polk's law partner. The New York *Courier and Enquirer* noted this relationship, and added, "and like him, was a good third-rate Country lawyer." There was a story current—fact or fiction?—that at Camargo, General Pillow had demonstrated his military genius by throwing up a breastwork in which the ditch was on the inside.

Polk, at this time, was still irritated with General Scott, who he said was not only "no aid" to the War Department but was, by his presence in Washington, "constantly embarrassing" to Secretary Marcy, already "overwhelmed with his labors and responsibilities." Already Polk and Marcy were thinking of an attack and landing at Vera Cruz, but the President was reluctant even to consider Scott for the assignment.

On October 2, the President learned that Taylor had left Camargo for Monterrey, and he surmised that "a battle would take place at the latter place." He also received word that General Kearny had taken possession of Santa Fé "without firing a gun or shedding blood," and had annexed New Mexico to the United States. One may infer from Polk's notation in his diary that Kearny was a Democrat: "General Kearny has thus far performed his duty."

President Polk was spending a quiet Sunday evening on October 11, when Secretary Marcy, Adjutant General Jones, and a dispatch bearer from General Taylor were ushered into the White House about dark. The President, if his diary reveals the true state of his mind, found no time to exult in Old Zach's victory at Monterrey because of the rapidity with which he found fault with the eight-weeks armistice Taylor had negotiated. Not a word of praise from the President—only this in his diary:

In agreeing to this armistice General Taylor violated his express orders and I regret that I cannot approve his course. He had the enemy in his power and should have taken them prisoners, deprived them of their arms, discharged them on their parole or honour, and preserved the advantages which he had obtained by pushing on without delay farther into the country, if the force at his command justified it.

At a cabinet meeting the next day, agreement was unanimous that Taylor had committed "a great error" in his terms of capitulation to General Ampudia and that had he captured the Mexicans, disarmed and paroled them, "it would have probably ended the war in Mexico." The cabinet agreed unanimously, too, that immediate orders should be sent Taylor to terminate the armistice and "to prosecute the war with energy and vigor." Ten days later the armchair strategist in the White House reversed himself, and the cabinet to a man agreed, "that under existing circumstances General Taylor should not advance beyond Monterrey. . . ."

One night, early in November, Senator Thomas Hart Benton dropped in at the White House, and he and the President conversed as length on the prosecution of the war. Benton felt that a bold stroke was needed, at once. And he suggested that it be made at Vera Cruz, which Polk and Marcy had already contemplated, and once the port was taken "a rapid crushing movement" against Mexico City should be launched. The Senator suggested that commissioners—"the first men of the country of both political parties" —accompany the army, authorized "to offer peace before a battle, during the battle, and after it was over."

"I am willing to accompany the army as one of these commissioners," volunteered Senator Benton.

"If it is thought expedient to institute such a commission," replied the President, "I will be most happy to avail myself of your services in that capacity."

A few days later, on November 10, Polk and Benton had another long talk about an attack on Vera Cruz. The Senator agreed with the President that "General Taylor . . . would not heartily cooperate with the government [on] such an expedition unless he commanded it himself" and also that, for all his bravery, Taylor was not "a man of capacity enough for such a campaign." The President then raised the name of General Scott. Senator Benton said he had no confidence in him. Then, after Polk had named several other officers, Senator Benton made his preposterous nomination of himself, as "a man of talents and resources," to be commissioned lieutenant general, should Congress create such a rank.

In the early days of November, the President began to denounce Taylor in his diary as "a bitter political partisan," and when the cabinet discussed possible leaders for the Vera Cruz expedition, Old Zach was discarded not only because of "a want of confidence . . . in his capacity" but also because his "partisan political feelings . . . render himself hostile to the administration." In the light of Taylor's successive victories one may wonder how Polk and the cabinet could agree that he was unfit for the command of the expedition against Vera Cruz.

The President suggested General W. O. Butler, but this didn't touch off any enthusiasm. Then the name of General Patterson was proposed for consideration, but his inexperience soon eliminated him. Inevitably, the name of Scott came up, and reluctantly, according to Polk, the cabinet came to the conclusion he should be chosen. On November 17, Polk wrote in his diary:

> General Scott it was known was hostile to the administration, and it was apprehended would have no sympathy with it in carrying out its plans . . . Yet . . . as he was the highest officer in command in the army, he should be entrusted with the conduct of this important expedition . . . I have strong objections to General Scott, and after his very exceptionable letter in May last nothing but stern necessity and a sense of public duty could induce me to place him at the head of so important an expedition. Still I do not well see how it can be avoided. He is General-in-Chief of the army. If I had the power to select a General I would select Col. Benton to conduct the expedition.

The cabinet meeting ended without any decision, but the next day Secretary Marcy told the President that, reluctantly, he had to admit that there was no other possible choice but Winfield Scott. And so, on the morning of November 19, Scott was summoned to the White House by President Polk.

By reference to Polk's diary and Scott's *Autobiography*, their conversation can be reconstructed:

Polk: "The capture of Vera Cruz is very important to secure peace. It is important that the officer entrusted to command the expedition should have confidence in the government, and that the government have confidence in him."

Scott: "Assuredly, sir."

Polk: "Without a cordial cooperation success can hardly be expected. If I could be satisfied of your proper confidence in the administration and that you would cordially cooperate with it, I would be disposed to assign the command to you."

Scott: "I have the utmost confidence in the administration and yourself, Mr. President, and I will cordially cooperate with you in carrying out your views in the prosecution of the war."

Polk: "I am willing to let bygones be bygones and I offer you the command."

Scott: "I am deeply grateful to you, Mr. President. I will show my gratitude by my conduct when I get to the field."

The President recorded that Scott was so much affected that he almost shed tears. The General later wrote that "every expression of kindness and confidence was lavished upon me. Such was the warmth and emphasis of his professions that he won my confidence."

General Scott left—"the most delighted man I have seen for a long time," noted the President—and though "oppressed with the labors of military preparation" he addressed a circular to the leading Whigs in Congress, revealing "how handsomely" President Polk had treated him.

Polk was not as "handsome" with Zachary Taylor. Two days after he had given the command of the Vera Cruz expedition to one Whig general he turned an angry pen loose on the other. Noting Taylor's hostility, Polk said he was a weak man "made giddy with the idea of the Presidency." He called Taylor "ungrateful" and "a narrow-minded, bigotted partisan . . . not fit for a higher command than that of a Regiment." Smugly, the President added: "I have no prejudice against him."

What provoked this last outburst against Taylor? Old Zach, understandably irked by orders that the Secretary of War had sent directly to General Patterson at Camargo to move against Tampico, had minced no words in replying. "While I remain in command of the army against Mexico, and am therefore justly held responsible by the government and the country for the conduct of its operations," Taylor wrote, "I must claim the right of organizing all detachments from it, and regulating the time and manner of their service." This letter Polk considered "in very bad taste and worse temper," and he must have been beside himself with anger, judging from the tirade he transferred to his diary.

During mid-December, Polk was still pushing for Congress to create the rank of lieutenant general so that he could name Thomas Hart Benton and thus supersede the two Whig generals. On the 14th, he met with a small group of House members to whom he confessed "embarrassment in conducting the war with the present officers." He explained his objections to Taylor and Scott—lack of sympathy with the government, not, of course, the fact that they were Whigs—and sought the solons' support to have Congress create the rank of lieutenant general. They all agreed it would be impossible to pass such a bill. On December 19, the President invited Senator Calhoun to the White House and repeated his story. Calhoun flatly refused to take part in the scheme.

On this day, General Scott arrived in New Orleans on his way to the Rio Grande. He had left Washington, basking, he thought, in President Polk's goodwill and warm professions of confidence. To have doubted Polk's sincerity, Scott wrote, "would have been . . . unmanly suspicion and a crime." But in New Orleans, he learned by a letter from Senator Alexander Barrow of Louisiana, an old friend, of Polk's intrigue to supersede him with Senator Benton in the rank of lieutenant general. "A grosser abuse of human confidence is nowhere recorded," Scott wrote in his *Autobiography*.

When, a few days later, the year 1846 came to an end, the military situation was as follows.

In northern Mexico, General Taylor was marching on Victoria, and General Wool, having ended his march from San Antonio, occupied Saltillo.

On the Gulf of Mexico, Tampico, captured by Commodore David Conner in November, was securely in American hands.

In Chihuahua, Colonel Doniphan occupied El Paso after the stirring victory of El Brazito.

In New Mexico, where Sterling Price was in command, a revolt against American rule was brewing.

In California, General Kearny, Commodore Stockton, and Lieutenant Colonel Frémont had almost completed its reconquest.

And at Camargo, General Winfield Scott waited patiently for a meeting with General Taylor, a meeting which Taylor had neither desire nor intention to attend.

20

"The Very Spot . . . for Battle"

From the goose quill of Secretary of War William L. Marcy there flowed on October 13, 1846, a letter of almost 3,000 words, but only forty-four of them thanked Zachary Taylor for his victory at Monterrey, and then only indirectly.

"The skill, courage, and gallant conduct displayed on that occasion by the troops under your command, both regulars and volunteers, have added glory to our arms," wrote the Secretary of War, "and merit from the government and people of the United States the warmest expressions of gratitude and praise."

That was all—no mention of Taylor, no word of praise for the General, personally—as Marcy's pen raced to relay President Polk's "regrets" over the terms Taylor had given Ampudia. The government did not contemplate any contingency when it would be "expedient to suspend hostilities" before peace negotiations. The continuation of the armistice is "extremely embarrassing" to the government's plans. Accordingly, General Taylor is instructed "to give requisite notice that the armistice is to cease at once, and that each party is at liberty to resume and prosecute hostilities without restriction."

Old Zach received this letter of censure, for such indeed it was, on November 2. His reply on November 8 did not conceal his irritation as he gave sound reasons of military necessity for granting the armistice terms, "cogent reasons, most of which occur of themselves to the minds of all who are acquainted with the conditions of things here."

Meanwhile, on November 5, Taylor informed Santa Anna that he had received instructions to terminate the armistice and that after November 13, he would consider himself "at liberty to cross the specified line." On November 10, Santa Anna received and answered Taylor's letter: "You may commence hostilities when you please and . . . I shall correspond to them."

163

Four days later, Commodore David Conner occupied Tampico without firing a shot. Unknown to Conner when he led the Home Squadron against the port, Tampico had been evacuated two weeks earlier on the orders of Santa Anna, who called for the troops and war materiel to join him at San Luis Potosí, where he was assembling an army.

On November 16, General Taylor took "peaceable possession" of Saltillo. Less than a month later, Taylor, with General Twiggs's regulars and General Quitman's volunteers, took the road to Victoria, leaving General Worth's command at Saltillo, while General William O. Butler held Monterrey. General Wool's force was at Parras, ninety miles west of Saltillo. On December 17, the fourth day of Taylor's march to Victoria, two Dragoons on foaming horses overtook him with an urgent message from General Worth. Santa Anna, Worth reported, was making a forced march north to strike both Saltillo and Parras.

Old Zach sent General Quitman on to Victoria to make a junction with General Robert Patterson's force, marching from Camargo to Tampico, and he hurried back over the trail. Meanwhile Wool had marched from Parras and Butler from Monterrey to strengthen Worth at Saltillo. Pushing on rapidly, Taylor passed through Monterrey, where another courier from Worth galloped up. It was all a false alarm, Santa Anna hadn't left San Luis Potosí at all. Taylor placed Butler in general command at Saltillo, and once again started out with Twiggs's troops for Victoria. It was on this second march that Taylor received a letter from General Scott announcing his coming to Mexico, "not . . . my dear general, to supersede you . . . My proposed theater is different. You may imagine it . . . But, my dear general, I shall be obliged to take from you most of the gallant officers and men (regulars and volunteers) whom you have so long and so nobly commanded."

One may imagine Old Zach's rage as he read on: "imperious necessity . . . for a time . . . stand on the defensive . . . infinitely painful to you . . . your patriotism to submit . . . temporary sacrifice with cheerfulness." Cheerfulness, indeed! Taylor wrote his son-in-law Dr. Wood: "I had been stripped of nearly the whole of the regular force & more than half of the Volunteers, & ordered here to act on the defensive . . . I cannot know what force will be left behind, until Genl S. completes his command." And later, Old Zach again expressed his bitterness to Dr. Wood: "We now begin to see the fruits of the arrangements recently made at Washington, by an intrigue of Marcey, [sic] Scott, & Worth to take from me nearly the whole of the regular forces under my command."

Taylor protested vigorously to the War Department, asking that his protest be brought to President Polk's attention, and he wrote a sharp letter to General Scott in which he did not "disguise my feelings" and Scott's reply was "somewhat tart." "He & myself understand each other perfectly, & there can for the future be none other than official intercourse between us," said Taylor.

Taylor's army was indeed depleted, for all told, Scott took 9,000 men from him, including General Worth's division of regulars at Saltillo. General Wool's command was already at Saltillo when Worth marched off on January 9, 1847, to join Scott. Nine days later, Worth reached Camargo—"General Worth moved his division with a rapidity that would have been commendable had he been going to the relief of a beleagured garrison," wrote Lieutenant U. S. Grant—and on January 22, he went into camp at Matamoros.

The next day, Taylor returned to Monterrey from the useless Victoria expedition, having bade farewell to troops who had marched and fought with him all the way from Corpus Christi. The diarists and letter writers in his command, Captain W. S. Henry and Lieutenant George G. Meade, left Old Zach with regrets. "Many a soldier's heart that had braved the battle's storm undaunted, now swelled with emotion," wrote Henry. "Many an eye that had flashed fire o'er glistening bayonets, filled with tears when the order announcing our separation was read." Meade was less sentimental, but no less sincere: "I must confess I regretted exceedingly parting with the old man. He has been most outrageously treated by the administration, which hopes to play off General Scott against him . . . to break him down and destroy his popularity."

After his army had been "shorn" by Scott, Taylor retained barely 500 regulars, including those of General Wool. Of the troops that captured Monterrey, there remained to Taylor only Brevet Colonel Charles May's two companies of the Second Dragoons, Colonel Jefferson Davis's Mississippi Rifles, and the two companies of the Third Artillery, now commanded by Captain Braxton Bragg, following the accidental death of the fearless Randolph Ridgely. While riding through Monterrey, about a month after its capture, Ridgely suffered a fractured skull when his mount stumbled into a hole and threw its rider. Three days later, on October 30 Ridgely died, a much lamented "soldier's soldier."

Old Zach took stock of his force, and found it a little more than 200 short of 5,000 troops. It was composed of the following commands:

Regulars

Unit	Strength
General Staff	41
1st Dragoons (Captain Enoch Steen)	133
2nd Dragoons (Brevet Colonel Charles May)	76
3rd Artillery (Captain Braxton Bragg)	150
4th Artillery (Captain John W. Washington)	117
Total Regular Troops	517

Volunteers

Unit	Strength
Mississippi Rifles (Colonel Jefferson Davis)	368
Arkansas Mounted (Colonel Archibald Yell)	479
Indiana Brigade (Brigadier General Joseph Lane) (composed of 2nd Indiana Infantry—Colonel William Bowles and 3rd Indiana Infantry—Colonel James H. Lane)	1253
1st Illinois Infantry (Colonel John J. Hardin)	580
2nd Illinois Infantry (Colonel William H. Bissell)	573
1st Kentucky Mounted (Colonel Humphrey Marshall)	330
2nd Kentucky Infantry (Colonel William McKee)	571
Texas Volunteers (Captain P. E. Conner)	61
McCulloch Spy Company (Major Ben McCulloch)	27
Total Volunteers Troops	4,242
Total Troops in command	4,759

While Taylor, who had joined Wool at Saltillo early in February, still inwardly burned over the "raid" on his army, he had no lack of confidence as to what would happen if Santa Anna did, in fact, launch the long-rumored attack. "I shall fight the enemy should he be disposed to give me battle; & altho nearly the whole of my command are volunteers, I have no doubt we will give a satisfactory acct of him," he wrote Dr. Wood. ". . . Confidence seems to be not only restored, but the greatest enthusiasm appears to pervade the whole of the force, & all express themselves desirous to come in collision with the enemy." In this same letter, dated February 9, Taylor said that Scott had "advised" him to fall back from Saltillo to Monterrey. "I informed him I could not think of doing [this] without peremptory orders to that effect from proper authority." Actually, Scott had not "advised" at all, he had ordered: "I must ask you to abandon Saltillo, and to make no detachments, except for reconnaissances and immediate defense, beyond Monterrey. I know this to be the wish of the government, founded on reasons in which I concur . . ." Advice or order, Taylor ignored it, and not only remained at Saltillo, but pushed nearly twenty miles south of it to Agua Nueva on the San Luis Potosí road.

Before Taylor returned from Victoria, a scouting party of Arkansas and Kentucky Volunteers, about eighty or ninety men, under Majors Solon Borland and John P. Gaines, failed to return. The inference, which proved correct, was that the party had been captured by advance elements of Santa Anna's army. Lieutenant Reynolds was disgusted with the unmilitary habits of the volunteers: "They had no precautions against surprise, had no pickets or sentinels and were taken asleep without firing a gun." This episode alerted Taylor to the imminence of battle.

Santa Anna for nearly four months had been building an army at San Luis Potosí. That the Napoleon of the West seldom, if ever, emulated his famous namesake in actual battle could not obscure the fact that he had great skill in raising troops, gathering materiel and stimulating morale. By the middle of January, 1847, Santa Anna had an army of more than 21,000 poised to march. The Mexican commander knew that General Scott was mounting an attack on Vera Cruz. He may have known, through the capture of a letter from Scott to Taylor, of the draining off of the latter's troops. Whatever prompted him, Santa Anna decided to march north and first crush Taylor, leaving Vera Cruz to defend itself. He was confident that later he could turn against Scott and contain his army within the fever belt near the coast, where the devastating *el vómito* would prove a powerful ally.

On January 28, Santa Anna began his march to attack Taylor, his force numbering 18,000 men. Rain, wind, and bitter cold lashed the Mexicans almost from the start, and the "ravages of the unpropitious season" began to take a toll. When the norther finally blew itself out and the sun returned, the weary soldiers soon were suffering from the other extreme of temperature. "The heat," states a contemporary Mexican account of the march, "became as intolerable as had been the cold on the days before." Long stretches without water, and a reduction in the rations made the march almost unendurable. By February 21, when his entire force had assembled at La Encarnación, fully 4,000 Mexicans had died or deserted or were ill or straggling. But even with his force reduced to 14,000 troops, Santa Anna had more than three times the men Zachary Taylor had at Agua Nueva.

Seeking specific information on the size of Santa Anna's force, General Taylor sent out Colonel May with the Second Dragoons and Major Ben McCulloch and his "spy company," as Taylor identified the twenty-seven Texans in his troop returns. May, from second-hand information, returned with the news that Santa Anna was at Encarnación in great force. McCulloch, who had penetrated with a single companion almost into Santa Anna's camp, was more specific. He estimated that the Mexican army was nearly 20,000 strong. The scouting parties also brought back word that Mexican cavalry, under General Vicente Miñón, was on the prowl, posing the threat of looping behind Taylor's army to block the Saltillo road or of launching a direct raid on Saltillo itself.

Taylor evacuated Agua Nueva on February 21, leaving Colonel Archibald Yell and the Arkansas cavalry to cover his withdrawal and to send along the wagons with foodstuff and supplies. Yell, on the approach of the enemy, was to fire the buildings, destroy whatever supplies remained, and fall back on the main army. At La Angostura (The Narrows), a defile about five miles below Saltillo, Taylor dropped off Colonel John J. Hardin's First Illinois Infantry and Colonel William R. McKee's Second Kentucky Infantry and continued about another mile and a half to the hacienda of Buena Vista. Here Old Zach left General Wool in immediate command of the army, while he, with a small complement, rode into Saltillo to inspect and reorganize the defenses of the city.

Late the same day, when it became evident to Colonel Yell that the enemy's arrival at Agua Nueva could not be long delayed, he put the remaining supplies, wagons, equipment, as well as the buildings, to the torch and rode off with his Arkansas cavalry to rejoin Taylor.

The smoke and flames told Santa Anna, as he approached Agua Nueva, that Taylor had escaped.

"Se fueron! Se fueron!" he cried. "They have fled! They have fled!"

From the destruction at Agua Nueva, and the signs of a frantic departure, Santa Anna inferred panic in Taylor's army, and he pushed his weary troops forward to fall upon a demoralized enemy and crush him.

When Taylor rejoined his army on the morning of February 22, General Wool had already disposed the troops in a defense line in La Angostura. Two months earlier, to the day, Wool and Captain James Henry Carleton were riding through the defile to their camp when Wool reined his horse and swept with his eye the terrain on both sides of the road.

"Mr. Carleton," said General Wool, "this is the very spot of all others I have yet seen in Mexico, which I would select for battle, were I obliged with a small army to fight a large one."

Wool then pointed to the network of deeply worn gullies on the right of the road and said that they would completely protect that flank. The heights on the left commanded the road, Wool declared, while deep ravines in front of them, extending back to the mountains, presented terrain which would hamper an enemy's movements.

Subsequently, topographical engineers examined the ground approvingly, and General Taylor himself had approved Wool's choice of the battle ground long before Santa Anna's brilliant array appeared on his front. No one since has improved on Old Zach's description of the ground over which the Battle of Buena Vista was fought:

> Our troops were in position occupying a line of remarkable strength. The road at this point becomes a narrow defile, the valley on its right being rendered quite impracticable for artillery by a system of deep and impassable gullies, while on the left a succession of rugged ridges and precipitous ravines, extends far back towards the mountains which bound the valley. The features of the ground were such as nearly to paralyze the artillery and cavalry of the enemy, while his infantry could not derive all the advantages of its numerical superiority. In this position we prepared to receive him.

Washington's battery of eight guns was posted on the road, while supporting it on the slopes and spurs to the left and rear were the First and Second Illinois, the Second Kentucky and Captain Conner's Texans.

On the extreme American left, along the base of the mountain, the Kentucky and Arkansas Mounted, both units on foot, guarded against a flanking movement by the enemy.

Immediately to the rear of Washington's battery on ridges overlooking the plateau that spread to the mountain were the Indiana Brigade, the Mississippi Rifles, the First and Second Dragoons, with Braxton Bragg's artillery, consisting of his own and Sherman's batteries, ready for dispatch to any part of the field.

Such was the disposition of Zachary Taylor's little army on the morning of February 22, 1847, when Antonio López de Santa Anna came thundering through the valley with an advance force of 2,000 or more cavalry, artillery, and a small detachment of infantry.

21

The Battle of Buena Vista

Psychologically, Santa Anna made a bad choice of the day on which to set out to crush an American army—Washington's Birthday.

An eager activity marked Zachary Taylor's camp on the morning of February 22, a morning as glorious in nature as the day was in tradition. Officers and orderlies galloped about, drums rolled, and flags whipped in the breeze. Regimental bands struck up "Hail Columbia" and "Yankee Doodle," and the troops cheered wildly as Old Zach rode along the lines. General Wool evoked enthusiasm as he passed from unit to unit, making a few "spirited and patriotic remarks" and exhorting the men to add luster to the glittering name of Washington. The watchword of the day, "Honor of Washington," passed from man to man, and there was more cheering.

The distant clouds of dust drew nearer the defile, and suddenly there burst into view the dazzlingly-attired Mexican cavalry, colors flying, and their bright spears gleaming in the morning sun. Soon artillery and infantry were discerned moving up, their bands playing and banners waving. Distinctly, in the American lines, the Mexican bugles were heard sounding a halt. In a moment, Santa Anna began his deployment. This was the signal for the engineers of both armies to busy themselves studying each other's positions and troop disposition.

About 11 A.M., three horsemen under a white flag galloped out from the Mexican lines, and shortly thereafter Santa Anna's surgeon general, a German named Pedro Vanderlinden, dismounted and handed General Taylor a peremptory summons to surrender. Old Zach snorted as he read the insolent note from the arrogant Napoleon of the West:

> You are surrounded by twenty thousand men, and can not in any human probability avoid suffering a rout, and being cut

to pieces with your troops; but as you deserve consideration and particular esteem, I wish to save you from a catastrophe, and for that purpose give you notice, in order that you may surrender at discretion, under the assurance that you will be treated with the consideration belonging to the Mexican character; to which end you will be granted an hour's time to make up your mind, to commence from the moment when my flag of truce arrives in your camp.

Dragoon Sam Chamberlain, who was not at the spot, recorded Taylor's reply as follows: "Tell Santa Anna to go to Hell! Major Bliss, put that in Spanish and send it back by this damned Dutchman."

Lieutenant Sam French, who was there, regretted not having written down "the exact words made by the General in his verbal reply," but he said they were "very forcible" and were "toned down" by Major Bliss. For Santa Anna, and history, Old Zach's official reply was neatly couched in twenty-eight words: "In reply to your note of this date summoning me to surrender my forces at discretion, I beg leave to say that I decline acceding to your request."

General Pedro de Ampudia, who had surrendered Monterrey to Taylor, began a flanking movement about two o'clock, marching toward the base of the mountain with four battalions of light infantry. To challenge this attempt to turn his left, Taylor ordered the Arkansas and Kentucky Mounted and a battalion of Indiana troops up the slope, and the two forces climbed opposite ridges, each trying to outflank the other.

Noting a movement on the Mexican left, suggesting the possibility of a wide enemy sweep to avoid the impassable gullies on the American right, Taylor sent Bragg's battery, supported by McKee's Kentucky Infantry, to occupy a position between the gullies and the mountains on that side, and slightly forward of Washington's battery on the road.

To provide artillery support for the soon-to-be-embattled left, two of Washington's guns were sent under Lieutenant Bryan, topographical engineer serving with the artillery, toward the mountain where Ampudia was trying to turn the American line. Deeming a third gun necessary, General Wool rode up to Captain Washington and asked if he could spare another.

"Yes," replied the artillerist.

"But what will become of this key to our position, if you are deprived of three of your guns?" asked Wool.

"I will defend it," said Washington.

Accordingly, Lieutenant John Paul Jones O'Brien was detached with a third gun, and when he joined the other two pieces he assumed command.

By now it was 3 o'clock and a Mexican heavy howitzer signaled the beginning of the battle. Immediately, Ampudia opened with a warm fire upon the American riflemen, the Mexicans discharging their muskets in rapid volleys, while Taylor's men, from behind the crest of their ridge, fired deliberately, "doing terrible execution with their unerring weapons." Captain J. H. Carleton, who was in the battle, and wrote the most complete account of it, described the duel:

> From that time until dark, these troops continued the conflict without changing their positions, except to approach each other by climbing still higher up the mountain, until, at last, there were two lines of combatants from near the plateau to its very summit.

Up and down the rest of the line, an occasional and ineffectual cannonade by the Mexicans broke the quiet, but there was no small-arms activity other than on the extreme American left. Nightfall ended the fighting there, and the two armies bivouacked on the field. No shooting, except a few exchanges between pickets and patrols, occurred during the night. With the end of hostilities, General Taylor left Wool in command, and accompanied by Jefferson Davis's Mississippians and a squadron of the Second Dragoons returned to Saltillo to look to the city's defenses.

At the close of action, Santa Anna made an impassioned speech to his men, and in the American lines the cheering was clearly heard:

"*Viva Santa Anna!*"

"*Viva la República!*"

"*Libertad o muerte!*"

That night, on the battlefield at La Angostura, both armies suffered dreadfully from the cold, made more biting by a wind-swept rain.

The battle was renewed at daybreak on February 23, with Ampudia still trying to envelop Taylor's left on the mountain. During the night, the Mexicans had pushed troops farther up the ridge, and they opened up furiously on the Kentucky and Arkansas troops on the opposite rise. The latter, heavily outnumbered, "maintained their ground handsomely." Although supported by a battery that poured grape and canister into the Americans, Ampudia was held at bay for more than a hour by their determined and deadly fire. But, in the unequal struggle, it became obvious to General Wool that the Mexicans became, by the moment, a more serious threat to his flank and rear.

At this critical moment, Wool sent two companies of the Second Illinois under Major Xerxes F. Trail, Captain Conner's Texans, and Lieutenant O'Brien and his three guns to support his outnumbered riflemen. Mexican sharpshooters on the side of the mountain harassed the defenders as Ampudia prepared to send a heavy column charging through the gorge between the two ridges to dislodge the Americans. O'Brien's four-pounder and six-pounder were out of range, but with his twelve-pound howitzer he delivered a staggering fire with spherical-case shot. "Six or eight . . . exploding just at the proper time, did immense execution," noted Captain Carleton. The Mexican musketry, which had been incessant, completely ceased as O'Brien's howitzer found its target. From the whole line, cheers went up as O'Brien blazed away, checking the column and causing it to move to the right to get out of range.

Meanwhile, on the road, about 8 A.M., Santa Anna made a strong demonstration against Captain Washington's battery, but the five guns the latter had retained dispersed the Mexicans with rapid and well-directed shots. Santa Anna now put cavalry and infantry under Generals Francisco Pacheco and Manuel M. Lombardini into motion against the American left—not the extreme left which was fighting valiantly against Ampudia—where the Second Illinois and the Second Indiana, with O'Brien's battery, held the line. As the Mexicans pushed on relentlessly, a battery of eight-pounders gave them hot support. General Joseph Lane, in command of that part of the field, sent O'Brien forward, supported by the Second Indiana, and within musket range, O'Brien opened with all three guns. The Mexicans wavered under his effective fire and the brisk musketry of the Indianians, but only for a moment and then the advance continued. Pacheco's and Lombardini's men showered mus-

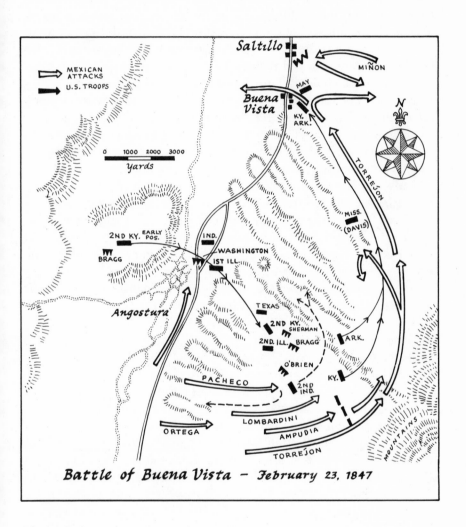

MEXICAN
ATTACKS
U.S. TROOPS

Saltillo

MIÑON

MAY

*Buena
Vista*

KY.
ARK.

N

0 1000 2000 3000
yards

TORREJÓN

MISS.
(DAVIS)

2ND KY. EARLY
POS.

IND.

WASHINGTON

BRAGG

1ST ILL.

TEXAS

2ND KY.
SHERMAN

2ND ILL. BRAGG

ARK.

Angostura

O'BRIEN

KY.

2ND
IND.

PACHECO

LOMBARDINI

ORTEGA

AMPUDIA

MOUNTAINS

TORREJÓN

Battle of Buena Vista – February 23, 1847

ket balls on O'Brien and the Second Indiana, and the latter troops were enfiladed by the Mexican battery.

O'Brien shifted his guns rapidly to the right, and took up the fire again, initially supported by the Second Indiana, which, after a splendid showing, suddenly fell back. Colonel William A. Bowles, a brave but unqualified officer, although ordered to charge to O'Brien's support, unaccountably gave a contrary order to his troops: "Cease firing and retreat!"

In vain did General Lane try to rally the Indianians as they broke and fled in disorder. O'Brien and his gunners, finding themselves alone, toiled heroically. "The intrepid little band of artillerists loaded their guns with double charges of canister and threw in handfuls of stones," declared Sam Chamberlain. On the battery, the Mexicans now concentrated their fire and seeing that O'Brien was unsupported by infantry they pressed forward eagerly to capture the American guns. O'Brien, firing until the last moment, limbered up two guns and retired. The third gun, the four-pounder, its entire crew and horses dead or wounded, O'Brien had to leave to the swarming enemy. "The Mexicans came out of the ravine in masses . . . The panic was contagious," said Sam Chamberlain. "Men left the ranks in all the regiments, and soon our rear was a confused mass of fugitives, making for Buena Vista ranch and Saltillo."

Meanwhile on the far left on the mountain side, things were going badly for the Americans, for Ampudia's weight of numbers, at least four or five to one, was beginning to roll up the line. Lieutenant Sam French, despite a musket ball in his right thigh, and Lieutenant George H. Thomas vigorously worked their guns against Ampudia. "Thomas and I used canister as rapidly as men (so well trained as ours were) could serve the guns," said French. On the effectiveness of their efforts, Captain Carleton noted: "Every discharge of Thomas' and French's pieces caused their immense masses to reel and waver, as the balls, opening a wide and bloody path, went tearing through them." But soon, French and Thomas were compelled to retire. The extreme American left, under the heavy pressure, was bent back so that it now faced the mountain.

Now brought into action for the first time was Braxton Bragg's battery, stationed to the right of the road. Bragg, along with McKee's Second Kentucky and Hardin's First Illinois, rushed to the plateau to bolster the Second Illinois, which was falling back under Pacheco's advance.

It was about this time, approximately 9 A.M., that General Taylor arrived on the field from Saltillo, bringing with him Colonel Jefferson Davis's Mississippi Rifles, Colonel Charles May and two companies of his Second Dragoons, Captain Albert Pike with a squadron of Arkansas Mounted, and a single gun from Bragg's battery. "The enemy was now pouring masses of infantry and cavalry along the base of the mountain on our left, and was gaining our rear in great force," reported Taylor.

The presence of General Taylor, calmly astride Old Whitey, had an electrifying effect on his troops. " 'Rough and Ready' was quite a reinforcement in himself," observed Dragoon Sam Chamberlain. General Wool galloped up, his spirit dampened by the impending disaster.

"General, we are whipped," exclaimed Wool.

"That is for me to determine," replied Old Zach calmly, as he took over the command of the battle.

Taylor ordered Colonel Davis to move forward with his Mississippi Rifles and that officer as he advanced begged and pleaded with the stragglers to fall in behind and return to the fight. "There were few, indeed, who heeded his call," observed Captain Carleton. One who did was the hapless Colonel Bowles, who had given the fatal order to retreat. He snatched up a rifle and cartridge box and moved forward bravely to fight with Davis's men as a private. The Third Indiana was summoned from the far right to support the Mississippians who, as they rushed on, made quite a sight with the tails of their red shirts out of their white duck pants. Black slouch hats completed the Mississippians' uniform. In addition to his rifle each man carried an eighteen-inch Bowie knife.

Holding their fire, until the range was close, Davis's men cut loose with "murderous accuracy" on Ampudia's infantry, supported by cavalry, which swept down from the mountain. Into a deep gully and up the other side dashed Davis's riflemen to gain the tongue of level ground over which Ampudia now charged. The Mississippians fired a volley as they spread out. A second volley and a third "poured slaughtering fire into the enemy." Slowed, then staggered, Ampudia's men fell back under cover of the ravines to reform.

Meanwhile, Mexican cavalry under General Torrejón, having passed along the base of the mountain, was about to sweep down upon Buena Vista hacienda. To oppose it were the Arkansas Mounted under Colonel Yell and Kentucky Mounted under Col-

onel Marshall, still fighting on foot, and two mounted companies of
Arkansas men under Captains Pike and Preston. It was not a formidable force, so Taylor dispatched Colonel May, with four companies of Dragoons to join the fight. And stragglers from the routed
companies were rounded up by Inspector General Churchill, the
paymaster, Major Dix, Major Monroe of the Artillery, and Captain
Steen, of the Dragoons, who was wounded.

The charge of the Mexican cavalry upon the ranch was met by
fire from many quarters, from the hurriedly gathered force in
front, from the ranch buildings and roofs, and from the fire of
Lieutenant John Reynolds's guns.

"The Mexican column, immediately divided," reported Taylor,
"one portion sweeping by the depot, where it received a destructive
fire from the force that had collected there, and then gaining the
mountain opposite under a fire from Lieutenant Reynolds's section,
the remaining portion regaining the base of the mountain on
our left."

The Mexican horsemen who had passed toward the mountains
to the west provided Reynolds with a good, if moving target, and
he sped them on their way, said Captain Carleton, continuing "to
play upon them with astonishing accuracy and great execution."
These Mexicans finally returned to their lines having made a ride
completely around the American position.

Meanwhile, throughout the day, General Miñón's cavalry had
threatened Saltillo, although his mission was to cut off Taylor's
retreat after Santa Anna had routed him. Approaching the city,
Miñón was met with heavy fire from Captain L. B. Webster's company in a redoubt guarding the road. Miñón moved in the direction
of Buena Vista. Captain W. H. Shover, with a single gun, moved
forward, supported by a mixed group of mounted volunteers, and
his determined firing drove Miñón's men into ravines for cover.
Fearlessly, Shover pursued, aided by a gun from Webster's battery
in the redoubt, and after breaking up a charge by the Mexicans
with his damaging fire, he finally drove them back in confusion.

The fighting was still furious on the main battlefield without,
as Captain Carleton put it, "any decided success on the part of
either army." When a powerful cavalry force descended upon
Colonel Jefferson Davis's Mississippians, he formed his regiment
and some Indiana troops into a "V" with the re-entering angle
presented to the Mexicans.

"The enemy . . . a body of richly caparisoned lancers came forward rapidly and in beautiful order—the files and ranks so closed as to look like a mass of men and horses," reported Davis. "Perfect silence and greatest steadiness prevailed in both lines of troops as they stood at shouldered arms awaiting an attack."

"Steady boys!" shouted General Taylor. "Steady for the honor of old Mississippi."

Colonel Davis, anxious "to obtain full advantage of a crossfire at short distance," repeatedly called to his men to hold their fire. The 1,500 brilliantly-arrayed Lancers, with flags and pennons flying, came down the slope at an easy hand-gallop. Progressively, their pace slackened and, when within about eighty yards of the opening of the "V," the horsemen drew up to a walk and were about to halt. A few itching fingers did not wait for Jefferson Davis's command to press the trigger, and this became the signal for both lines to blaze away with a destructive fire that emptied many saddles and sent the survivors reeling back in confusion. "It was appalling!" noted Captain Carleton. "The whole head of the column was prostrated."

As the Mississippians sprang forward in pursuit, one of Sherman's field pieces came into line and "followed their retreat with a very effective fire, until they had fled beyond the range of his gun."

"Well done, Jeff!" cried Old Zach, swinging his cap above his head. "Hurrah for Mississippi!"

Captain Carleton, witness to this exciting incident of the battle, provided an interesting critique:

In this affair, had it not been for that unaccountable and suicidal pulling up to a halt before a body of the best marksmen in the world, and distant only eighty yards;—had this compact mass of cavalry . . . dashed at speed into the angle before them, they would have lost many men, no doubt, but it is difficult to conceive what would have saved the Mississippi and Indiana troops from total destruction. And, had so large a force broken through our lines, and, at this time, gained the road between Buena Vista and La Angostura, the fortunes of the day would again have been placed in a jeopardy most painful to contemplate.

The stout resistance at the Buena Vista ranch and the dispersal

of Miñón's cavalry afforded Colonel May's Second Dragoons, reinforced by the First Dragoons and portions of the Arkansas and
Indiana troops, the chance to apply great pressure on the Mexican
right at the base of the mountain. With effective fire they held the
Mexicans in the narrow gorges and ravines while the artillery
blasted away at the huddled masses. "The position of that portion
of the Mexican army which had gained our rear was now very
critical," reported General Taylor, "and it seemed doubtful
whether it could regain the main body."

Then occurred a strange incident of battle—"a trick of Santa
Anna," said Sam French—as from the Mexican lines came an officer
with a white flag, with an astonishing question from Santa Anna:
"What did General Taylor want?" Taylor immediately dispatched
General Wool, under a flag, to parley with the Mexican commander, and ordered a cease-fire. When Wool reached the
Mexican lines and noted that they continued firing, he returned
to the American position without having seen Santa Anna. During
this lull on the American side, the entrapped Mexican troops
hastily extricated themselves from their precarious position and
rejoined their main body. (The Mexican version of the incident
is that a lieutenant, separated from his command and about to be
captured or killed, "availed himself of a stratagem to feign a parley." When he returned to the Mexican lines with Wool, he simply
disappeared.)

Defeated by the American left, Santa Anna now sent his reserves
under General Ortega to follow the same route that Pacheco and
Lombardini had traversed in the morning against the American
center on the plateau. It was the most powerful attack column of
the day, for the troops who had escaped during the lull quickly
rallied upon it, and moved forward again. Captain Carleton, who
estimated the strength of this assault group at 12,000, said it advanced "in a perfect blaze of fire." Facing it were the Illinois regiments of Hardin and Bissell and McKee's Kentuckians, who despite support from the sizzling fire of the guns of O'Brien and
Thomas, were compelled to give way, and seek shelter in a ravine.
Taylor's report stated these brave volunteers "had been overwhelmed by numbers."

"The moment was most critical"—these were Old Zach's exact
words—for O'Brien, fighting his two unsupported guns with extraordinary energy and skill, could not blunt the Mexican charge.

Two horses had been shot from under this gallant artillerist and the one he rode was limping from a wound, and O'Brien himself had received a leg wound. With all the cannoneers dead or wounded and only some green recruits left to man the pieces, O'Brien hung on grimly to the last, until none remained to load or fire the guns.

Not until the Mexicans came within a few yards of his position did O'Brien retire. "I was . . . delighted to find that I had maintained my ground sufficiently long to cause the victory to be secured," O'Brien reported, "for, at this moment, the rest of our artillery arrived and came into action."

Braxton Bragg, with his own and Sherman's battery, roared up, the horses urged forward at breakneck speed by whip, spur, and even the flat of the sword. Supporting them were Dragoons and the Mississippi Rifles and Lane's Indianians. Unlimbering rapidly, Bragg immediately went into battery under the watchful eye of Zachary Taylor. Legend quickly grew about Old Zach's order to Bragg. It may have been, as the country soon delighted in retelling:

"Give them a little more grape, Mr. Bragg."

Or, more in keeping with Old Zach's personality:

"Double-shot your guns and give 'em hell!"

Or, perhaps, more accurately, if less picturesquely, as Captain Carleton reported:

"Maintain the position at every hazard."

Whatever version is correct, Bragg fulfilled all three. His withering fire of grape did, indeed, give the Mexicans a taste of the warmth of Hell, and he maintained the position. Bragg's battery, wrote Carleton, "belched forth a storm of iron and lead which prostrated everything in its front. Nothing could stand its terrible fury."

Meanwhile the Illinois and Kentucky troops, who had taken refuge in the ravine leading to Washington's battery, were being shot to pieces. The Mexicans swarmed the ridge, pouring a deadly fire into the Americans. Colonel Hardin, Colonel McKee, Lieutenant Colonel Henry Clay, Jr., and many more fell heroically. The only escape from the rain of bullets from above was through the open end of the gorge, near the road. To it the shattered troops, constantly deluged with lead from the crests, scrambled over the loose stones. And then, to block their only exit, there rode into the gorge with their long weapons poised, a large squadron of Lancers.

Extermination was at hand for these hapless troops when, suddenly, above the rattle of musketry and triumphant cries of the Mexicans, the surrounded Americans heard a roar from the road. It was Captain Washington's battery drawing a bead on the Lancers. "I've heard many sweet sounds, the voices of lovely women & the melodious breathings of sweet instruments," Lieutenant W. H. L. Wallace, who was in the gorge, wrote a friend in Illinois, "but the whistling of that shell was the most grateful sound that ever greeted my ear. I turned, as fatigued as I was, to see the effect. It was terrible. The main body of Lancers scampered back over the hill." The repeated explosions of spherical-case shot broke over the Lancers and they gave way and retired. As the Kentuckians and Indianians ran panting out of the gorge to the battery, Washington delivered "a flight of iron . . . over their heads into the retreating cavalry."

Elsewhere on the field, the tide of battle had turned. Zachary Taylor, sometimes riding Old Whitey to threatened points, sometimes sitting calmly with one leg hooked around the pommel of his saddle and directing fire or troop movements, was the calmest man on the field. With his clothes ripped in many places by bullets, Old Zach was in the thick of the hottest of the fighting. No less fearless, the energetic General Wool rode everywhere, encouraging the men.

As darkness neared, the Mexicans almost everywhere had given ground under the fire of Washington's batteries from La Angostura, and the gallant work on the plain of Bragg's and Sherman's batteries, Davis's Mississippi Rifles, and Lane's Indiana Volunteers. Their concentrated fire broke the charge of Ortega's reserves and forced it to retire. The firing died down, and Santa Anna made no further attempt to force Taylor's position. "The smoke, which had enveloped the two armies like a thick veil, then lifted slowly up," declared Captain Carleton, "and there was the field, blue with the uniforms of the dead."

Taylor's weary men bivouacked on the bloody battlefield, suffering intensely from the cold. During the night the wounded were taken to Saltillo, fresh companies from the town were sent to replace the exhausted, even decimated, companies that had stood the brunt of the fight, and the men in the field were supplied with ammunition.

All were ready for a resumption of the battle in the morning, but when the morning mists lifted, the Americans saw, with surprise and delight, that Santa Anna had abandoned his position and that the Mexicans were in retreat. Captain Carleton recorded the moment:

> Then it was that a sound went along our lines ever to be remembered. It was but a single cry at first; then a murmur, which rose and swelled upon the ear like the voice of a trumpet; then a prolonged and thrilling shout: "Victory! Victory! Victory! The enemy has fled! The field is ours!"

Old Zach and General Wool fell into each other's arms, tears in their eyes. To the troops, remarked Sam Chamberlain, "it was a sight more lovely than the fairest woman in the world," which was quite a concession from a self-proclaimed expert on women. Sergeant John D. Duncan of the First Illinois added to his "satisfaction" in the Mexicans' departure his conviction that "they had us nearly whipped if they had known it." Another Illinois officer, Lieutenant Wallace, looked up from his blanket in the morning and saw distinctly the dust of the retreating column. "Oh, what a feeling of relief came over me," he wrote in a letter back home. "I set up a shout of *victory*. It was a mockery, however. I had the day before felt very much as I should suppose a *whipped* man would feel & I've no doubt, *inter nos* had it been just as convenient for us, as for Santa Anna to *vamos,* we would have been off to Monterrey."

Santa Anna hurried back to San Luis Potosí to claim victory, while his dejected, weary army straggled behind him, death, sickness, and desertions so thinning the ranks that barely half the force that had set out so confidently finally returned. However, one Mexican historian asserted that "the troops received with much disgust the order to retreat" despite losses of 591 dead and 1,037 wounded. When prisoners were added, the enemy loss was doubtless close to General Taylor's estimate of 2,000.

Buena Vista was costly for the Americans, with 267 dead, 456 wounded, and 23 missing for a total of 746. The battle was essentially a vindication of the volunteer as an American fighting man. It took some time for the young West Pointers to realize it, and often during the Mexican War their criticism of the volunteers' lack of discipline was just. But before the Mexican War was over, just as West Point proved itself a producer of professional officers, the volunteer soldiers proved themselves worthy to be led by such leaders.

He didn't know it at the time, of course, but Buena Vista was Old Zach's last fight in Mexico. The next fight for the victor of Palo Alto, Resaca de La Palma, Monterrey, and Buena Vista would be in the field of politics. And his next victory, twenty months away, would place him in the White House.

22

The Missouri Xenophon

It was William Cullen Bryant, poet, classical scholar, and editor of the New York *Post,* who first compared Doniphan and Xenophon as "two military commanders who have made the most extraordinary marches known in the annals of warfare of their times."

Noting that their "names are in sound so similar," Bryant expressed the hope that Doniphan would emulate Xenophon and "give the world as charming and as perfect a history of his expedition as the latter has done."

This, Colonel Alexander W. Doniphan never did, but the Missouri Mounted Volunteers did not want for observing and willing pens to chronicle the saga of what Bernard De Voto aptly called the "anabasis in homespun." At least half a dozen intelligent and educated members of Doniphan's command provided vivid memoirs of the long trek through unknown enemy country, with its hazards, hardships, brushes with hostile Indians and battles with superior Mexican forces.

When General Kearny headed for the Pacific on September 25, he left orders with Doniphan to march his troops to Chihuahua to join General Wool, just as soon as Sterling Price's Missouri Volunteers reached Santa Fé. However, when Kearny received word on the march that the Navajos had gone on a rampage and had attacked settlements, destroyed crops, driven off cattle, and carried off women, he sent orders to Doniphan on October 2 to march against the Indians before conforming to his original instructions.

Nothing of a disturbing nature had occurred in Santa Fé after Kearny's departure. Colonel Doniphan and Private Hall, who learned he had been elected to Congress during the march from Missouri, completed the basic law for New Mexico, and the first elements of Price's troops arrived on October 3. It was not until October 11, however, that Doniphan received Kearny's order to move against the raiding Navajos. Not only Doniphan's desire quickly to accomplish this mission so that he could join Wool, but the exigencies of approaching winter, with its difficulties of snow-swept trails and the scarcity of forage for the animals, prompted immediate implementation of his new orders.

Invading the Navajo country by three different routes—Doniphan took the center one, with Major William Gilpin on his left and Lieutenant Colonel Congreve Jackson on his right—the punitive force was faced with tremendous difficulties during a five-weeks struggle against the terrain and the elements. Doniphan summed up these hardships in a few words: "We . . . traversed a country of mountains and valleys amid the intense cold winter. Our daily march was through snows, and over snow-capped mountains . . ." Private Jim Hughes was more specific. The men had "little else than their summer clothing" which served them poorly "in the midst of snow, and ice and rocks." Only pack-mules could travel the route, "so steep and abrupt are the rocks, hills and mountains." Tents were discarded so that "light armed and unembarrassed, they might make their marches with expedition." To top off the discomforts of the campaign, the men hadn't been paid a penny after four months of service.

In spite of all difficulties, Colonel Doniphan was able to penetrate into all portions of the Navajo country and to collect "three-fourths of their tribe" at Ojo Oso, or Bear Spring, where, on November 22, 1846, a treaty was signed. Not, however, before Sarcilla Largo, a young Navajo chief, "very bold and intellectual," made a powerful speech:

American, you have a strange cause of war against the Navajo. We have waged war against the New Mexicans for several years . . . You have lately commenced a war against the same people . . . We can not see why you have cause of quarrel with us for fighting the New Mexicans on the west, while you do the same on the east . . . This is our war. We have more right to complain of you for interfering in our war than you have to quarrel with us for continuing a war we had begun long before you got here. If you will act justly, you will allow us to settle our own differences.

To this Indian logic, Colonel Doniphan responded with remarks

that having surrendered, the New Mexicans were now entitled to
the protection of the United States and that when the Navajos stole
from the New Mexicans "they were stealing from us and when
they killed them they were killing our people." Doniphan pointed
out to the Navajos the advantages of peaceful coexistence—the term
would not be invented for another hundred years—and the promise
of "a valuable trade with us." The Navajo chief was won over.
"Let there be peace between us," he said, and the treaty was signed.

By mid-December, Doniphan was back at Valverde on the Rio
Grande and ready to march to Chihuahua. His command, reinforced by the Chihuahua Rangers, a company of 103 volunteers
drawn from the various commands at Santa Fé, now numbered
856. Also at Valverde, waiting since October to join the march,
were traders with 315 wagons of goods to sell in Chihuahua.

On December 14, Major Gilpin began the march with 300 men,
and two days later Lieutenant Colonel Jackson followed with 200
more. On the 19th, Colonel Doniphan led the remaining 356
troops on to the trail. Between the units, the traders' heavily laden
wagons rolled. Three trying days and nights were spent crossing
the forbidding desert track called *Jornada del Muerto,* or "Journey
of the Dead," a ninety-mile waterless stretch across a big bend in
the Rio Grande. One of the troopers remembered this as "a dreadful desert" without water to drink or wood for fire. The men arrived at last at the village of Santa Ana, "fatigued with marching,
faint with hunger, and benumbed by the piercing winds."

But at Santa Ana, their troubles were over for the time, and
men and animals had both rest and sustenance while the command
closed up and concentrated at the village, which was about sixty
miles from El Paso del Norte. There, Doniphan learned, a Mexican
force of 2,000 awaited them. The march, having been resumed
on December 23, brought Doniphan by Christmas Day to within
twenty-five miles of El Paso. The men skylarked on the march,
firing off salutes and singing "Yankee Doodle" and "Hail Columbia." They went into camp on the east bank of the Rio Grande, in
an open, level prairie, with the mountains to the east, and chaparral north and south of the camp. The place was called El Brazito,
or Little Arm, for an island in the river divided the stream into
unequal widths at this point.

The troops scattered in all directions in search of wood, and
grass for the animals. Colonel Doniphan and some officers engaged

in a friendly card game. Within fifteen minutes, a trooper from the advance guard galloped up to inform the Colonel that the enemy was advancing on him. Doniphan jumped up, tossed his cards down, and reached for his saber. "Boys, I hold an invincible hand," he cried "but I'll be damned if I don't have to play it out in steel now."

The bugles sounded assembly, and the men, dropping wood and buckets of water, rushed to their arms. Confusion reigned in the camp, while horsemen galloped up and down the road announcing the enemy's approach. The scene, wrote an eighteen-year-old soldier, "would do credit to the pen of any author to describe." Private Marcellus Ball Edwards then undertook to describe it and he did quite well:

> The bugles sounded the assembly over and over again. The jingling and rattling of arms, the cries "Fall into line!"—"Get your horses!"—"Fall in on foot here!" etc., drowned every other sound and caused about as mixed an affair in camp as can well be conceived. Men, of course, had misplaced some of their arms, and they could be heard asking of others, "Do you know where my gun is?"—"You've got my saber!" etc., etc.

Barely half a mile away, forming in line of battle, were 500 Mexican Dragoons and infantry and militia numbering another 700, all commanded by Lieutenant Colonel Antonio Ponce de León. Had the Mexicans charged at once they would have had a decided advantage over Doniphan's troops, who were thus taken by surprise. As his men fell into line under the most convenient company colors, Colonel Doniphan and his staff, "as calm and collected as when on drill," surveyed the enemy Dragoons, "gallant and imposing . . . in a uniform of blue pantaloons, green coats, trimmed with scarlet, and tall caps plated in front with brass, on the tops of which fantastically waved a plume of horse hair, or buffalo's tail."

From this dazzling array, with swords and lances glittering in the sun, an officer "on a foaming steed" rode forth to the American lines, a black flag in his hand. On one side of the flag were two skulls and crossbones; on the other the motto, *"Libertad o muerte"* —Liberty or death. Halting within twenty yards of the troops, the horseman waved his black banner in salute, indicating he desired a parley.

Colonel Doniphan and his interpreter, Thomas Caldwell, advanced toward the Mexican herald, and Caldwell approached to inquire the purpose of the visit.

"The Mexican general summons your commander to appear before him," the horseman replied insolently.

"If your general desires peace, let him come here," answered Caldwell on Colonel Doniphan's behalf.

"Then we will break your ranks and take him there," declared the Mexican.

"Come then and take him," replied the interpreter.

"Curses be upon you," shouted the messenger. "Prepare then for an attack—we neither ask nor give quarter."

Doniphan's reply to this was, in his words, more abrupt than decorous: "Charge and be damned."

The Mexican wheeled his horse, waved his black flag, and then galloped back to his battle line. In his official report of the Battle of Brazito, Doniphan indicated that there were many impatient trigger-fingers in the command as the Mexican officer rode off. "With my permission a hundred balls would have pierced the insolent bearer of the pirate flag," wrote Doniphan, "but I deemed it most proper for the honor of our country to restrain them."

The Mexicans launched their attack, opening fire on the Americans when they had moved into a range of 400 yards. Five rounds the Mexicans fired, with no response. One soldier-diarist said "the sound of bullets over our heads reminded me of a hail storm," as he and his mates waited impatiently for the word of command. The Mexicans were now within 150 yards of the American position, when finally the word came: "Fire!" Like a peal of thunder, the Missouri rifles roared. The withering volley threw the attackers into confusion, checking their advance, and forcing it to veer to the right toward the wagons on Doniphan's left. "Our line," wrote a soldier, "had been numbered off—one, two—with orders that number two would reserve its fire while number one fired . . . reloading . . . alternately." The effect was deadly, and "consternation and dismay" seized the Mexicans as the wagon company joined in the fight. As the teamsters poured in a hot fire, Captain John W. Reid, who had managed to mount twenty men, charged the Mexican Dragoons, who were preparing to assault Doniphan's left. For twenty minutes, although outnumbered three to one, Reid's little mounted band kept up a warm fight.

Meanwhile, pressure on Doniphan's right increased as cavalry and infantry, under cover of the chaparral, closed in behind three unanswered rounds of fire. "Lie down on your faces, and reserve your fire until the Mexicans come within sixty paces," ordered Doniphan. The Mexicans, apparently believing they had silenced their adversaries, pushed forward with excited cries of *"Bueno! Bueno!"* Then, on signal, Doniphan's whole right wing rose up and delivered a galling volley into the oncoming Mexicans. They reeled and broke, the mounted men giving spur to their horses and the infantrymen fleeing in their wake.

The action was over a half hour after it started, and in the repulse the Mexicans left 43 known killed on the field and reportedly more than a 150 were wounded. Only seven Americans were wounded in the fight at El Brazito, none fatally. One soldier explained the light casualties: "They always overshot us, both with their howitzer and small arms."

Some wine was found among the spoils of victory, and Doniphan's men celebrated their victory, as well as Christmas Day, by drinking it immediately. Also taken after the battle were ammunition, baggage, provisions, blankets, lances, guns, several standards, and the single howitzer which the Mexicans took into battle.

Two days later, unopposed by Mexican troops but with considerable municipal oratory, Colonel Doniphan led his command into El Paso del Norte, the present Ciudad Juárez, where it remained until early February, 1847, awaiting the arrival of the artillery from Santa Fé.

El Paso proved an oasis of delight for the weary Missourians, and its fruit trees, shrubs, orchards, and vineyards were a vast relief from the desert wastes that they had traversed. Bountiful were food, fruit, wine, beer, pulque; frequent were fandangoes and horse and mule races; continuous was street gambling, until Colonel Doniphan forbade the *al fresco* gatherings for monte, chuck-luck, twenty-one, faro, and other games of chance. Agreeable were the people, once they realized that Doniphan had not come to plunder and that all foodstuffs would be purchased. In some instances, hospitality extended to the "charms and unpurchased kindness" of the señoritas. There were, as might be expected, fights, an occasional free-for-all, and considerable dissipation. And often during the stay, when sentries shot at prowling wolves, there were false alarms of enemy attacks.

After a house-to-house inspection, Doniphan's men confiscated

20,000 pounds of power, ammunition, and lead, 500 small arms and four cannon, the taking of which not only removed a threat but provided war materiel for the command.

During January, Doniphan learned of a revolt against the Americans in New Mexico and the murder of Governor Charles Bent. General Kearny's bloodless conquest of the summer had, in less than six months, changed its complexion. After campaigning for nearly two months, Colonel Sterling Price succeeded in suppressing the rebellion and restored the authority of the United States in New Mexico.

Colonel Doniphan lingered only a week after the artillery—117 men and six pieces under Major Meriwether Clark and Captain Richard H. Weightman—arrived on February 1, and his command of 924 men, exclusive of two companies later formed from among the helpers with the traders' wagon train, marched out of El Paso on February 8 to join General Wool at Chihuahua.

It was on the march, not many days later, that Colonel Doniphan learned that General Wool was not at Chihuahua. Instead, he had marched to join Taylor. Wool left San Antonio the day Taylor occupied Monterrey—September 25—and he crossed the Rio Grande unopposed. A Mexican officer appeared and stated that Monterrey had fallen and that a two-months armistice then prevailed. Wool then marched to Monclova, construing that the armistice line was beyond that point.

After sitting out the armistice at Monclova, Wool decided it was much more important for him to join Taylor than to march on Chihuahua, and he wrote the General seeking permission for the change in his orders. Taylor promptly ordered him to occupy Parras, ninety miles west of Saltillo, and "Old Granny" Wool, or the "Woolly Devil," as his men unfondly called him, pushed on. One of the major complaints against Wool by his men was voiced by a sergeant: "He has showed more friendship to the Mexicans than he does to the volunteers." One historian of the Mexican War, conceding that General Wool would have won no popularity contests with his troops, declares that "no soldiers were better cared for, none suffered less from camp disease, none were better behaved and none fought better . . ." It was on December 5 that Wool moved into Parras with his 3,000 troops.

The startling information that he would not find Wool at Chihuahua presented Colonel Doniphan with two alternatives, each of them hazardous. One was to retrace steps to Santa Fé, the other to join Wool at Parras or Saltillo. He put it to a vote of the troops, and almost to a man they voted to move forward. "Our situation is rather critical," observed one soldier, "leaving an enemy in our rear, marching into the heart of their country, expecting to meet a powerful one in front, depending upon them for subsistence, and our strength not exceeding one thousand."

The trials of the march were tremendous—the first enemy Doniphan's men met were the long waterless stretches of wasteland. On one occasion, men and horses went two days and nights without water. When it was encountered, there was a scramble. "Horse, mule & man vied with each other in drinking out of the same puddles," declared Private Jim Hughes. When the occasion presented, the troops took their swords from their scabbards and filled the latter with water. Rain, when it came, was a blessed event. So parched was most of the area that careless handling of fire by the men often set the prairie ablaze. On one occasion, the wind created an ocean of flame, "gaining new strength from every puff . . . raging and sweeping like a wave." The wagon trains, the ammunition and artillery narrowly escaped engulfment by the fire.

On February 28, about eighteen miles from Chihuahua, Doniphan came into view of a strong Mexican force behind fortifications on the Río Sacramento, where the road from El Paso crossed the stream. Doniphan moved due south into a broad plain between two ranges of mountains, the 400 military and traders' wagons in parallel columns of 100 each. In the spaces between the wagons, the troops and artillery marched. Across his entire front, Doniphan spread three mounted companies to shield his approach.

The Mexicans, estimated at 3,500 to 5,000 men by the Americans and conceded by Mexican sources to have totaled 2,000 with ten cannons, had a strong position. Their right wing was firmly anchored on a hill, where two redoubts with a single gun commanded the road and the plain to the right of the road. On either side of the road, and in line with the redoubts on the hill were two breastworks, with four guns. Paralleling a forty-five degree bend in the road to the southwest, three more strong positions blocked the river crossing. The Mexican line of fortifications—Doniphan reported that "they had 27 redoubts dug and thrown up and extending at intervals across the whole ground"—ended with their left on a high hill, south of the Río Sacramento and to the left of the road. Its guns commanded the plain and the crossing. In addition to ten

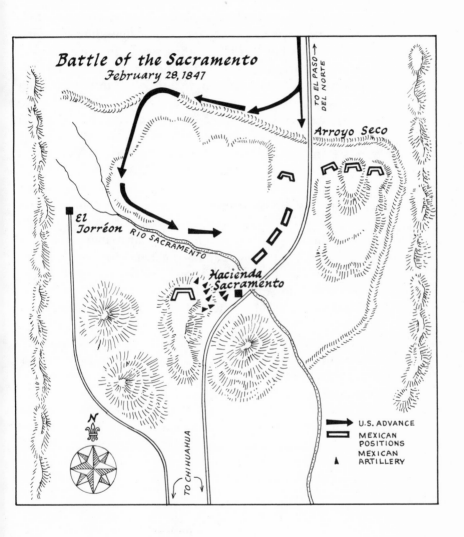

Battle of the Sacramento
February 28, 1847

TO EL PASO DEL NORTE →

Arroyo Seco

El Torréon

RIO SACRAMENTO

Hacienda Sacramento

N

TO CHIHUAHUA

➤ U.S. ADVANCE
▭ MEXICAN POSITIONS
▲ MEXICAN ARTILLERY

cannons, the Mexicans had six culverins (small pieces) mounted on carriages, which were placed on the slopes of the latter hill.

General José A. Heredia and his officers were confident that their position was impregnable and that they would smash Doniphan and capture those that survived the battle. "So certain of victory were the Mexicans," wrote Private Hughes, "that they had prepared strings and handcuffs in which they meant to drive us, prisoners, to the city of Mexico, as they did the Texans in 1841."

As the Americans came within a mile and a half of the Mexican lines, they crossed a deep ravine with sloping banks, the Arroyo Seco. Here, the Mexicans made their first mistake in not attacking Doniphan during the crossing. Once the command reached the high ground, Doniphan advanced his cavalry and then diverged the rest of the force to the right, away from the road. The Mexicans, taken by surprise at this movement, rushed forward about a thousand cavalry, under General García Condé, and four pieces of artillery. "Nothing could exceed in point of solemnity and grandeur the rumbling of the artillery, the firm moving of the caravan, the dashing to and fro of the horsemen, and the waving of banners and gay fluttering guidons, as both armies advanced to the attack . . ." recorded an American soldier.

Suddenly the wave of Mexican cavalry halted, but Doniphan pushed on to within 1,200 yards of them, and ordered Major Meriwether Clark's battery of six-pounders and Captain Richard Weightman's section of twelve-pound howitzers to open fire. The American guns threw "a well directed and most destructive fire," and the Mexicans fell back to bring their own guns into action. For the better part of an hour, the cannonading continued hotly, with Clark's and Weightman's gunners discharging twenty-four rounds to the minute. The Mexican fire did little damage, for the troops dismounted and maintained full open order of ranks, but many horses and mules were killed and a number of wagons were shattered.

Having lost about twenty-five men and many horses, General Condé retired—"in some confusion," Doniphan reported—into the Mexican entrenchments. At this point the bugles sounded, and the Americans, still diverging to their right to avoid the Mexican batteries and the strongest redoubts on the enemy's right near the road, advanced boldly to the attack. When Doniphan's men had reached within a quarter of a mile of the Mexican line, he ordered Captain Weightman to charge with his howitzers, supported by three companies of cavalry. "The howitzers charged . . . and were gallantly sustained by Captain Reid; but by some misunderstanding, my order was not given to the other two companies," reported Doniphan.

The Mexican guns on the heights now opened furiously on the Americans, but as they were compelled to deliver a plunging fire, little damage was done. Within fifty yards of the central redoubt, Weightman's guns roared. The companies of Captain Hudson and Captain Parsons, having received their orders late, now galloped forward to support the busy howitzers. Then, dismounted, the whole of Doniphan's line rushed forward on foot, sweeping determinedly up to the redoubts on the plain, with Major Clark's six-pounders scattering grape and canister among the defenders while the troopers blazed away with hot musket fire.

This was too much for the Mexicans. After obstinately resisting for a while, they leaped from the entrenchments and fled, some toward Chihuahua and others to the redoubts still engaged with the Americans. Meanwhile, a body of mounted irregulars, trying to reach the American rear, met stubborn fire from the teamsters, and when Clark's guns joined in, the enemy horsemen retired hastily.

The battle raged for three hours and came to an end at sunset when the last Mexican position was carried, the hill on the Mexican left. "The field was literally covered with the dead and wounded from our artillery and unerring fire of our riflemen," Doniphan reported. The Mexican loss was 300 killed and as many more wounded and about 40 prisoners were taken. Doniphan's losses were slight. Major Samuel C. Owens of the wagon companies was the only fatality, while a second American was mortally wounded. Seven others received wounds from which they recovered, to quote Doniphan, "without any loss of limb." The Mexicans lost their entire artillery, ten wagons, and a large quantity of provisions and supplies.

In his report, Colonel Doniphan made a statement which, in the light of another American war, fifteen years later with its John Pelhams and Willie Pegrams, is most interesting:

> It is abundantly shown, in the charge made by Captain Weightman with the section of howitzers, that they can be used in any charge of cavalry with great effect. Much has been said, and justly said, of the gallantry of our artillery, un-

limbering within 250 yards of the enemy at Palo Alto; but how much more daring was the charge of Captain Weightman, when he unlimbered within fifty yards of the redoubts of the enemy.

On March 1, an advance force of 150 men under Lieutenant Colonel D. D. Mitchell marched into Chihuahua, and the next day Colonel Doniphan led his "rough, ragged and ready" soldiers into the town. Their term of enlistment had only three more months to run. For fifty-nine days, Doniphan occupied Chihuahua. On March 13, a bi-lingual newspaper, *Anglo Saxon,* was started. March 20, Doniphan learned of Zachary Taylor's great victory at Buena Vista and he ordered a salute fired in celebration.

Doniphan considered his position "ticklish," and to General Wool he described it as "exceedingly embarrassing," for not only was he in a hostile country, with no American troops close to him, but his soldiers, unpaid since June, were in desperate need. He sent a courier to Wool at Saltillo asking for instructions. Wool sent the message to Taylor at Monterrey, and Old Zach ordered Doniphan to join the main army, preparatory to discharge of the regiment. Taylor's order reached Doniphan on April 25, and three days later the First Mounted Missouri Regiment began the 600-mile march to Saltillo, which distance they covered in less than a month.

On May 22, Doniphan's troops were reviewed by General Wool, whose order for the occasion stated: "No troops can point to a more brilliant career than those commanded by Colonel Doniphan." Five days later, at his Walnut Springs camp at Monterrey, General Taylor reviewed the Missourians. On the last day of their enlistment Doniphan's men were at Camargo. Ten days later they sailed from Brazos for New Orleans where they arrived on June 15.

This was not only homecoming for the Americans, but it meant their first payday after a year of service. "The regiment of Missourians now in the city are obviously the heroes of the town," declared the *Picayune.* "They excite unusual attention by their appearance."

In thirteen months Doniphan's command covered more than 3,500 miles by land and more than 1,000 miles by water. The march of the Missouri Xenophon might well have been, as Private Jim Hughes, who made it, declared, "the most extraordinary and wonderful Expedition of the age."

23

The Second Front

If there was one thing the officers and men of Commodore David Conner's Home Squadron wanted more than anything else it was action. And now, as the year 1847 began, with General Winfield Scott assigned to open a second front at Vera Cruz, action at last was promised.

Blockade duty was irksome. Confined to the ships, living off ship's rations, cruising during "the parching heats of summer and the long and boisterous nights of winter," the officers and crews welcomed any diversion from the routine. Mexico had no navy to challenge the American squadron, and the unremitting blockade had swept the Mexican merchant marine from the sea. The war, complained Commodore Conner's flag lieutenant, Raphael Semmes, had become "a war, for the navy, of toils and vigils, without the prospect of either excitement or glory."

At the time of the annexation of Texas in July, 1845, the Home Squadron had been ordered into Mexican waters, prepared to establish a blockade if Mexico declared war. When John Slidell went to Mexico on his futile mission, the American flotilla was ordered to withdraw so as not to jeopardize by its presence the expected negotiations. When Slidell was rejected by two Mexican presidents, Commodore Conner was ordered once again to cruise off the Mexican coast.

With the outbreak of hostilities in Texas, Commodore Conner immediately offered General Taylor the navy's cooperation. Not only did his gunboats effectively blockade the Rio Grande, but the old Commodore landed 500 sailors and Marines at Point Isabel to secure Taylor's depot, while Old Zach marched off to fight at Palo Alto and Resaca de la Palma.

The Home Squadron welcomed expeditions which broke, for some of the blocking vessels, the monotony. Abortive attempts to capture Alvarado, south of Vera Cruz, were frustrated in August by the inability of some of the vessels to cross the bar, and again in October, by the inability of light steamers with gunboats in tow, to make headway against the current of the river. On October 25, Commodore Matthew C. Perry—he was the younger brother of the Perry of Lake Erie and the very Perry who would open Japan—was sent by Commodore Conner on a successful expedition to Tabasco. An expedition against Tampico resulted in the occupation of the city by the navy, although Conner's ships didn't have to fight for the town, the Mexicans having evacuated it before the navy arrived. It was not until January 23 that the army moved into Tampico, which became, with Brazos Santiago at the mouth of the Rio Grande, a staging area for Scott's expedition against Vera Cruz.

From New Orleans on December 23, 1846, Scott had written Commodore Conner that he looked forward with "great pleasure" to their "forthcoming joint operations against the enemy" at Vera Cruz. "I shall do all in my power to render the combined service cordial and effective," said the General. "Of your hearty reciprocation I am entirely confident."

Three days later, while at sea heading for Brazos Santiago, Scott wrote the Commodore again about "the attack we are jointly to conduct." The General declared that the landing point would be determined when "I shall have looked at the coast, and had the benefit of full conference with you," but he assumed that the nearer the city the better. "Your knowledge of the beach (its shoals and surf) is probably already sufficiently minute," wrote Scott. "I, however, throw out the suggestion that you may, if necessary, make a particular study of the subject before my arrival." Scott told Conner of the special landing boats that had been ordered and built under the supervision of naval officers, and he added, "I may need important aid from your squadron in this particular, as in many others."

Thus was established, more than two and a half months before Scott was prepared to attack Vera Cruz, the basis for the smooth and effective completion of the first major amphibious operation in the military annals of the United States—an operation which, a century and a quarter later, had never been surpassed in the efficient cooperation between the army and the navy and in the achievement of the objective.

General Scott fussed and fumed—he wasn't named "Old Fuss and

Feathers" for nothing—over delays in the arrival of transports to carry troops to the Isle of Lobos, the designated rendezvous off the mainland, about midway between Tampico and Vera Cruz. The General was also piqued by the failure of supplies, ordnance, casks of water, and many other things to arrive on schedule. With all his concerns for the Vera Cruz expedition, Scott now had tossed into his lap a disciplinary problem involving a high-ranking officer of the regular army, Colonel William S. Harney.

Scott had bypassed Colonel Harney, commander of the Second Dragoons, by assigning him to stay with General Taylor's army while his command was given to Major Edwin V. Sumner, "a much safer and more efficient commander," according to the General. Harney was furious and refused to give up his command. "As long as I am a colonel, I shall claim the command of my regiment," he wrote Scott indignantly. "It is a right which I hold by my commission and the laws of the land, and no authority short of the President of the United States can legally deprive me of it."

Charges of disobedience of orders and insubordinate conduct were brought against Harney, and he was tried by a court-martial, found guilty, and sentenced to be reprimanded. General Scott generously remitted the sentence and restored Harney to his command. In Washington, President Polk saw the incident as Scott's persecution of an officer who was a Democrat, and, of course, heartily disapproved. Scott's "arbitrary and tyrannical conduct . . . to this gallant officer" matched Taylor's "same proscriptive spirit . . . towards . . . gallant Democratic officers," the President confided to his diary. Having reassured himself so often of his own fairness, Polk doubtless believed what he next entered into the diary: "I have myself been wholly uninfluenced by any reference to the political opinions of the officers of the army in the conduct of the War."

It was during all the harassments at Brazos Santiago that Scott received two communications from Commodore Conner, which, after pledging "the cordial cooperation of the naval forces," provided the general with valuable information. Vera Cruz and the Castillo de San Juan de Ulúa were garrisoned by about 3,800 troops. Neither town nor fortress ever had more than four days' supply of provisions. The Commodore was unaware of any "regular force of any consequence" between Mexico City and Vera Cruz at that time, January 11, and he did not believe the Mexican Government could assemble a force sufficient for Vera Cruz's protection. The Isle of Lobos provided good shelter, but Conner warned Scott that sudden storms were frequent during the present season.

In his second letter, dated a week later, Conner stated that "the present would be the most favorable time" for the attack. He had no reason to change his views as to the garrison and provisions at Vera Cruz. It was his opinion that if 4,000 or 5,000 troops were landed at Vera Cruz by the end of January or early in February, so as to completely invest the place, "its surrender, in less than 10 days, with that of the castle, would be certain, and probably without the necessity of firing a gun." (Time would prove the old sailor's shrewd estimate of the situation, and even in the matter of the shooting, he *could* have been right if Vera Cruz were invested in January instead of March.) Perhaps the most significant point of information the Commodore gave Scott was his first choice of the beach due west of Sacrificios Island as the point of landing.

It was not until February 15 that General Scott left the Brazos for Tampico where four days later the troops encamped along the Panuco River gave the General a rousing welcome. Scott's stay at Tampico was brief, just a few hours more than a full day, but during this time he issued on February 20, his momentous Order No. 20. In extending the jurisdiction of military courts over crimes not covered by the Articles of War—crimes which in the United States would be punishable in civil courts—Order No. 20 established the base upon which the American military government of the future would be constructed. It was a bold, unauthorized stroke by General Scott, but it was an effective means of controlling troop discipline and protecting the people in the occupied territory.

The next day Scott reached Lobos, where he found many new volunteer regiments had arrived, but he chafed at further delay in waiting for Worth's regulars from Brazos Santiago, Twiggs's regulars and Patterson's volunteers from Tampico, and the artillery batteries, Harney's Dragoons and the Tennessee Mounted, none of which had transportation. Moreover, barely a third of his ordnance supplies had arrived and fewer than half of the surfboats, with which the assault on the beach would be made, had come. A new concern for the General was the outbreak of smallpox in the Second Pennsylvania regiment. He landed the exposed troops on Lobos, but kept the patients aboard ship and the threat of epidemic soon passed.

By February 28, Scott could not conceal his impatience. "Perhaps no expedition was ever so unaccountably delayed," he wrote the Secretary of War. "By no want of foresight, arrangement, or energy on my part, as I dare affirm." But even as Scott fussed, ships from New Orleans and other ports arrived daily, loaded with supplies and equipment. "Coming down before the gale like race horses," the transports from Tampico and Brazos also reached the rendezvous. The anchorage at Lobos soon became, in the words of one soldier, "a wilderness of spars and riggings."

At last, on the morning of March 2, many weeks behind his hopes, Scott ordered Signal No. 3, a yellow flag, run up the mizzenmast of the steamer *Massachusetts:* "All vessels; proceed to Antón Lizardo." This was the harbor below Vera Cruz, where Commodore Conner's Home Squadron lay at anchor.

At noon on March 5, the *Massachusetts* dropped anchor at Antón Lizardo and by the afternoon of the sixth the army fleet, more than eighty vessels, had joined the navy in anchorage.

General Scott, conscious that the approach of the yellow fever season made necessary an early attack, conferred immediately with Commodore Conner, who pointed out that the beach should be stormed during calm weather, that is between the ever-recurring northers, which blew up suddenly.

On March 6, Commodore Conner and General Scott made a reconnaissance cruise in the little steamer *Petrita*, a vessel captured at Tabasco, and with them were their staffs, Generals Twiggs, Worth, Patterson, and Pillow, Colonel Totten and such bright young engineers as Robert E. Lee, Joe Johnston, P. G. T. Beauregard, and George Gordon Meade, among others. The *Petrita* turned the point of the long reef on which San Juan de Ulúa stands, when Colonel Totten, his glass to his eye, exclaimed: "They are manning their batteries." Colonel Persifor F. Smith took a look and agreed. "They are using their sponges," he said. "We shall have a shot presently." A white puff from the castle announced the first shot—a shell that fell short. A second shot was short, a third burst in the air not far from the ship and a fourth sailed over and fell a hundred yards beyond. "We were in a ridiculous position . . . in danger with no adequate object, with no means of defense, with all of our officers of rank on board," wrote Inspector General Ethan Allen Hitchcock. "If a chance shot had struck our engine we should have cut a pretty figure!" Lieutenant Meade, who said the castle threw eleven

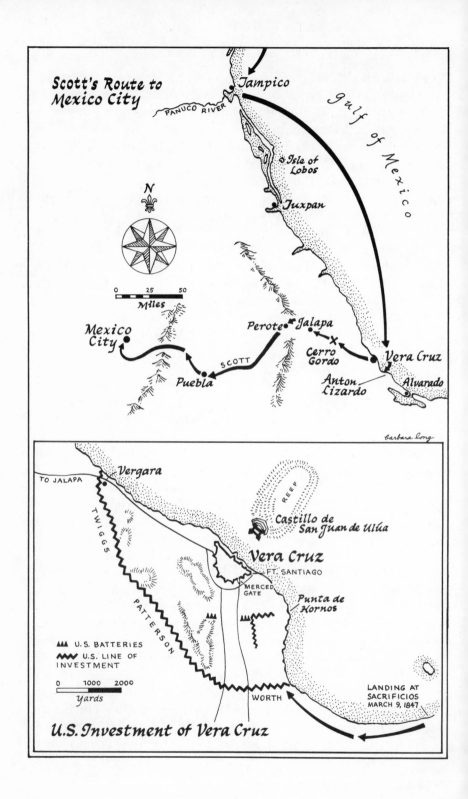

Scott's Route to
Mexico City

Tampico

PANUCO RIVER

Gulf of Mexico

Isle of Lobos

N

Tuxpan

0   25   50
Miles

Mexico
City

Perote Jalapa

Cerro
Gordo

X

Vera Cruz

SCOTT

Puebla

Anton
Lizardo

Alvarado

barbara long

Vergara

TO JALAPA

REEF

Castillo de
San Juan de Ulúa

T W I G G S

Vera Cruz

FT. SANTIAGO

MERCED
GATE

Punta de
Hornos

P A T T E R S O N

▲▲▲ U.S. BATTERIES

〰 U.S. LINE OF
INVESTMENT

0   1000   2000
Yards

WORTH

LANDING AT
SACRIFICIOS
MARCH 9, 1847

U.S. Investment of Vera Cruz

shots at the *Petrita*, agreed: "This operation I considered very foolish; for, having on board all the general officers . . . one shot . . . might have been the means of breaking up the expedition."

Such a shot, indeed, would have effected the waging of two wars, and undoubtedly would have changed, to some degree, the course of American history.

As a result of the reconnaissance, Scott agreed with Commodore Conner that the beach opposite Sacrificios, within three miles of Vera Cruz, was the best place to land. He also decided to scrap his plan of embarking the troops in the surfboats directly from the transports. He adopted the Commodore's suggestion that the troops be transferred first to the large warships at Antón Lizardo and transported in them to Sacrificios, and then to the landing boats for the assault on the beach.

General Scott designated March 8 as "D-Day," but during the night a norther blew up and the operation was postponed for twenty-four hours. Accordingly, on the morning of March 9, between sunrise and 11 A.M., Scott's army transferred from the transports to the navy vessels. By noon, Commodore Conner aboard the *Raritan* and General Scott aboard the *Massachusetts* threaded their way through the narrow pass leading from the anchorage. Everything, as the fleet filed out one by one, was propitious, noted Lieutenant Semmes, Conner's flag lieutenant. The sky was cloudless, the breeze gentle from the southeast and favorable for the landing. "Every step of our progress was frought with the association of three hundred years," declared Lieutenant Semmes, as he imagined Cortés on a sand dune gasping in wonderment at the strange and wonderful armada.

Only 65 of the 141 surfboats that Scott had ordered had reached Antón Lizardo, and these were in tow as the fleet made its way to Sacrificios. The surfboats were in three sizes— forty feet by twelve feet, thirty-seven feet nine inches by eleven feet, and thirty-five feet nine inches by ten feet two inches—and were transported from the United States in "nests." The boats were fitted and equipped, respectively, for eight, seven, and six oarsmen, which Commodore Conner supplied. Built with both pointed ends alike, the boats were steered by oar, and the helmsmen were young officers or petty officers, assigned by the Commodore.

General Scott had organized the army into three main groups: The First Brigade, under General Worth consisted of the Fourth,

Fifth, Sixth, and Eighth Infantry Regiments, with a company of Louisiana Volunteers attached to the Fifth and a company of Kentucky Volunteers attached to the Sixth; and the Second and Third Artillery. This force numbered 3,065 men.

The Second Brigade, under General Twiggs, consisted of the First, Second, Third, and Seventh Infantry; the First and Fourth Artillery; and Colonel Persifor F. Smith's regiment of mounted riflemen, temporarily dismounted. Twiggs's command numbered 2,917 men.

The Division of Volunteers, under General Patterson, was composed of three brigades, but as the brigades of General James Shields and John Quitman had not yet arrived, only General Pillow's brigade of about 3,500, made up of two regiments each from Tennessee and Pennsylvania and a South Carolina regiment, was immediately available.

The Dragoons—the companies of the First and Second were consolidated—under Colonel Harney, and the Tennessee Mounted, under Colonel Jonas E. Thomas, were to be held under direct orders of General Scott.

Guns of twice-promoted Lieutenant Colonel James Duncan, Captain Francis Taylor, and Lieutenant E. J. Steptoe, when not detached, were to serve, respectively, with Worth, Twiggs and Pillow.

Such was the force which on the late afternoon of March 9, 1847, awaited the signal to storm the beach below Vera Cruz. In addition to arms and ammunition, each soldier carried nothing but a greatcoat, a haversack with two days supply of bread and cooked meat, and a canteen of water.

The honor of going ashore as the first wave was bestowed upon Worth's brigade, and the operation began on the instant the naval vessel dropped anchor. Each of the surfboats accommodated about forty to fifty men in addition to their crews. As they filled, they attempted to form a line about a quarter of a mile offshore, but confusion among the landing crafts caused by a strong current coming from Sacrificios, was only partially remedied by the *Princeton* throwing out a hawser to which the surfboats made fast. "This was an interesting moment," noted Captain Ephraim Kirby Smith, "and must have been a grand spectacle from the yards and tops of the shipping."

Meanwhile the steamers *Vixen* and *Spitfire* and five gunboats, under Commander Josiah Tatnall, anchored in a line parallel to the shore and close enough in for effective grape range with their thirty-two-pounders to cover the landing.

Everything was now ready for the great adventure. In the surf-boats the men waited, with fixed bayonets. On the navy ships, the regimental band played "Yankee Doodle," "Hail Columbia," and "The Star Spangled Banner." Troops in the second and third waves mingled eagerness with apprehension. "I believe there were few of the army who did not envy their position," wrote George Ballantine, an English volunteer, "or would gladly have incurred the hazard of the enterprise, for the shadow of glory which the distinction conferred."

Among the 10,000 spectators of the drama, on which the curtain was about to rise—American soldiers and sailors and the officers and crews of the foreign warships in the harbor—was George Wilkins Kendall of the New Orleans *Picayune*. When, about 5:30 P.M., General Scott gave the signal—a cannon shot from the *Massashusetts* —Kendall informed the *Picayune* readers that "a more stirring spectacle has probably never been witnessed in America." Under the strong pull of the sailors, each boat's crew eager to land its troops first, the landing craft sped shoreward. As the keels grated on the sand, officers with swords in hand and men, their muskets and cartridge boxes held above their heads, leaped into the waist-deep water and splashed ashore. But as the line of surfboats neared the sand, a naval gig had forged ahead and from it, gesturing with his sword, jumped General Worth, the first to land at Vera Cruz.

Regimental colors were planted in the sand, and the troops quickly formed on them. In a matter of moments, Worth's line moved forward with a rush for the first ridge of sand hills "scarcely a pistol shot distance" from the landing spot. To the wonderment of all—Worth's men as they pounded across the sand, the thousands who blackened the rigging of all the ships in the anchorage, the men and gun crews on Tatnall's covering flotilla—not a shot was fired during the entire landing operation.

As the surfboats had passed, Tatnall's men had broken forth with a wild cheer and this was picked up by the thousands aboard the vessels and by the landing troops themselves. "We took it up and such cheering I never expect to hear again," wrote Lieutenant George B. McClellan, "except on the field of battle. . . . Our company . . . ascended the sand hills and saw—nothing."

Immediately after Worth's brigade went ashore, the surfboats returned for General Patterson's Volunteer Division and "without waiting to form again in order of battle they continued to pour the troops upon the beach in successive trips as fast as they could come and go." By 10 o'clock that night, the United States Navy had completed its finest hour in the Mexican War. It put ashore more than 10,000 troops, and stores and provisions for several days without a casualty or even the slightest accident of any kind during the six-hour operation. Old Commodore David Conner, who would be relieved by Commodore Matthew C. Perry in a few days, had done his work well. None knew and appreciated this more than General Scott, who officially reported: "To Commodore Conner, the officers and sailors of his squadron, the army is indebted for great and unceasing assistance, promptly and cheerfully rendered. Their cooperation is the constant theme of our gratitude and appreciation."

Why General Juan Morales did not oppose the American landing is as good a question today as it was on March 9, 1847. From General Scott down, virtually everyone in the army expected that the landing would be challenged, and that American casualties would be high. "If the Mexicans had concealed themselves behind the sand hills until our boats were nearly in the surf, and then had come down and opened fire, it is my belief that half the men would have been killed or wounded before reaching the beach," wrote Captain William H. Parker of the navy. "Why the Mexicans did not meet us on the beach when they might have annoyed and cut us up most unmercifully, is most unaccountable," wrote Captain Robert Anderson of the Third Artillery. ". . . Had they planted a battery on the beach where they must have thought we intended landing, they might, with the unimportant loss of their cannon, have killed and drowned a thousand of our men."

General Scott immediately set about investing the walled city, with its nine forts on the landside and the formidable San Juan de Ulúa guarding the sea approach. The garrison of Vera Cruz totaled approximately 4,000 troops and the armament included an excess of 200 guns.

Slight resistance was experienced on March 10 from Mexican guerrillas, and now and then sharp musket fire suggested minor skirmishes while Scott extended his line and began the unloading of ordnance and supplies. A norther swept in on the 11th and made landings of materiel impossible for almost an entire week. The encirclement of Vera Cruz was completed on March 12. Worth's brigade held the right, from the beachhead. Patterson's volunteers, which had been reinforced on the 10th by the arrival of Quitman's brigade, held the center of Scott's line, while Twiggs's regulars pushed on to Vergara on the Gulf of Mexico, more than two miles north of the city. The American line, from beach to beach, extended for almost eight miles. On March 13, the aqueduct, which provided Vera Cruz with water, was cut, thus worsening conditions within the town.

Before the landing at Vera Cruz, officers and men had read in Mexican newspapers of Santa Anna's "smashing victory" over General Taylor, and to a man, nobody believed it. On March 15, Scott announced in a general order to the troops receipt of "authentic information of a great and glorious victory . . . by . . . General Taylor at Buena Vista. . . ."

The northers did more than prevent Scott from landing his guns and mortars, his draft horses and pack-mules, his ammunition and supplies; they provided torment for the men in the line and the work parties under the "indefatigable engineers," as the General called them, preparing emplacements for guns. Captain Kirby Smith complained of "the fine sand pricking our faces like needles and nearly putting out our eyes." Another irritation—seemingly more so than the occasional brushes with enemy guerrillas and cavalry patrols and the hundreds of shells fired daily from Vera Cruz's forts—were the assaults of wood ticks, red bugs, and sand fleas. Two young engineers, Lieutenant Gustavus Smith and Lieutenant George B. McClellan, developed a ritual to outwit the sand fleas. They greased themselves with salt pork and slept in canvas bags drawn tight around their necks.

As the siege of Vera Cruz continued, some of Scott's generals and other high-ranking officers were impatient with the investment of the town. They expressed willingness to lead storming parties, their urging of such a move being implicit criticism of Scott's caution. Lieutenant Cadmus Wilcox heard some regular officers say: "Monterrey, a strong place, was taken in three days, and we have confronted Vera Cruz for two weeks and not a gun has been fired."

General Scott, after reconnoitering the walled city, said he preferred taking Vera Cruz "by head work, the slow, scientific process," than by storming "at the cost of immense slaughter to both sides." To Colonel Totten, Scott declared: "Vera Cruz must be taken with a loss not to exceed one hundred men; for every one over that number I shall regard myself as his murderer."

Painstakingly, the engineers prepared the installations for the mortars and guns, when the weather permitted them to be put ashore. Often they were under enemy fire, while occasionally some of them were in jeopardy from their own troops. One night, returning from a work party, Captain Robert E. Lee and Lieutenant P. G. T. Beauregard were challenged:

"Who comes there?"

"Friends," called Captain Lee.

"Officers," shouted Lieutenant Beauregard.

The sentinel, despite this exchange, fired from only three or four paces. "We were both blinded and stunned by the explosion," recorded Beauregard. "For . . . fearing he might have been armed with a revolver, at one spring we had grasped him and disarmed him." Inspector General Hitchcock, in noting the incident in his journal, said the ball passed between Lee's left arm and body, singeing his coat.

The Mexican guns were active, but generally ineffectual in trying to halt the building of the batteries. By March 22, Scott was ready to begin firing. Before, however, opening the bombardment, he summoned the city to surrender and received, as expected, a prompt refusal. At 7 P.M., the first mortar shell was lobbed into the city. Six more mortars took up the fire, and soon the roar of guns from the American batteries, from the city, from San Juan de Ulúa and from Commander Tatnall's gunboats, "from a position too daringly assumed," produced a continuing man-made thunder.

As Scott's heaviest guns were twenty-four-pounders, much too light for breaching the walls of Vera Cruz, the General asked Commodore Perry if he could supply some heavy navy guns.

"Certainly, General, but I must fight them," replied the Commodore. And so six heavy guns were put ashore and with 200 sailors and volunteers attached to each piece, the guns were dragged three miles through the loose sand, sometimes knee-deep, and across a wide lagoon. Finally, "after incredible toil and perseverance," the pieces were in place in General Patterson's secton of the line— three sixty-eight-pounder shell guns and three thirty-two-pounder solid-shot guns.

On March 24, the naval battery, under Captain John H. Aulick, opened up with terrific effect, crumbling the walls on each side of Fort Santa Bárbara. "The enemy was astonished at the vigor and power of this new assailant," wrote Lieutenant Raphael Semmes. Courageously, the defenders replied with "spirited and obstinate" fire, and they tried to concentrate upon the tormenting navy guns.

That night, Scott received a message from the consuls of England, Spain, and Prussia, asking for a truce to remove foreign families and the Mexican women and children. The General replied the next day that he had offered the foreigners a chance to escape the siege on the day he landed and that until he began firing the opportunity was still open. Now, Scott stated, the only truce he could entertain must be based on the application of the Vera Cruz commander, accompanied by his agreement to surrender. "In the meantime," declared the General, "the siege will go on with increased means and vigor."

On March 26, General Juan Morales, commander of both city and castle, fell conveniently ill and turned the command over to General José Juan de Landero. The new commander immediately wrote to Scott "to invite your excellency to enter into an honorable accommodation with the garrison" and asked that three American commissioners be appointed to treat with a similar number of Mexicans.

Firing was suspended on both sides, while Generals Worth and Pillow, Colonel Totten, and Captain Aulick of the navy negotiated with Colonels José Gutiérrez de Villanueva and Pedro Manuel Herrera and Lieutenant Colonel Manuel Robles at Punta de Hornos, outside Fort Santiago on the coast. After the usual haggling, terms of capitulation were agreed upon on the night of March 27, and ratified by both commanders the next day.

Under the terms, the garrison was to march out with military honors and stack arms, and the men were to be released on parole given by their officers not to serve until exchanged. The security of person and private property was guaranteed, freedom of religion was pledged and the Americans promised fair compensation for the use of buildings by the army.

At ten o'clock on the morning of March 29, Mexican batteries fired a salute, and the Mexican flags came down in the city and castle. As the garrison marched out of the Merced Gate in the south wall, American flags ran up the poles from which the Mexican standards had been lowered, while the guns of the army and the fleet joined in a mighty salute.

Two hours after the American troops garrisoned the city, Winfield Scott began a report to Secretary of War Marcy:

"The flag of the United States of America floats triumphantly over the walls of this city and the castle of San Juan de Ullúa."

Scott captured Vera Cruz at a cost of only nineteen American lives—twelve soldiers and seven sailors—while the wounded reached only fifty-seven, for a total of seventy-six casualties—about one-fifth of Zachary Taylor's loss at Monterrey and about one-tenth of the casualties at Buena Vista.

The news of Vera Cruz followed fast upon that of Buena Vista in the United States, and Scott's victory, being so cheaply purchased, was not rated a very formidable achievement. In his *Autobiography*, Scott relates how a friend in New Orleans spread the news of Vera Cruz:

"Someone in the crowd . . . called out: 'How many men has Scott lost?' 'Less than a hundred.' 'That won't do . . . Taylor always loses thousands. He's the man for my money.'

"Only a few faint cheers were heard for Vera Cruz. The long butcher's bill was wanted . . . The keynote sounded in New Orleans was taken up all over the land."

24

Scott Moves Inland

Winfield Scott had successfully gained, by April 1, 1847, two of the first three objectives of his invasion of Mexico.

The first objective was to land his army on the beach near Vera Cruz, and this had been expeditiously performed.

The second objective was to reduce and occupy the city and its formidable fortress, San Juan de Ulúa, to provide a port of entry and a base for reinforcements, equipment, and supplies.

There remained the third immediate objective—to get the army out of the hot and coastal fever belt before the dreaded *vómito* paid its annual visitation. In this, Scott's patience was sorely tried, for his deficiencies in wagons, draft animals, and pack-mules were staggering. He had requisitioned 800 wagons and he had only 180 on hand (300 more were at sea, at the time, but Scott did not know it), and although he had asked for 7,500 horses and mules to draw the wagons and pack supplies, he had received only 1,100. While Scott fretted, he could not place all the blame for the shortage of animals on the Quartermaster Department. Many hundreds were lost when ships carrying them foundered or cracked up on the shoals during the recurring northers.

Wagons or no wagons, mules or no mules, the General was determined soon to move the army to the healthful altitude of Jalapa, a picturesque town seventy-five miles from Vera Cruz, which reared its roofs more than 4,000 feet above the pestilential seacoast. But there were affairs to be transacted, arrangements to be made, which occupied the General's time during the first week of April.

A joint army-navy expedition was sent out to capture Alvarado and round up some much-needed horses. General Quitman marched along the shoreline, while Commodore Perry moved by sea. The plan was for the navy to hold its fire until Quitman's troops were in position to prevent the people from driving off their horses into the chaparral. As Quitman approached the fort at the mouth of Alvarado, an engineer party in advance of the main body had its attention drawn by "a curious-looking Mexican flag," flying over the fort. They edged closer to identify the banner.

"Surely I can't be mistaken," exclaimed one of the party, "that must be the American flag."

"The American flag! How the devil did it get there?" said another.

"That's more than I can tell," replied the first speaker, "but the American flag it is, and no mistake."

It was, indeed, the American flag, and it was also a mistake. At least Commodore Perry thought it was and ordered Lieutenant Charles G. Hunter, commander of the one-gun steamer *Scourge,* who had exceeded his authority, to appear before a court-martial. Having arrived at the fort ahead of Perry, Lieutenant Hunter decided to throw a shot or two at the works. This brought immediate surrender. Hunter raised the American flag, left six of his forty men as a garrison, and moved up the river to capture the towns of Alvarado and Tlacotalpan. Quite an achievement for a vessel with only one gun. But it frustrated the plan and when Quitman came up, the horses that they had come for were safe in the chaparral.

Hunter was found guilty and sentenced to be reprimanded by the Commodore, the reprimand to be read on the quarterdeck of every ship in the squadron. "This was done," noted an officer of the squadron, "and the reprimand was very bitter in tone and unnecessarily severe."

About a week later, Scott sent out an army detachment in search of horses, and this was more successful than Quitman's frustrated march. The navy, too, went expeditioning on its own, and on April 7 captured Tuxpán, north of Vera Cruz, after brief resistance by the shore batteries.

Meanwhile, in Vera Cruz, Scott had reissued his Martial Law Order No. 20, first promulgated at Tampico. Prices of foodstuffs were regulated. The General distributed 10,000 rations of meat, beans, and bread, and imposed a duty on merchandise, the proceeds of which were to be applied to the sick and wounded of the army and navy and the poor of the city. By April 5, Scott could report to Secretary of War Marcy that "the inhabitants of this city . . . are beginning to be assured of protection and to be cheerful," although five days earlier, the General had excoriated the "few worthless soldiers, both regulars and volunteers" responsible for the "un-doubted atrocities."

Scott did not concentrate all his time and efforts in establishing an effective military government for Vera Cruz. He reorganized the army for its march inland, forming it into three divisions. General Worth led the First, consisting of the brigades of Colonel John Garland and Colonel N. S. Clarke. General Twiggs commanded the Second, composed of the brigades of General Persifor F. Smith and Colonel Bennett Riley. The Third, commanded by General Patterson, contained the volunteer brigades of Generals Shields, Pillow, and Quitman.

On March 8, Scott's movement inland began when Twiggs's Second Division took the National Road for Jalapa, supported by a squadron of the Second Dragoons and the field batteries of Taylor and Talcott. Each soldier carried forty rounds of ammunition and in his haversack hard bread for four days and cooked bacon or pork for two days. Twenty-four hours later, Patterson's division of volunteers, minus Quitman's brigade and the Tennessee Mounted, whose horses hadn't arrived, took up the march.

Scott learned, on the day that Patterson marched, that General Santa Anna, now the President of Mexico, was at Jalapa with 6,000 troops. Scott felt that the size of Santa Anna's force was "exaggerated by rumor," but he forwarded the information to Twiggs and to the commanders in Twiggs's rear.

What had happened after the "victory" of the Napoleon of the West at Buena Vista? Shortly after his return to San Luis Potosí, Santa Anna learned of the uprising against Acting President Valentín Gómez Farías in Mexico City. It was a struggle between the clerical and anticlerical parties, the former resisting recent levies on Church property. The clerical party, or Polkos, enlisted the support of the National Guard in the capital, and defied the Puros, as Gómez Farías's party was called. Even as Scott's expedition bore down on Vera Cruz, civil war broke out in the capital, and no troops left the city to assist Vera Cruz to resist the American invasion.

Just about the time that Scott had completed the investment of Vera Cruz, Santa Anna began his "triumphant" march to Mexico City, his apparent purpose being to support Gómez Farías. Delegations from the contending parties met Santa Anna on the way at several stops, and by the time he reached Guadalupe Hidalgo in the

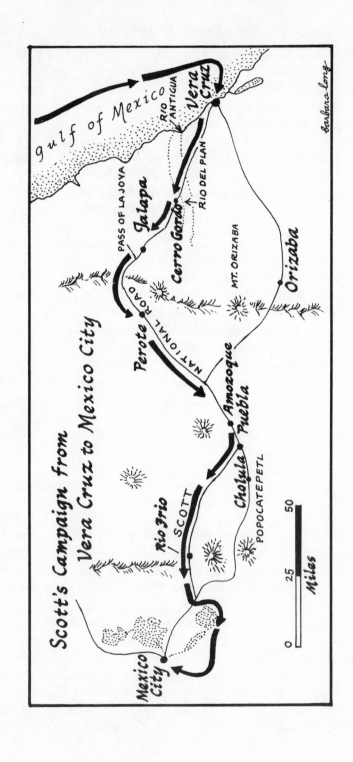

Scott's Campaign from Vera Cruz to Mexico City

gulf of Mexico

RIO ANTIGUA
Vera Cruz
RIO DEL PLAN
PASS OF LA JOYA
Jalapa
Cerro Gordo
RIO
Perote ROAD
NATIONAL
MT. ORIZABA
Orizaba
Amozoque
Puebla
Cholula
POPOCATEPETL
Rio Frio
SCOTT
Mexico City

Miles
0   25   50

barbara long

suburbs he was prepared to sacrifice Gómez Farías in his own interests. He refused to enter the capital until hostilities ended between
the rival parties. A committee of Congress called on Santa Anna
and invited him to assume the office of president. On March 21, as
Scott made final arrangements to begin the bombardment of Vera
Cruz, the Napoleon of the West took the oath of office. Within a
week Congress had given Santa Anna sweeping powers, so flexible
that he could increase the levies on the Church or repeal them as
he saw fit. After exacting a "voluntary" contribution of about
$2,000,000 from the Church, Santa Anna canceled the legislation.
As the President intended to move eastward to challenge Scott's
advance, he did not wish to leave Gómez Farías in office as acting
president. So Congress, obligingly, abolished the office of vice-
president, Gómez Farías's regular post. To the newly created position of interim president, General Pedro María Anaya was elected.

Santa Anna was now free to engage the Americans. He had
ordered troops at San Luis Potosí and other garrisons to concentrate at Jalapa where shortly he would have twice the 6,000 men
that Scott considered an exaggeration. And then, on April 2, he left
Mexico for the front. Writing that day to a friend, Foreign Minister José Fernando Ramírez said Santa Anna's departure was "particularly touching" and "bystanders were deeply moved," and that
one felt "as if he were watching someone bid his final farewell."
"Even S. A.'s opponents shed tears," wrote Ramírez. "S. A. disclosed the fact that he had evil presentiments of the future." For
his own opinion, Ramírez declared: "He did not leave to repel the
invasion, for this I believe to be impossible. He left to prevent the
Yankees from getting into Mexico City without firing a shot."

At Perote, less than a hundred miles from the coast, Santa Anna
augmented his army by compelling many of the troops paroled at
Vera Cruz to reenter the service. Thus it was that while Twiggs's
lead division, retracing the path of Cortés, marched first through
endless expanses of sand on either side of the ancient road and
gradually into a land of flowers, shrubs, and trees, Santa Anna had
built up an army of at least 12,000 men.

The intense heat and toil of the march, to which the annoyances
of diarrhea were added, created considerable straggling among
Twiggs's division. Although marching conditions steadily improved,
it was not until the third day that the column crossed the famed
stone-arch National Bridge over the Antigua River. It was past

noon on April 11 when Twiggs led his command across the Río del Plan over another fine stone bridge and went into camp just beyond the village of Plan del Río. Here first contact with the enemy was made when Twiggs's advance guard of Dragoons came upon a small body of Lancers which they almost captured. The Mexicans sprang into the saddle and, their horses being fresh while the mounts of the Dragoons were weary from the march, they soon found safety after an exchange of a few ineffectual shots.

The next day, Twiggs sent a strong reconnaissance force up the National Road into the hills, and in a sharp brush with enemy pickets, Captain Joseph E. Johnston was severely wounded. The meeting with the Lancers the day before and the clash on April 12 were clear indications to General Twiggs that Santa Anna's main force was not far away. Twiggs decided to push forward well before dawn on the 13th and attack the enemy's fortified positions, which the reconnaissance had revealed. Meanwhile, during the day, the brigades of Pillow and Shields, of Patterson's division, arrived, General Patterson himself being ill. Twiggs, who assumed command of both divisions, acceded to the urging of Pillow and Shields to postpone the attack twenty-four hours to permit their troops to recoup their energies after the hard march.

Santa Anna, who had reached Jalapa on April 5, considered several strong defensive places along the National Road to make his stand against Scott's advance. He decided upon the pass of Cerro Gordo where the highway is hemmed in between the almost perpendicular gorge of the Río del Plan and two high hills, Cerro Gordo and Atalaya. The distance to this position from the American camp at Plan de Río was about five miles by the road, which made a wide loop from the river in its climb to the pass and descent to the tableland between Cerro Gordo and the river. The road made, roughly, half of a figure eight, from Plan del Río to Santa Anna's camp.

Lieutenant Colonel Manuel Robles, a distinguished Mexican engineer officer, found Cerro Gordo "advantageous for harassing the invading enemy . . . but not the best point to dispute their passage and much less to attempt a decisive victory." His view was that the Americans might turn Santa Anna's left, by moving over the rough terrain north of the road, get to the Mexicans' rear and cut the National Road. Robles also pointed out the Mexican force would suffer from lack of water. The first objection, Santa Anna brushed aside. Indicating what he considered impassable ground on his left, Santa Anna declared: "A rabbit could not pass there." To the second objection, he ordered a ditch dug from his estate at Encero to bring water to his troops.

General Patterson, his indisposition having passed, rejoined the army on the 13th and assumed command of both divisions. He countermanded Twiggs's attack order for the morning of the 14th, to await General Scott's arrival before bringing on a general engagement. Scott, meanwhile, upon receiving word that Twiggs had encountered opposition, had left Vera Cruz on April 12, with orders for Worth to follow with his division. The General reached Plan del Río at noon on the 14th.

Scott's brilliant young engineers had been active during the lull. Lieutenant Zealous B. Tower had reconnoitered Santa Anna's right, which consisted of three batteries with strong infantry support established upon three fingerlike ridges which projected into the plain between the river and the road. Deep ravines separated the ridges. The first ridge, nearest the river, had six guns and 500 troops. The next, or middle, "finger" was the most formidable of the three, with its eight guns and 1,000 troops. Five guns and 300 infantry were on the third ridge, nearest the road.

Meanwhile Lieutenant P. G. T. Beauregard and Lieutenant W. T. H. Brooks, General Twiggs's aide, had independently reconnoitered a mule path which led off to the right from the road, and they had pushed through the maze of gullies, seeking a route to the enemy's left. Beauregard reported to Twiggs that though difficult, an advance on the enemy's rear was practical that way. Twiggs's attack plan had called for assaults on both flanks of the enemy at the same time, which in effect amounted to two unrelated attacks.

Beauregard then asked Twiggs if he might "make a few remarks relative to his plan?" "Certainly, sir, and I will be happy to listen to you," responded Twiggs. Beauregard then outlined a proposed move through the wilderness of ravines and growth to strike Santa Anna in the rear.

"You may be right, sir, but it is already late," replied Twiggs. "I have given all my orders, and to change them now might occasion too much confusion and uncertainty. Don't you think we will succeed anyhow?"

"Certainly, sir, but I think we ought to throw all the chances in our favor," said Beauregard.

When General Patterson called off the proposed attack, the

engineers continued their reconnoitering. On April 15, Captain Robert E. Lee, accompanied by Beauregard and several other engineer officers, set out over the mule path Beauregard and Brooks had examined. Beauregard wrote later:

> When we arrived at the foot of Atalaya they ascended to its crest and I went around its base to the foot of the Cerro Gordo, about one-half mile farther than on the 13th . . . In the afternoon of that day, having another attack of fever which I had taken at Vera Cruz, I was compelled to return to Plan del Río, marking, however, with a hatchet, as I went along, the road which was afterwards made on the 17th . . .

Long after dark, Lee had not returned, as Inspector General Ethan Allen Hitchcock noted as he wrote at 7 P.M. in his journal: "Captain Lee had been out all day searching for a path or passes by which the forts on the heights can be turned." It was only by luck that Lee ever returned from that mission. As he made his way over the rough ground, concluding as he went that a road could be improvised by which troops and guns might pass, Captain Lee came upon a spring, around which the bushes were trampled and from which a newly worn path led to the south. Lee immediately concluded that he had reached the rear of Santa Anna's left.

Suddenly voices in Spanish approached and Lee, with no escape possible, quickly dropped behind a giant log, which fortunately was screened by thick undergrowth. His companion, John Fitzwalter, hid himself in the growth nearby. Lee, scarcely daring to breathe, lay hour after hour behind the log as Mexican soldiers came to the spring almost constantly. Several times, soldiers sat down on the log, and once a Mexican stepped over it, inches from Lee. The forty-year-old captain, who long had considered duty the sublimest word in the English language, suffered in enforced silence the assaults of insects who crawled over him, as he pressed against the fallen tree and the damp ground.

By dusk, the steady flow of Mexicans to the spring had dwindled and pitch-black darkness finally brought safety. Lee and his companion struggled back to camp. Despite Lee's belief that the army could pass around Santa Anna's flank and a similar view held by Major J. L. Smith, who commanded the Engineers, further reconnaissances were undertaken on the 16th during which Lee ap-

proached, but did not reach, the National Road to Jalapa in the
rear of Santa Anna. To his wife, Lee explained Scott's problem:

> The right of the Mexican line rested on the river at a per-
> pendicular rock, unscalable by man or beast, and their left on
> impassable ravines; the main road was defended by field works
> containing thirty-five cannon; in their rear was the mountain
> of Cerro Gordo, surrounded by intrenchments in which were
> cannon and crowned by a tower overlooking all—it was around
> this camp that it was intended to lead our troops.

Lieutenant John G. Foster, with a pioneer company, went to
work early on the 16th and cut out a path for the army as directed
by Lee. Late that day, Scott had formulated his plan. Early on April
17, Twiggs's division, guided by Captain Lee, would move over
the new trail around Santa Anna's left flank, but the battle would
not begin until the 18th, when Worth's division and part of Scott's
siege train had arrived.

Scott's plan of battle was for Twiggs to strike the enemy left
before daylight and "take up position across the National Road in
the enemy's rear," while Pillow demonstrated against the three
fortified ridges on Santa Anna's right. Pillow exhibited reluctance
to his assignment, according to Colonel Hitchcock, who noted:

> General Pillow . . . intimates very clearly that he considers it
> a desparate undertaking. General Scott told him that the at-
> tack in the rear would distract the attention of the enemy and
> make an opening for him. General Pillow said he would go
> where ordered if he left his bones there, but asked the General
> to consider that two of his regiments were raw and without
> service. General Scott said that the regulars were very much
> "diluted" with raw recruits, not so good as raw militia just
> from home. Saying something about discipline, General Scott
> insisted that the attack in front must be made.

Up and down the ravines, Twiggs's men followed Captain Lee.
The artillery was lowered, a piece at a time, down the steep slopes
by hand and by ropes, and pulled up the opposite sides by the same
method. As the enemy was approached, the order for strict silence
was passed down the line. But a moment later a soldier slipped, his

musket clattering against his mess kit. His captain (the men called him Blunderbore) came bellowing up, sword in hand: "You infernal scoundrel, I'll run you through if you don't make less noise." Whether the Mexicans heard the outburst or not, the incident provided a hearty laugh for the column and eased the tension.

Shortly before noon, Mexican lookouts atop Atalaya, about 700 yards away, detected Twiggs's movement. There was a rattle of musketry, answered by American rifles, and then Lieutenant Frank Gardner with a company of the Seventh Infantry went charging up the hill. Soon he was sharply engaged at the crest, and Twiggs ordered the First Artillery and the rifle company under Colonel Harney to move at once to Gardner's support.

"I beg your pardon, General, how far shall we charge them?" asked a captain.

"Charge them to hell," roared Twiggs.

Away Harney's men went and, joining Gardner, they delivered a furious fire upon the Mexicans, who retired. However, the Mexicans did not yield Atalaya without a fight, and three countercharges were sent up its slopes, but all proved futile. When the third wave of Mexicans rolled back, Harney's men swept down the hill in close pursuit, and actually started up the slopes of Cerro Gordo itself. Here the Americans encountered heavy showers of grape and canister, and having insufficient forces to push forward in the face of the Cerro Gordo batteries, Harney retired, not without damage by the Mexican artillery, to the crest of Atalaya. Security of the position was provided by light artillery under Lieutenant Jesse L. Reno.

During the night, under Robert E. Lee's direction, three twenty-four-pounders from Captain Steptoe's battery were hauled up Atalaya and installed in emplacements Lee had hastily constructed. Assisting in this arduous operation were men from General Shields's brigade which, sent to reinforce Twiggs, had arrived after the fight had been broken off.

Before sunrise on April 18, Twiggs ordered the brigades of Shields and Colonel Riley to move well out to the right—they were led into position by the indefatigable Captain Lee—to strike the National Road at or beyond Santa Anna's camp. Colonel Harney was to sweep down Atalaya, cross the valley between the two hills, and then storm the Mexican positions atop Cerro Gordo. And, on the American left, Pillow's demonstration before the Mexican

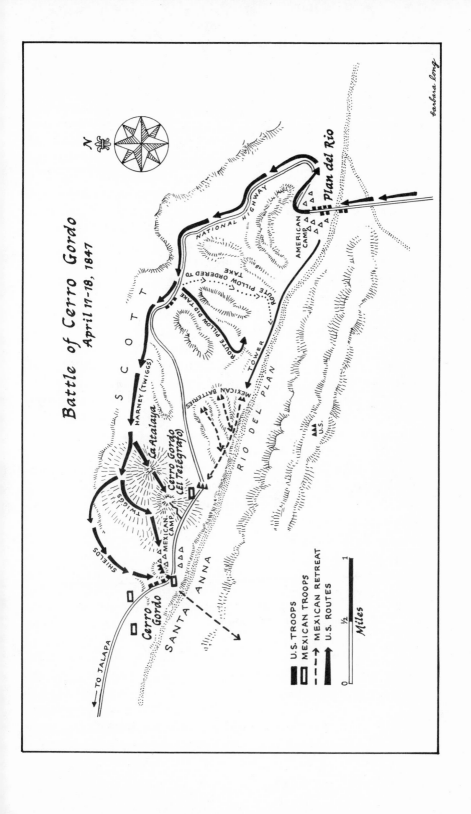

Battle of Cerro Gordo
April 17-18, 1847

Plan del Rio

AMERICAN CAMP

NATIONAL HIGHWAY

ROUTE PILLOW ORDERED TO TAKE

ROUTE PILLOW DID TAKE

TOWER

MEXICAN BATTERIES

U.S.

RIO DEL PLAN

SCOTT

HARNEY (TWIGGS)

La Atalaya

TWIGGS

Cerro Gordo
(El Telégrafo)

MEXICAN CAMP

SHIELDS

SANTA ANNA

Cerro Gordo

TO JALAPA

Barbara Long

U.S. TROOPS
MEXICAN TROOPS
MEXICAN RETREAT
U.S. ROUTES

Miles
0   ½   1

batteries on the three "finger" ridges was to begin when the sound of Twiggs's guns was heard.

An artillery duel from the two crests initiated the action, as Shields and Riley moved their columns over the prescribed route. During the turning movement, Shields continued in a wide arc to the west of Riley, whose troops diverged to the left, working their way around the base of Atalaya to that of Cerro Gordo, all the while under heavy fire. Here half of Riley's command moved resolutely against the Mexican battery of five guns on the plain near the Mexican camp, while the rest dashed gallantly up the steep hill to take the Mexican guns in the rear.

Meanwhile, about 7 A.M., Colonel Harney got Twiggs's order to assault Cerro Gordo. Down the slopes of Atalaya raced the Americans, yelling their heads off as they ran, and across the hollow and up the rugged side of Cerro Gordo. "Charge! Charge!" shouted the officers, and the red-headed Harney, sword in hand, gallantly led the way. A halt, about seventy yards below Cerro Gordo's crest, gave the panting troops a breather. Then Harney, waving his sword toward the Mexican position, drove forward again. "The enemy, pressing upon our troops with superior numbers, successively gained possession of the lower works of the position," states a Mexican account, "and without losing an instant, rapidly ascended to assault the last crest of the hill."

Bursting over the top, Harney's men used pistols, bayonets, and swung their muskets as clubs to rout out the Mexicans. Even as Harney's men swept to the top, some of Riley's troops appeared on the crest in rear of the Mexicans, who broke and fled. Captain John B. Magruder quickly turned the Mexican guns on the fleeing enemy. The Mexican officers bravely tried to stem the rout. General Ciriaco Vázquez was killed. Gallantly did General J. N. Baneneli attempt a coun009charge with the Mexican reserve, which finding itself precipitated into a hand-to-hand struggle with the blue-coated enemy were, according to Mexican sources, "panic-struck in an instant [and] fell into disorder."

By now the American flag had been raised over Cerro Gordo, just about the time that Shields, after a rugged march, burst out of the chaparral, upon the Mexican battery by the road. He was greeted by two of the five guns which were not playing upon Riley's troops, advancing upon the position. General Shields was struck down, and for a moment, his troops hesitated. But the Mexicans, astonished at their appearance and not knowing how many more were behind them, had had enough. "The Yankees! The Yankees!" they cried. "They have come out on the road!" And each man struck out for himself, as Shields's men pushed forward again, joining Riley's troops in sweeping through Santa Anna's camp.

The Napoleon of the West, who in a proclamation to his troops, which the Americans captured, had pledged: "My duty is to sacrifice myself and I will know how to fulfil it! . . . I am decided . . . to die fighting!" fled with the rest. George Wilkins Kendall in a battlefield report to the New Orleans *Picayune* scribbled on April 19 "amid confusion of all kinds and with no other table than knees," told his readers that "Santa Anna, himself, instead of intombing himself as he threatened, escaped by cutting the saddle mule of his team from the harness of his magnificent coach, mounting him, and then taking to the chaparral."

While a glorious victory was being won on General Scott's right and center, a fiasco was being enacted under the misdirection of General Pillow on the left of the American line. Pillow, who had less than four miles to march, was ordered to start at 6 A.M., but it was not until nine o'clock that he reached his preassigned position before the enemy batteries on the three ridges. And then, over the protest of Lieutenant Tower of the Engineers, Pillow changed his route so as to come under the full fire of all three positions, instead of turning the battery nearest the river, where there was considerably more cover and where the batteries on the other two ridges were unable to reach the Americans effectively.

Confusion on the march had placed attack groups and their support a considerable distance apart, and when the incompetent Pillow began to deploy his troops, according to Lieutenant George Gordon Meade, some of the stragglers were "literally shoved into their places one by one." The injudicious law partner of President Polk impatiently cried out: "Why in the hell don't Colonel Wynkoop file to the right?" Lieutenant Meade, who was obviously scandalized by Pillow's incompetence, wrote: "This yell of the General's was at once followed by the blast of a Mexican bugle and within three minutes after that their fire opened upon us."

Colonel William T. Haskell's Second Tennessee Regiment caught the full blast of the galling fire of grape, canister, and musketry, and some men bolted, some jumped for cover, and the rest were ordered to charge. Emerging into the clearing, they were

mowed down by the frightful fire, about eighty falling dead or
wounded in the space of several minutes. The remnant fled to
safety. Lieutenant Meade said Pillow, during this slaughter, was
"squatting down with his back to the work." He was wounded,
Meade noted, in the arm, and when his aide came up, "they together went off to the rear on the run." The Tennesseans had been
cut up terribly and the Pennsylvania regiment, which was to support them "had kept so well in reserve that they could not be
found," as Meade remarked with more than a tinge of his usual
contempt for volunteers.

In vain, Meade tried to rally Pillow's men. Seeking out the General, he suggested that regulars were needed. Pillow directed him
to go to General Scott and ask, in his name, for some regular reinforcements. Meade galloped off in search of Scott, finding him on
a ridge over which Worth's reserve division was crossing to the
Jalapa road.

"I told the General my message," wrote Meade, "and he directed
me to say to General Pillow that he had no regulars to spare."
After quickly relating to the young lieutenant the result of the
battle, Scott added, "finally that General Pillow might attack again,
or not, as he pleased. He evidently was not much surprised and
not much 'put out' that Pillow was thrashed, and attached no importance to his future movements."

Meade hurried back to Pillow, where he found the Pennsyl-
vanians had finally been persuaded to attack, but the attack never
came off. White flags were raised over the Mexican batteries, which
were hopelessly isolated by the course of battle on the other end
of the line.

Scott's victory was a dazzling one. At the cost of 63 killed and
367 wounded he had routed Santa Anna, and captured five generals, including the distinguished La Vega, who was captured at
Resaca de la Palma and exchanged, 199 officers and 2,837 rank and
file. Another 1,000 Mexicans were believed to have escaped after
capture.

More than forty cannons, which were soon rendered unservice-
able by the Americans, and 4,000 stands of arms were among the
spoils of battle. Santa Anna, in his haste to "sacrifice" himself, left,
wrote Kendall of the *Picayune* "his service of massive silver, nearly
all of his papers, his money [about $25,000], everything in his car-
riage, even to his dinner." In a subsequent dispatch, Kendall stated

that Santa Anna's "most excellent dinner, together with delicious
wine, and some highly-flavored cigars" came as a perfect windfall,
after a hard morning's work, to Captain Justus McKinstry and
Captain [Seth or Thomas (?)] Williams. "To say that they did not
sit themselves comfortably down on his richly cushioned seats, par-
take of his sumptuous dinner . . . would be departing farther from
the truth than I care about doing right now," added Kendall.

The hero of the battle, according to the official reports, was Captain Lee. Scott in his report was "impelled to make special mention
of Captain R. E. Lee" who was "again indefatigable . . . in reconnaissance as daring as laborous and of the utmost value. Nor was
he less conspicuous in planting batteries, and in conducting columns to their stations under the heavy fire of the enemy." Colonel
Riley, although it was not "appropriately within the range" of his
report, could not "refrain from bearing testimony to the intrepid
coolness and gallantry exhibited by Captain Lee . . ." General
Twiggs reported Lee's "invaluable service . . . his gallantry and
good conduct on both days deserve the highest praise." Twiggs said
he consulted Lee "with confidence, and adopted his suggestions
with entire assurance." Lieutenant Isaac I. Stevens of the Engineers
summed it all up: "Captain Lee has won golden opinions."

As for Lee, he wrote his son Custis after Cerro Gordo, "You
have no idea what a horrible sight a field of battle is."

25

The Feuding Conquerors

Sixty-eight days after United States troops had landed on the beach at Vera Cruz, the American flag flew over Puebla, second city of Mexico, less than 100 miles from the capital.

By May 15, 1847, one year and one week after the first American victory of the war at Palo Alto, unbroken success had crowned American arms in the twofold invasion of Mexico under Zachary Taylor and Winfield Scott.

Elsewhere, American occupation was firmly and peacefully established in California, and American warships were, within the limitations of their number, blockading Mexican Pacific ports. In New Mexico, General Sterling Price's occupation faced minor raids and occasional threats of a new revolt, but the American domination was secure. On Mexico's Atlantic coast, Commodore Perry had seized or neutralized all of the significant ports.

The war was going well, but General Scott's claim to General Taylor after the victory at Cerro Gordo—"Mexico has no longer an army"—was quite premature if Scott's implication was that the end of the war was at hand. For one thing, Santa Anna, having escaped to Orizaba, had rallied a new force about him with that organizational magic that went hand-in-hand with battlefield ineptitude. For another, the Mexican Congress, the very night it received word of the disaster at Cerro Gordo, decreed that while the government "has power . . . to carry on the war" it was not authorized "to make peace with the United States" and, moreover, "every individual is declared a traitor who . . . shall treat with the government of the United States."

On the same day, April 21, General José Mariano Salas issued a proclamation calling for volunteers for "a guerrilla corps with which to attack and destroy the invaders in every manner imaginable." The motto for this guerrilla "warfare of vengeance," was: "War without pity, unto death!"

General Scott had, moreover, a number of problems with which to contend. The most pressing, for the moment, was a lack of money —"hard" money, the only kind acceptable by the Mexicans. The troops could and, more often than not, did miss their paydays, but the purchase of supplies for the army required that considerable specie be available to quartermasters and commissaries. Often, the situation became so critical that Scott would have been justified in seizing supplies or levying a loan on the Mexicans.

Two weeks after his arrival at Jalapa—the army had occupied that garden spot the day after Cerro Gordo—Scott had received authority from Washington to collect customs at the ports and to levy a contribution on the people. The former project he turned over to the port commanders and the latter he chose not to invoke, because "we may ruin and exasperate the inhabitants and starve ourselves." General Scott was certain the Mexicans would remove or destroy their animals and products rather than permit them to fall to the Americans without compensation. "Not a ration for man or horse would be brought in, except by the bayonet," declared Scott, and this would occupy the troops "in search of subsistence and stop all military operations."

The next problem Scott faced was an approaching manpower shortage caused by the expiration of the terms of the twelve-months volunteers. The General's exasperation was intense when he learned at Jalapa that General George Cadwalader and about 3,000 troops intended for his army had been diverted by Secretary of War Marcy to General Taylor "to avert . . . a calamity." Washington had not yet learned of Buena Vista.

Scott hoped that many of the volunteers would reenlist, but his hopes did not coincide with reality. Out of seven regiments, whose enlistments would expire between the end of May and the end of July, only one company of four officers and sixty-four men could be recruited by Captain Chatham Roberdeau Wheat, destined to become one of the famed soldiers of fortune of the nineteenth century, and the dashing leader of the notorious Louisiana Tigers in the Confederate Army.

Because it would have been foolish to march the volunteers deeper into Mexico with their time so nearly up, and with the yellow fever season fast reaching its height at Vera Cruz, Scott decided to release the volunteers immediately. Accordingly on May 3, he ordered transports for 3,000 troops, and three days later, under command of General Patterson, who was returning to the United States, the volunteers marched out of Jalapa. In the party was Gideon Pillow, recently promoted to major general—"Why?" was a universal question in the army—who was going home to bring out a newly formed division of regulars.

A third concern for General Scott at this time was transportation. Wagons were accumulating, at last, at Vera Cruz, but the shortage now was not in vehicles but in wagonmasters and teamsters, who were civilian employees of the army. Scott tried to induce departing volunteers to sign up for these jobs without much success.

Meanwhile, Scott had not kept the army idle at the idyllic Jalapa. Almost immediately, Worth's division had pushed on over the ever-climbing National Road which led to the great Mexican plateau and Puebla. At the pass of La Joya, ten miles beyond Japala, Worth found a strong position abandoned, its guns spiked. Continuing his march into Perote, with its formidable eighteenth century castle, Worth on April 22 not only took the town without the slightest opposition but found a Colonel Velásquez ready to surrender with an inventory of artillery, and arms and munitions. These Captain R. E. Lee and Captain W. C. De Hart verified, and the General signed a receipt.

General Quitman, who had recently been promoted a grade, was assigned the four remaining volunteer regiments with Scott's army, two Pennsylvania regiments and those of New York and South Carolina. Quitman left the Second Pennsylvania, with a company of artillery, to garrison Jalapa and moved on to join General Worth at Perote. Here Quitman dropped off the First Pennsylvania as a garrison for the fortress, and with the New York and South Carolina troops he took up the march behind Worth.

On May 14, Worth was camped at Amozoque, about twelve miles from Puebla, not only to "spruce up" the army for an impressive entry into the city, but to permit Quitman, a day's march in the rear, to close up. About 8 o'clock in the morning the alarm came. "The long roll sounded," wrote Captain Ephraim Kirby Smith, "a call that always thrills to the marrow a soldier, as it never beats on light occasions and is the usual prelude to a battle." Mexican cavalry, about 2,500 strong, had been sighted approaching the town.

The leader of this mounted force was none other than the Napoleon of the West, himself, Antonio López de Santa Anna. Having raised about 4,000 infantry at Orizaba, Santa Anna had marched to Puebla, where he hoped to add more troops and obtain money and ammunition. Puebla received him coolly, so he ordered the infantry to march to Mexico City, while he rode out on a purposeless mission, it appears, against the advancing Americans. A few rounds from Worth's artillery threw the mounted force into confusion, and without returning the American fire with any of its three pieces, the Mexican cavalry veered off to their left, passing around Worth's right and apparently moving on Quitman. The latter, having heard Worth's guns, was ready, and once again the Mexicans moved to the left and disappeared into the hills. Noting in his journal that Santa Anna led the Mexicans, Kirby Smith added: ". . . but no one can devise what could have been the object of his movements."

The next day, as Worth approached Puebla, he was met with cordiality by city officials, and in the ensuing negotiations of surrender, the General gave Puebla more generous terms than Scott had given Vera Cruz. In doing so, Worth actually sabotaged Scott's Martial Law Order, by permitting Mexican authorities to settle difficulties between Americans and Mexicans.

Four days earlier, General Scott had prepared a proclamation— it was suggested by a representative of the Bishop of Puebla and urged by Colonel Ethan Allen Hitchcock—which in part read:

> We have not profaned your temples, nor abused your women, nor seized your property . . . The Army of the United States respects, and will ever respect, private property of every class and the property of the Mexican church . . . The government and people of the United States desire peace—desire your friendship . . . The system of forming guerrilla parties to annoy us, will I assure you, produce only evils to this country, and none to our army, which knows how to protect itself against such cut-throats . . . I shall march with this army upon Puebla and Mexico. I do not conceal this from you. From those capitals I may again address you. We desire peace, friendship, and union; it is for you to choose whether you prefer continued hostilities.

In an unofficial letter to Scott on May 19, Worth said he had had three editions struck off, such was the demand of the people of all classes for the proclamation. "It takes admirably and my doors are crowded for it," Worth wrote. "It . . . has produced more decided results than all the blows from Palo Alto to Cerro Gordo. I have scattered them far and wide, and taken three chances to get them into the capital."

Among the United States leaders, the Mexican War was characterized by dissension, distrust, envy, jealousy, ambition, rivalry, and even hatred. In a round robin of animosity, Polk hated Scott and Taylor; Taylor hated Polk and Scott; and Scott hated Taylor and Polk. Scott and Ethan Allen Hitchcock started out avowed enemies and wound up sincere friends; Scott and Worth started out as warm friends and wound up bitter enemies. Worth held a consistent relationship with Hitchcock with whom mutual hostility existed before, during, and after the war. And Worth and General Twiggs maintained between them a formal coolness, backed by mutual contempt. Twiggs, for his part, did not have happy relations with General Patterson who, by now, had returned to the United States.

By this time, General Scott, thanks in part to his irascible pen, was involved in feuds with Nicholas P. Trist, President Polk's special envoy to Mexico, and with Commodore Perry and his flag lieutenant, Raphael Semmes. And, moreover, Scott and General William Jenkins Worth were on the verge of breaking up their close friendship of many years.

On April 15, President Polk had appointed Trist, friend and protégé of Thomas Jefferson, as his envoy to be attached to General Scott's army "to conclude a treaty of peace with the Mexican Government, should it be so inclined." Trist, a West Pointer, had served President Andrew Jackson as his private secretary and for eight years was United States Consul in Havana. Neither his $2,000 salary nor title of chief clerk in the State Department did justice to his talents and his importance in the administration, for he was, indeed, next in authority to Secretary of State Buchanan and often served as acting secretary.

Assured of the President's confidence in his "ability, patriotism, and integrity," Trist left at once on his great mission—so "secret" that the New York *Herald* printed four days after he left the full story "with remarkable accuracy & particularity." Traveling incognito by way of New Orleans, Trist reached Vera Cruz on the revenue cutter *Ewing* on May 6. In his papers was a draft of a treaty prepared by the Secretary of State, a dispatch to the Mexican Minister of Foreign Affairs, and a letter from Secretary of War Marcy to General Scott.

Instead of proceeding at once to Jalapa to present himself to Scott—Trist could have secured an escort, or gone up in the train scheduled to march on May 8—the envoy wrote a letter to the General enclosing a sealed packet to be forwarded to the Mexican authorities (without revealing to Scott the contents), and Marcy's letter to Scott.

On receipt of Trist's letter on May 7, Scott went into a rage and immediately replied. He was furious that a " (sealed!)" document should have been sent him, and he vented his anger on Marcy as well as Trist: "I see that the Secretary of War proposes to degrade me by requiring that I, the commander of this army, shall defer to you, the chief clerk of the Department of State, the question of continuing or discontinuing hostilities." Had he calmly read Marcy's letter, instead of going off half-cocked, Scott would have realized that although Trist "was clothed with such diplomatic powers as will authorize him to enter into arrangements with the government of Mexico for the suspension of hostilities," his own authority as commander-in-chief was in no way impaired. Two conditions which qualified Trist's diplomatic powers seemed lost on the irate General: First, Trist must inform Scott in writing that "contingency has occurred in consequence of which the President is willing that further active military operations should cease"; and, second, Scott would be the sole judge as whether to hold or retire from any positions "necessary to the health and safety of the troops."

The incident, which would have been ludicrous were it not so preposterous, need never have developed had Trist approached Scott a little more tactfully, had the General read Marcy's letter more carefully, and had not pen and ink been readily available to each.

Scott's outburst drew from Trist a thirty-page acrimonious reply which lay unopened for several days—and probably unread in its entirety—before Scott returned to the attack. The General, on May 29, wrote from Puebla, expressing his "contempt and scorn" for Trist's latest "farrago of insolence, conceit and arrogance," and told him that in future communications "be brief and purely official."

General Scott found time to complain bitterly to Marcy of "an attempt to place me under the military command of Mr. Trist" and voiced the desire to be recalled because of "many cruel disappointments and mortifications" he had experienced and "the total want of support and sympathy on the part of the War Department which I have so long experienced."

When President Polk saw the copies of the correspondence he recorded in his diary: "Gen'l Scott has written very foolish & bittei letters to Mr. Trist & Mr. Trist has written as foolish a letter to him." At a cabinet meeting, the question of recalling both Scott and Trist was discussed and dismissed as inappropriate, but the Secretaries of War and State were instructed to write the embattled letter-writers condemning both and ordering them "to cease their . . . personal controversy and to act in harmony."

But before either received the reprimand, they had "buried their pens" and were on terms of cordiality. A gift of guava jelly from Scott when Trist suffered an indisposition; the good offices of General Persifor F. Smith, a friend of both; and the activity of Edward Thornton of the British Embassy, in achieving communication with Santa Anna, who agreed to accept the American dispatch, opened the door to amiable relations between Scott and Trist. Before the end of July, Trist wrote Buchanan that he had "entirely misconceived" the General's character and asked that their correspondence not be brought "to the notice of the public," but that he be permitted "to withdraw it from the files of the department." Similarly, Scott wrote Marcy "the happy change" in relations with Trist, whom he found, on better acquantance, to be "able, discreet courteous and amiable," and such was his "present esteem" that he wished that "all I have heretofore written to the department about Mr. Trist should be suppressed."

Scott's dispute with the navy came when Lieutenant Raphael Semmes arrived at Jalapa early in May with orders from Commodore Perry to negotiate with Mexican authorities for the release of Passed Midshipman R. C. Rogers, who had been captured.

"I called on General Scott . . . and presented him with my letter of credence from Commodore Perry," wrote Lieutenant Semmes. "The General did not appear at all pleased with my mission." General Scott was not pleased and expressed his doubt to Semmes of "the expediency of more than one channel of communications with the Mexican Government." The General regretted that "Com-

modore Perry has thought it necessary to send you, as his special
messenger to treat with the Mexican Government on the subject
of Mr. Rogers . . . a note from the Commodore would have been
sufficient to have interested me officially and personally in his fate."

Scott then told Semmes of Trist's arrival and suggested "you . . .
refer the business of your mission to him. I only make the suggestion." Because of guerrillas and rancheros, a flag of truce, sent
ahead of the army, was unsafe, Scott said; therefore he could not
comply with the request for an escort. Perhaps later, when the
army neared the capital. "In the meantime, you can remain here,
return to Commodore Perry's squadron, or advance with the army,
as may seem to you best," wrote Scott. "I have no advice to offer
on the subject."

Later Semmes wrote he could not understand how his mission
"could be construed into an infringement of the prerogatives of
General Scott." Neither could President Polk, when the matter
reached his desk. "Gen'l Scott arrogates to himself the right to be
the only proper channel through whom the U.S. Government can
properly communicate with the Government of Mexico on any
subject," the President noted in his diary on June 12, "which is an
assumption wholly unwarrantable & which I will not tolerate."

Lieutenant Semmes attached himself to General Worth as an
aide, and this naval officer, who would gain fame in another war,
fought with the army for the rest of the Mexican War.

Meanwhile, in Puebla, General Worth apparently was in a jittery
state of mind. Lieutenant U. S. Grant recalled that almost contin-
uously, Worth "had the enemy hovering around near the city in
vastly superior numbers to his own." Grant's brigade changed
quarters three times in a week and once, "General Worth had the
troops in line, under arms, all day," while "he galloped from one
command to another proclaiming the proximity of Santa Anna . . ."
To cap this, Worth issued to his division a circular warning that
the Mexicans in the markets might be poisoning foods which they
sold American soldiers. The circular denounced "the habit of cow-
ards, to poison those from whom they habitually fly in battle, a
resource familiar in Spanish history, legitimately inherited, and
willingly practiced by the Mexicans."

This highly impolitic scare handbill was repugnant to Scott, and
he ordered Worth to round up all the copies he could. Worth's
response was to demand a court of inquiry both for the poison

incident and the terms of surrender, disapproval of which Scott showed by issuing his Martial Law Order. The court agreed Worth should be censured, which censure Scott made very light and with publication limited to brigade and division commanders and staff officers. This consideration for his old friend was lost on Worth who, from that time on, limited himself only to official communication with Scott.

When General Twiggs marched his division of regulars into Puebla on May 29, Scott had concentrated there about 6,000 troops, of which fully 1,000 were on the sick list. He awaited reinforcements before marching on Mexico City. These were not too long in arriving. On June 2, Colonel J. S. McIntosh started from Vera Cruz with 700 new troops, 400 pack-mules, 700 horses, and 128 wagons, of which ten carried silver coins for the army to pay the troops and pay its bills. McIntosh was joined by General George Cadwalader with 500 men, and on June 15 the combined force reached Jalapa, where the garrison joined the column on the march three days later for Perote.

On June 16, General Gideon J. Pillow started from Vera Cruz with 1,500 more men, and he sent word ahead to Cadwalader to await his arrival. When Pillow reached Perote, the reinforcements for Scott now exceeded 4,000 men with 500 wagons. The column was a welcome sight when it marched into Puebla on July 8, bringing the strength of Scott's army up to 10,000 troops. The General now made plans to begin the long-awaited march on Mexico City, but when word came that General Franklin Pierce, with more than 2,400 troops had left Vera Cruz on July 19, Scott deferred his departure from Puebla. During his march, Pierce was attacked five or six times by guerrilla bands and was delayed by the destruction of the bridges over the Río San Juan and the Río del Plan, but on August 6, he reached Puebla.

The very next day, the movement on Mexico City began. "Leaving, as we all feared, inadequate garrisons at Vera Cruz, Perote and Puebla," wrote Scott, ". . . we marched from Puebla with only 10,738 rank and file." On the 7th Colonel Harney's brigade, composed of detachments of the First, Second, and Third Dragoons, rode out as an advance guard, while Twiggs's division had the post of honor, leading the march. As his two veteran brigades under Persifor F. Smith and Bennett Riley formed in the grand plaza Twiggs waved his hat to his men and cried: "Now, my lads, give them a Cerro Gordo shout," and with a roar the troops fell in behind Davy the Bengal Tiger and took the road to the capital.

On August 8, but only about five marching hours behind Twiggs,
Quitman's division moved out. It was composed of Shields's brigade
of New York and South Carolina Volunteers and a brigade commanded by Lieutenant Colonel S. E. Watson of the Marine Corps,
composed of 300 Marines and a portion of the Second Pennsylvania Volunteers.

Worth's division, consisting of the veteran brigades of Colonel
John Garland and Colonel N. S. Clarke, took up the march on the
9th, while on the 10th, Pillow's division, composed of the brigades
of Cadwalader and Pierce, formed the rear of Scott's column.

". . . No division," wrote General Scott, ". . . was ever separated
more than seven or eight miles from support, or rather half that
distance by a double movement—one division advancing and the
other falling back." Accordingly, in the event of a formidable attack on an interior division, Scott could have united three divisions
in a little more than two hours.

Enjoying the drama of his situation to the fullest, Scott had written the Secretary of War: "Like Cortez, finding myself isolated
and abandoned . . . I resolved no longer to depend on Vera Cruz,
or home, but to render my little army a *self-sustaining machine.*"

In faraway England, the old Duke of Wellington, who had moved
pins on a map of Mexico ever since the American landing at Vera
Cruz, exclaimed when he heard of the march on Mexico City:
"Scott is lost. He has been carried away by successes. He can't take
the city, and he can't fall back on his base."

26

"That Splendid City . . . Ours!"

Winfield Scott, having already cast himself in the role of a latter-day Cortés, was equal to the occasion when the army struggled up the more than 10,000-foot pass of Río Frío and began the descent into the Valley of Mexico.

It was then, wrote the General, that "the object of all our dreams and hopes—toils and dangers;—once the gorgeous seat of the Montezumas . . . first broke upon our enchanted view." Under a dazzling sun, the surrounding lakes in the distance sparked "like pendant diamonds" and the towering giant, Popocatepetl, in the clear air, seemed "near enough to touch with the hand." For a moment, the General's mind, "filled . . . with religious awe," was caught up in a "sublime trance." Recovering, Winfield Scott thought, and assumed that every man in the column thought so, too: "That splendid city soon shall be ours!"

The eastern and southeastern approaches to Mexico City were screened by three lakes and extensive marshes, the only passages through the latter being over defendable causeways of earth raised above the level of the swamps. Immediately to the east of the city, and extending for a considerable distance north was Lake Texcoco. Lake Chalco and Lake Xochimilco were both south of Lake Texcoco and southeast of the city, Xochimilco being closer to the capital than Chalco. The National Road, the most direct route to the city, passed through the village of Ayotla, on the northern shore of Lake Chalco, crossed the marsh, and passed between Lake Texcoco and the strongly fortified hill of El Peñón, which rose 300 feet above the marshes, and then continued into the city

During the three months stay in Puebla, Scott's "indefatigable engineers" had collected and studied maps and had charted potential approaches to the Mexican capital. Four possible avenues of attack were available to Scott. The first was to march some thirty miles around the northern end of Lake Texcoco and approach the city from the north. The second route was along the main road, formidably defended by El Peñón. A third choice was by a causeway branching to the left off the National Road to the village of Mexicalcingo at the northern tip of Lake Xochimilco and then north to the city. The fourth possibility was a circuitous route along the south shores of Lake Chalco and Xochimilco, and thence to the village of San Agustín on the Mexico City-Acapulco high road.

Twiggs's division went into camp at Ayotla on August 11, and before the other divisions had come up and pitched their tents in the villages in the vicinity, Major John Lind Smith of the Engineers and his brilliant octet of subordinates—Captains R. E. Lee and James L. Mason; First Lieutenants P. G. T. Beauregard, Zealous B. Tower, and Isaac I. Stevens; Second Lieutenants George B. McClellan, Gustavus W. Smith, and John G. Foster—were busy reconnoitering the ground.

The march around the northern edge of Lake Texcoco was soon discarded by the engineers as impracticable. (Lieutenant Sam Grant, in a personal and unofficial terrain study, suggested this route and submitted it to his superiors. "I know not whether General Scott was put in possession of the information," he wrote home. But Grant insisted in his letter that "his" route "avoided all the fortified positions until we reached the gates of the city at their weakest and most indefensible as well as most approachable points . . . We would have been on solid ground instead of floundering through morass and ditches and fighting our way over elevated roads, flanked by water where it is generally impossible to deploy forces.")

The first object of reconnaissance was El Peñón, about midway between Ayotla and Mexico City. Captain Lee, Captain Mason, and Lieutenant Stevens started out with escort on the morning of August 12 to inspect the hill, and they found it bristling with guns and troops. Their observations that day and the next satisfied the engineers that El Peñón was a formidable position, strongly held. Lee described it: "The hill of El Peñón . . . stands in the waters of Lake Texcuco [sic]. Its base is surrounded by a dry trench, and its sides arranged with breastworks from its base to its crest. It was armed with thirty pieces of cannon, and defended by 7,000 men . . . The causeway passed directly by its base; the waters of the lake

Guadalupe
Hidalgo

LAKE
TEXCOCO

N

Mexico City

Chapultepec

Molino del
Rey

Tacubaya

San Antonio Abad
Garita

RIO CHURUBUSCO

Coyoacan

Mexicalcingo

EL
PEÑON

NATIONAL ROAD

San Angel

Churubusco

San Geronimo

Pedregal

San
Antonio

Ansaldo-
Padierna

ZACATEPEC
HILL.

Ayotla

TO PUEBLA

Contreras

San Agustin

LAKE XOCHIMILCO

ACAPULCO ROAD

Xochimilco

LAKE
CHALCO

Chalco

0 1 2 3 4 5
Miles

Valley of Mexico

washed each side of the causeway for two miles in front and the whole distance, seven miles, to the city."

The next day, Lieutenant Stevens returned to reconnoiter El Peñón. Accompanied by only two Dragoons, he spent seven hours studying the position. "I went half way round the Peñón . . . within almost point-blank range of its guns, examining the different batteries, determining the various approaches, and particularly the character of the innundation," Stevens wrote his wife. "Frequently I was in the water up to the belly of my horse."

When Lee reported to Scott that the position at El Peñón, strong in itself, was also protected by four batteries on the causeway—one about 400 yards in front of the hill, another at its side, a third a mile from the entrance to the city, and the fourth at the entrance— Scott concluded that a better way into Mexico City must be found. "No doubt it might have been carried," reported the General, "but at a great disproportionate loss."

While Lee, Mason, and Stevens were studying El Peñón from close range on the morning of the 12th, Major Smith with Lieutenants Beauregard and Tower climbed Calderón Hill in front of El Peñón for a general view of the valley. That afternoon, Lee and Beauregard skirted the northern shore of Lake Chalco where, Beauregard stated, they learned of "the road on the other side of these lakes, which was reported as quite good, although narrow and rough."

On the 13th, the day Stevens made his study of El Peñón, Mason, Beauregard, and Lieutenant McClellan reconnoitered the village of Mexicalcingo, where Lee and Tower, who had followed the road above Lake Chalco, joined them. "We found the position of Mexicalcingo naturally a strong one and pretty well fortified," wrote Beauregard, "but with few guns in position and a small force to defend it." The engineers agreed, Beauregard stated, that "if immediately, properly and boldly attacked, it could have been taken without much loss."

General Scott felt so, too, particularly as Mexicalcingo was isolated from El Peñón, which could not supply timely assistance, especially if the hill was itself under threat of attack. However, as Captain Lee pointed out, the causeway to Mexicalcingo extended two miles past the town before it "opened upon terra firma at the village of Churubusco." To Scott, the carrying of the village offered few difficulties but, having captured it, "we should have found ourselves . . . on a narrow causeway, flanked to the right and left by water, or boggy ground."

So before committing himself to an attack at that point, Scott awaited word of a reconnaissance around the south end of Lake Chalco which Colonel James Duncan, Worth's artillery chief, undertook on the morning of August 14. Duncan returned in the early afternoon with information that the road south of Lakes Chalco and Xochimilco, while extremely rough, was not impassable for artillery and the trains. On the basis of Duncan's report—which actually was half a report, for he reconnoitered only halfway to the village of San Agustín—Scott decided to bypass El Peñón and Mexicalcingo, and take the southern approach to Mexico City.

On August 15, Worth's division, which was at the village of Chalco, led off the march, with Harney's Dragoons in the van. The same day, the divisions of Pillow and Quitman followed closely, while Twiggs remained at Ayotla until the 16th as a threat to El Peñón and Mexicalcingo, "to deceive the enemy," reported Scott, "as long as possible." The deception didn't last long, for on the march, Mexican cavalry and infantry challenged Twiggs briefly. He deployed for battle, but a few rounds of artillery dispersed the Mexicans.

Worth reached San Agustín on the 17th, while Pillow and Quitman were at hand on the 18th, with Twiggs closing up. "The army moved around [Lake] Chalco with considerable difficulty over a road thought by the Mexicans to be absolutely impracticable," wrote Inspector General Hitchcock in his journal. A captured Mexican letter explained how the Americans had marched over the impassable trace of a road: ". . . Each man of eight or ten thousand Americans who had to pass that way took a bag of sand on his shoulders, so that on the way they mended the road as they went along with eight or ten thousand bags of sand!"

San Agustín lay on the Acapulco road, about nine miles from Mexico City. Three miles nearer the capital was the hacienda of San Antonio, strongly fortified and whose guns swept the road effectively. This Worth discovered on the 18th on a reconnaissance in force before the field works. The first Mexican fire killed Captain Seth Thornton of the Second Dragoons, whose ambush and capture on the Rio Grande sixteen months earlier had started hostilities. Scott's "daring engineers," Mason, Stevens, and Tower, determined that San Antonio could be attacked only frontally. To the right of

the road was a vast bog, while on the left was the *pedregal,* an extensive lava field, five miles wide, east and west, and three miles
long, north and south.

The *pedregal* was, wrote Lieutenant Stevens, "a perfect honey-
comb of lava projections." Great blocks of jagged volcanic rock,
deep cuts and fissures, ridges and mounds and slopes made the
lava field an impossible barrier. "I cannot better describe the
pedregal," wrote Lieutenant Raphael Semmes, "than by comparing
it to a sea, which having been lashed into a fury by a tempest, had
been suddenly transformed . . . into stone."

It was the general opinion that, the terrain being what it was,
the Acapulco road, so formidably guarded at San Antonio, and with
a strong bridgehead at the Río Churubusco and the fortified convent of San Mateo nearby, was out of the question as the avenue of
attack. Scott now looked to the west of San Agustín, across the
seemingly impassable *pedregal* toward the San Angel road. This
road ran from Coyoacán, a village situated north of the lava field,
midway between San Antonio and San Angel, and it continued
from the latter village past the ranches of Ansaldo and Padierna,
skirting the western edge of the *pedregal,* and on to the village of
Contreras, after which it trailed off into a mule path which lost
itself in the mountains.

The terrain and the roads favored Santa Anna, who, with his
peculiar genius for organization, had gathered an army of 20,000
men and ninety guns to meet Scott's 10,000 at the gates of Mexico
City. By massing his troops at San Antonio, Coyoacán, and San
Angel, within less than five miles, he could move easily to threatened points of attack. When Scott unobligingly refused to attack El
Peñón, and moved south, Santa Anna quickly regrouped his forces.
Leaving General Manuel Rincón at El Piñón and General Nicolás
Bravo to defend the Mexicalcingo-Churubusco area, Santa Anna
shifted his headquarters to the convent of San Mateo at Churubusco. General Francisco Pérez, with a brigade of 3,000 men, was
stationed at Coyoacán and General Gabriel Valencia, who had been
north of the capital, marched through the city to San Angel.

Such was the disposition of Santa Anna's army, twice as large as
the American force grouped around San Agustín. Inspector General
Hitchcock thought the situation presented "rather an uncomfortable aspect." Forage for the horses was gone, the hard bread for the
troops was getting musty, and in the entire army there were only

four days' rations, plus some beef on the hoof. Colonel Hitchcock noted that General Scott appeared discouraged as he passed along the road lined with men, horses, and wagons, "the men without tents, the evening almost cold and a menace of rain." With the defenses of San Antonio appearing much too strong to assault, Hitchcock contemplated how Scott's "prospects . . . darken every moment." Into his diary at 9 A.M. on August 19, Hitchcock wrote: "Now is the time for the General to keep cool!"

27

Seventeen Minutes at Padierna

A decade and a half before the Civil War revealed Robert E. Lee to the world as a military genius, discerning officers in General Scott's army in Mexico had already discovered this fact.

Writing to his wife, during the campaign before Mexico City, Lieutenant Isaac I. Stevens said of Lee: "He is one of the most extraordinary men in the service. In the very prime of manhood, of remarkable presence and address, perhaps the most manly and striking officer in the service, of great grace of manner and great personal beauty, he has established an enduring reputation. His power of enduring fatigue is extraordinary, and his strength of judgment and perfect balance are conspicuous. For counsel, General Scott relies more upon him than any other man in the service."

Lieutenant Raphael Semmes, the naval officer turned soldier, in his *Service Afloat and Ashore in the Mexican War*, published in 1851, wrote of Captain Lee and his "invaluable" services: "Endowed with a mind which has no superior in his corps, and possessing great energy of character, he examined, counselled, and advised with a judgment, tact, and discretion worthy of all praise. His talent for topography was peculiar, and he seemed to receive impressions intuitively, which it cost other men much labor to acquire."

To Captain Lee on August 18, General Scott assigned the important mission of finding a way through the *pedregal* for the army to reach the San Angel road. Accompanied by Lieutenant P. G. T. Beauregard and supported by the Eleventh Infantry and two companies of Dragoons under Captain Phil Kearny, Lee struck off into the lava field.

The party soon picked up a rough but passable road on the edge of the *pedregal*. "We found the road pretty good for about half the distance," wrote Beauregard, "but the rest was quite rough, hilly, and partly covered with *pedregal*, but I saw it could be made practicable (with a little trouble and labor) for artillery." As the road reached Zacatepec Hill, a little more than three miles west of San Agustín, it trailed off into a mule path, which itself disappeared in the broken, uneven and rough sea of lava. Here the escort ran into a strong advance party of Mexicans who, after a sharp exchange of shots, retired to the western fringe of the *pedregal*.

Lee and Beauregard climbed to the top of Zacatepec while their supporting troops, thwarted in the immense mass of jagged rocks and chasms, gave up their brief pursuit of the retreating Mexicans. From the hill, the two officers clearly saw the San Angel road, about a mile and a half to the west, and the village of Padierna, which the Americans assumed was Contreras, with the result that they gave the wrong name to the forthcoming battle.

What was more important, Lee and Beauregard noted a formidably fortified hill, strongly held, beyond the road, but close to Padierna. It was obvious to the two engineers that if the Mexican troops could advance and retire over the *pedregal*, then Scott's army assuredly could cross it, too. When Lee presented their findings and recommendations that a road be chipped out of the rock for the artillery to pass to within range of the Mexican works, General Scott assigned the task to him.

Meanwhile, at Padierna, General Valencia, who had disobeyed Santa Anna's instructions, prepared for a frontal attack by the Americans. Santa Anna had placed Valencia at San Angel, with permission to fall back on Tacubaya, if Scott attacked in force, but otherwise to maintain his position. Valencia, instead, advanced down the San Angel road to Padierna on the morning of August 18, with a portion of his force. There, on a hill which overlooked the *pedregal*, he dug trenches, raised breastworks, installed twenty-two guns and encamped, bringing in the rest of his 4,000 troops.

Santa Anna, on the evening of the 18th, had sent orders to Valencia, with whom he had no bonds of friendship, to return on the morning of the 19th "with the whole force of the army under your command" and take a position at Coyoacán, sending his artillery to Churubusco. Valencia, who had ambitions to oust Santa Anna as President, refused to comply with the order, "both because of my military and patriotic conscience." Santa Anna, disgusted at Valencia's insubordination, replied: "Do what you like and let each one bear the responsibility that pertains to him."

Such was the situation when Lee, assisted by Lieutenants Beaure-

gard, Stevens, Tower, McClellan, Foster, and Smith, started out on
August 19 with 500 men from General Pillow's division "to open a
practicable road . . . for the siege and other trains, in the direction
of San Angel." Worth's division was left in front of San Antonio,
while Quitman's division remained at San Agustín to guard the
wagons. The rest of Pillow's division, supported by Twiggs's division, which followed, were to protect the road builders. According to Beauregard, the road construction began about 9 A.M. and by
1 P.M. its work had advanced "to within reach of the enemy's guns."
Lee had located the road on a direct line to Padierna, and progress
was good despite skirmishes with Mexican pickets and patrols which
attempted to harass the Americans. However, when the Mexican
batteries opened within range of the work party, Lee called off
the operation, returned Pillow's men to their regiments, and packed
up the tools. Before more work could be done to complete the
road, the Mexicans had to be dislodged.

The light batteries of Captain John B. Magruder and Lieutenant
Franklin D. Callender and Lieutenant Jesse Reno's rockets were
ordered forward and Captain Lee placed them into position to
answer Valencia's much more potent fire. From 2 P.M. to 10 P.M.,
the American guns, outranged and outpowered, remained in action,
after which they were withdrawn. Captain Lee, who stayed with
the guns for some time, may have noticed a young lieutenant with
Magruder's battery. His name was Thomas Jonathan Jackson.

Early in the afternoon Twiggs ordered General Persifor Smith's
brigade to advance toward the American batteries. He then sent
Colonel Bennett Riley's brigade to the right, to cross the ravine and
its swift stream, which separated the positions of the two forces, and
occupy the village of San Gerónimo. This move was "for the
purpose of cutting off the retreat of the enemy," after Valencia had
been driven from his works by frontal attack. Riley, as he neared
the village, had two brushes with bodies of Lancers, but they were
driven off. To his dismay, however, Riley saw advancing from the
direction of the city, a tremendous force of Mexicans—it was Santa
Anna himself, with perhaps 5,000 or more troops—but for some
mysterious reason they halted and deployed on high ground before
San Angel. Meanwhile, from Valencia's works, more than 2,000
troops had emerged to block the road, which Riley had recently
crossed. His position, between two stronger Mexican forces, was
precarious.

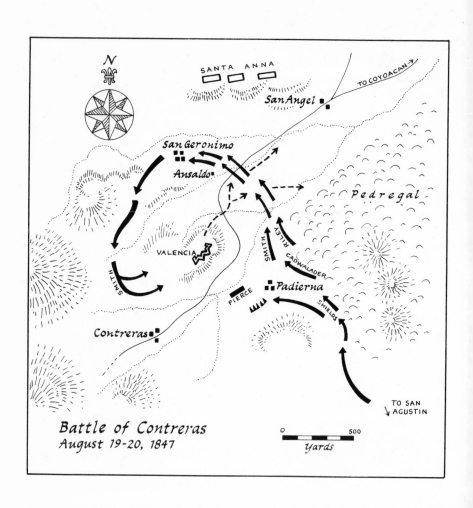

N

SANTA ANNA

TO COYOACAN

San Angel

Pedregal

San Geronimo

Ansaldo

SMITH

RILEY

CADWALADER

VALENCIA

SMITH

Padierna

PIERCE

SHIELDS

Contreras

TO SAN
AGUSTIN

Battle of Contreras
August 19-20, 1847

0   500

Yards

Meanwhile, on the American side of the ravine, Persifor Smith realized his brigade would be slaughtered by Valencia's twenty-two guns if he attacked frontally. Accordingly, Smith decided to move to the right out of range of the Mexican batteries and get to Valencia's left and rear. Calling for diversionary fire from Magruder's guns to mask his movement, Smith led his brigade "with great difficulty . . . crossing the rock for near a mile." As he approached the village or ranch of Ansaldo, he saw, as Riley had, the huge Mexican force on the slopes below San Angel. Lieutenant Beauregard, who had piloted Colonel George W. Morgan's Fifteenth Infantry across the lava field to join Cadwalader's brigade in support of Riley, started his "painful and fatiguing trip across the *pedregal*." In the ravine, Beauregard heard his name called; it was General Smith. With permission, Beauregard attached himself to the General ("I disliked exceedingly the idea of recrossing the *pedregal*," wrote Beauregard, "my shoes and pantaloons being already very badly torn") and he led Smith to General Cadwalader.

"I suppose, sir, you assume the command here?" asked Cadwalader.

"Certainly, with pleasure," responded Smith.

After consulting with Cadwalader and learning that Riley's brigade was at San Gerónimo, Smith turned to Beauregard and said: "Let us look at our position, and at that fellow's, Santa Anna, whilst my brigade is coming up." They started out and, recorded Beauregard, "stumbled upon Lee, who had just arrived *on his own hook*," whereupon the three continued the reconnaissance. Smith, studying the Mexican position at Padierna and the deployed troops of Santa Anna near San Angel, needed little time to evaluate the serious predicament of his much outnumbered brigades.

"We had now in our front, and on our left flank, eighteen thousand Mexicans, with between twenty-five and thirty guns—among the troops, six or seven thousand cavalry," he reported. "We were, at most, three thousand three hundred strong, and without artillery or cavalry . . ."

Although the day was drawing rapidly to a close, General Smith planned to attack Santa Anna in two columns at once. But before the troops could form, darkness fell, making it impossible to see the enemy's lines, and Smith called off the operation. The troops bivouacked without fire or shelter, under miserable conditions throughout an all-night rainstorm.

Shortly after nightfall, General Smith learned from Lieutenant Zealous B. Tower that a deep ravine led directly to the rear of Valencia's fortified position. The ravine, Tower reported, was "practicable for infantry, though very difficult."

Persifor Smith, as bold as he was efficient, greeted the news with characteristic promptness. "If that be the case," he said, "we will attack it before daylight." Later, Tower returned to the ravine and found it "knee-deep with water from the rain which was then falling in torrents."

General Smith felt that if General Scott could make a substantial demonstration in front in coordination with his attack on the Mexican rear, the chance of inflicting a crushing defeat on Valencia would be considerably greater. Despite the pitch-blackness, scattered but briefly by the occasional lightning streaks, and the torrential downpour, Captain Lee volunteered to cross the hazardous *pedregal,* inform General Scott of Smith's plan to march out at 3 A.M., and urge a diversion at the same time across the ravine.

Lee left at 8 o'clock, with a few men, and groped and stumbled over the jagged terrain. His only landmark was the outline of Zacatepec, etched for occasional instants by the lightning. The sound of marching feet reached Lee's ear, and soon a flash revealed Shields's brigade advancing to support Smith. Lee provided Shields with a guide, and pushed on, tired, bruised, with his uniform in tatters, to reach Scott's headquarters at Zacatepec, only to find that the General had returned to San Agustín. Once again, Lee sent his weary feet and tired body over the rough terrain and, nearly exhausted, he reached Scott's headquarters at 11 P.M.

While Lee was making his report, Pillow and Twiggs arrived, having hours before lost their way in the *pedregal* trying to reach San Gerónimo. Both were fatigued and Twiggs had injured his foot, but Scott instructed the latter to round up troops for the demonstration. Lee, for all his own near exhaustion, volunteered to help Twiggs. At Zacatepec, they found General Franklin Pierce's brigade and the batteries of Magruder and Callender. This demonstration force, under Colonel Trueman B. Ransom of the Ninth Infantry—Pierce had been painfully injured when his horse fell— marched out of its bivouac at 1 A.M., with Lee guiding them to the position.

Meanwhile, Shields had arrived at San Gerónimo at about 11 P.M. with between 500 and 600 men. "General Shields reported and received his orders from General Smith," wrote Beauregard, "neither at the time suspecting that the former was the ranking officer." As Smith formed his column at 2:30 A.M., Shields was assigned to remain at San Gerónimo and cover Smith's rear.

"At precisely 3 o'clock in the morning . . . the troops commenced their march," reported Smith. Rain was still falling on the well-drenched troops and the night was so dark an object six feet away could not be seen. As they marched, "the men were ordered to keep within touch of each other, so that the rear could not go astray." "After wading knee-deep in mud and water," wrote Beauregard, "we arrived unperceived, just about daybreak within 500 yards in the rear of [Valencia's] position."

Riley had led the way, followed by Cadwalader, while Major Justin Dimick, with Smith's brigade, closed the rear. After waiting for his column to close up, Smith gave the signal for Riley to attack. Riley moved farther up the ravine, turned to the left and climbed the slope to the crest where, on being detected, a warm fire greeted him. Throwing out skirmishers, Riley rushed down the slope to the attack. A rifle company, reinforced by the engineer company, poured in a hot fire from a sheltered position under the brow of an intervening ravine, sweeping the ground ahead of Riley. Then, scrambling over the top, these troops joined in Riley's attack.

Meanwhile Cadwalader had followed in Riley's path and rushed down the hill in close support. Major Dimick's brigade, which was to follow the same route, was now ordered by Smith to change direction and approach Valencia's position from the left. Until Riley had stormed down the hill, the Mexican attention was focused upon Ransom across the ravine, on the edge of the *pedregal*. He was demonstrating admirably with his guns, and the threat of an infantry charge was ever present. And then Smith struck suddenly from three sides. "The circle of American fire," states a Mexican source, "coiled like a serpent around our forces, and stifled them, now in disorder and lost."

Frantic efforts to turn their guns were of no avail; while some Americans rushed in with the bayonet, others continued to shower the defenders with lead. The Mexicans, abandoning the position, fled, each man for himself. The cavalry, in its haste to escape, trampled on the infantry, and all was chaos and confusion. Among the first to leave was General Valencia, but others were not so fortunate. For as the Mexicans retreated in disorder up the San Angel road, General Shields pounced upon them in San Gerónimo, and hundreds of prisoners were taken.

Now in possession of the Mexican works, General Persifor Smith looked at his watch. Seventeen minutes after the first shot was fired, the Battle of Padierna (which Americans still call Contreras, although that village didn't see a Mexican or American soldier) had ended in a dazzling American victory. Valencia's Army of the North was shattered, with 700 dead and 813 captured, including four generals and 84 other officers. Twenty-two guns, thousands of small arms, an immense quantity of ammunition, powder and shells, and 700 pack-mules and a number of horses were also taken. American losses were only sixty killed and wounded. "One of the most pleasing incidents of the victory," wrote Scott, "is the recapture in the works by Captain [Simon] Drum, 4th artillery . . . of the two brass six-pounders, taken from another company of the same regiment, though without loss of honor, at the glorious victory of Buena Vista . . ." These were the guns so gallantly served by Lieutenant John Paul Jones O'Brien. They are on display in the Administration Building at West Point to this day, with the citation: "Lost without dishonor, recovered with glory."

About 6:30 A.M., General Smith sent Lieutenant Beauregard to tell General Scott of the victory. Beauregard mounted a horse and rode into the *pedregal* in search of the General. He came upon Scott and General Worth and their staffs, about halfway to San Agustín. On hearing the glorious news, they sent up a cheer.

"Young man," said Old Fuss and Feathers to Beauregard, "if I were not on horseback, I would embrace you."

28

Churubusco and an Armistice

Before the sun had fairly risen on that August 20 morning, Winfield Scott had won a great victory at a trifling cost. Before the sun went down that day the American army had smashed its way to the very gates of Mexico City, but this time there was "the long butcher's bill."

When General Scott learned of Persifor Smith's sweeping victory at Padierna, he immediately ordered General Worth to attack San Antonio from the front, while the victors over Valencia moved to take the place in the rear. At the time, one of Worth's brigades and some of Quitman's troops were moving to reinforce General Smith, but when the latter's victory made support unnecessary, Scott hurried them back to their commanders.

Meanwhile, General Smith organized an immediate pursuit of the retreating Mexicans. This was underway when General Twiggs arrived and took command. At San Angel, General Pillow joined the pursuers and took the overall command of the force, which pushed on to Coyoacán. General Scott reached Coyoacán sometime after 9 A.M. and took full direction of the operation.

Scott has been criticized by both American and Mexican historians of the war for fighting a bloody battle that need not have been fought. "If Scott and Worth had halted at the village of Coyoacán and the hacienda of San Juan de Dios [in front of San Antonio] they could not . . . have failed to occupy the entrenchments of the hacienda of San Antonio and the bridge and church of Churubusco, only a few hours later and without the slightest resistance," wrote a Mexican historian. Lieutenant Raphael Semmes asked four years later in his book: "Why was the battle of Churubusco fought? . . . An isolated fortress, four miles from the city, it is impossible to point out a single reason why it should have been assaulted; and if assaulted at all, why it should have been assaulted in front . . ."

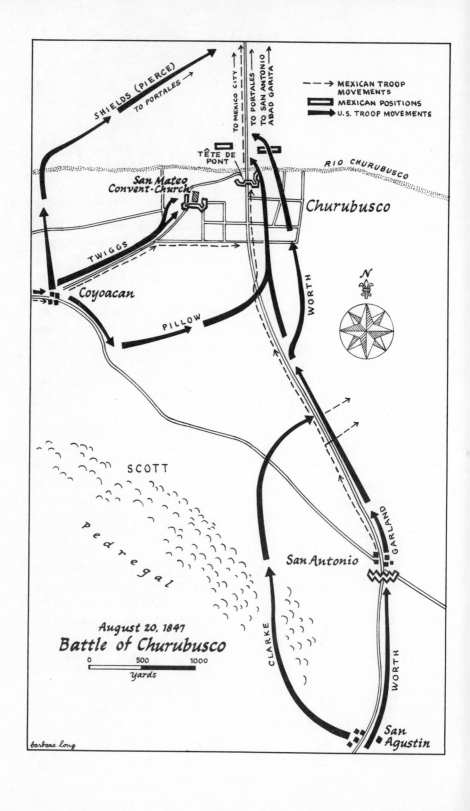

SHIELDS (PIERCE)

TO PORTALES

TO MEXICO CITY

TO PORTALES

TO SAN ANTONIO
ABAD GARITA

MEXICAN TROOP
MOVEMENTS

MEXICAN POSITIONS

U.S. TROOP MOVEMENTS

TÊTE DE
PONT

RIO CHURUBUSCO

San Mateo
Convent-Church

Churubusco

N

TWIGGS

WORTH

Coyoacan

PILLOW

SCOTT

P e d r e g a l

San Antonio

GARLAND

CLARKE

August 20, 1847
Battle of Churubusco

0   500   1000

Yards

WORTH

San
Agustin

barbara long

Both criticisms smack of hindsight. How could Scott, in hot pursuit of a retreating foe, possibly know that the enemy would have evacuated shortly a strong position which he soon defended so valiantly? But where Scott was open to criticism was in moving against prepared positions without having had his "indefatigable engineers" make a thorough reconnaissance of the southwest approaches to Mexico City or of the Mexican positions at Churubusco.

Rightly or wrongly, General Scott did what most successful generals would have done under the same conditions: he pursued determinedly an enemy which had retreated in disorder. Having instructed Worth to assault San Antonio, Scott now hurried Pillow, with Cadwalader's brigade, down the road from Coyoacán to San Antonio to take the place in the rear. Twiggs's brigades under General Smith and Colonel Riley were ordered to attack the fortified convent-church of San Mateo, less than a quarter of a mile from the strongly constructed and powerfully defended *tête de pont* at the south end of the bridge over the Río Churubusco. Pierce's brigade, with Captain Lee as its guide, was sent up the road that led north from Coyoacán with orders to cut diagonally to the right after crossing the river in order to get to the main road above the bridgehead. When Shields came up, his brigade was ordered to follow Pierce closely, and Shields, who ranked Pierce, took command.

Meanwhile, about an hour earlier, Worth had gotten the attack on San Antonio underway. Colonel N. S. Clarke's brigade, guided by Captain James Mason, made a wide arc through the eastern edge of the *pedregal* to get to the rear of San Antonio, while Colonel John Garland's brigade attacked up the high road to Mexico City.

But the garrison of about 3,000—"much shaken by our decisive victory at Contreras [Padierna]," General Scott said—did not wait to be attacked. It was in motion, falling back to the Churubusco bridgehead, when Clarke's men exploded out of the *pedregal* and hit the retreating column at its center. The Mexicans, in confusion, scurried for safety, while Clark and Garland, whose men had stormed through San Antonio, took up the pursuit.

From the steeple of a church in Coyoacán, Lieutenant Stevens of the Engineers, turned his glass upon the San Antonio road, "and observed the enemy in full retreat, the causeway for more than a mile being filled with troops, packmules, and baggage-wagons." He immediately reported this fact to Scott, who ordered Twiggs to advance on the convent. By this time, Pillow, with Cadwalader's brigade, had discovered that the Mexican garrison from San Antonio was withdrawing hastily into the Churubusco *tête de pont*. Veering sharply to the left, Pillow sent his troops across ditches and splashing through swamps as he hastened to support Worth's rejoined brigades in the attack on Churubusco.

North of the bridgehead, Lee had led Shields and Pierce to the Portales ranch, about three-quarters of a mile from the Mexican position, where they soon were "hotly engaged and somewhat pressed." Lieutenant Reno's howitzer battery, called up at once by Lee, brought down effective fire. However, Shields and Pierce, being outnumbered by infantry and cavalry, the latter menacing the American left, needed reinforcements. Lee hurried to Scott to secure them.

The Battle of Churubusco was now raging in three separate and, in effect, unrelated areas—Shields and Pierce holding on grimly at Portales; Smith's and Riley's brigades of Twiggs's division attacking the convent; and Worth and Pillow assaulting the bridgehead.

To the right of the road, from which the heavy fire from the bridgehead had forced them, the men of Worth and Pillow advanced through cornfields which crackled as lead rained upon them. "An occasional cannon ball sang through the corn as it tore its path along our front," wrote Captain Ephraim Kirby Smith. ". . . The roll of the Mexican fire exceeded anything I have ever heard . . . The grape, round shot and musketry were sweeping over the ground in a storm which strewed it with the dead and dying."

The time now was about 12:30 P.M. In front of the convent, Persifor Smith was finding it a formidable work, while Colonel Riley, who attacked the flank of San Mateo, was equally impressed by its strength and the vigorous defenses of its garrison. Behind the thick ten- or twelve-feet-high adobe walls of the convent enclosure, firing platforms for infantry had been constructed, and outside the walls were entrenchments and emplacements for seven guns. Within the enclosure, the fortified church and convent were mutually supporting. Across the river, behind its raised banks, lines of infantry also supported San Mateo.

From the convent and its exterior works came destructive fire, and Twiggs ordered up Taylor's battery to support Smith. Quickly positioned by Lieutenant Stevens, Taylor "came into action in most gallant style," and he drove the Mexican troops from the roof of the

convent. "But so destructive was the return fire of the enemy behind his earthern breastworks," wrote Stevens, "that in a short time
his battery was cut up, and he was obliged to withdraw, losing many
men and horses. . . ." Severe showers of grape, canister, musketry,
round shot and shell poured upon the Americans, but the battery
unflinchingly continued to return a heavy fire on the entrenchments.

Captain Lee, meanwhile, had reached Scott, and the General had
sent a rifle company and a squadron of Dragoons under Major
E. V. Sumner to join Shields and Pierce at Portales. Shields now
moved forward to the attack.

For nearly three hours the three battles continued, and, despite
the brave and stubborn Mexican resistance, the Americans in all
three areas had edged in close for the final assault.

When the time seemed right, Worth ordered the storming of the
tête de pont. Down the high road raced the Sixth Infantry "with a
steadiness worthy of its established reputation," but a galling fire
checked its advance. Meanwhile Clarke's Fifth and Eighth Regiments, in the face of "a terrible fire" dashed across the deep and
wet ditch around the bridgehead and carried it with the bayonet.
Quickly the captured pieces were turned on the Mexicans in the
town, while Garland's brigade were engaged in furious hand-to-
hand fighting with the troops to the left and rear of the bridgehead. "The main body of the enemy," reported Worth, "was soon
discovered in full and confused retreat."

Some of the cannon in the *tête de pont* were trained upon the
convent, and Duncan, galloping up with two of his guns, quickly
blazed away at the church tower, from which Mexican sharp-
shooter fire had come throughout the obstinate contest. About
twenty minutes after the bridgehead had been stormed, Twiggs,
noting a slackening of fire from the convent and its outer works,
ordered Smith in for the kill. Captain Edmund B. Alexander, in
command of the Third Infantry, cleared the ramparts and then
rushed over the bastion to carry it in hand-to-hand fighting. Almost
immediately, a white flag fluttered on the convent, which surrendered to Captain James Madison Smith. The count of prisoners
taken in San Mateo revealed 104 officers, several generals, among
them Interim President Anaya, and 1,155 rank and file.

The hard-won successes south of the Churubusco River were
matched by Shields and Pierce north of the stream at Portales. Al-

though outnumbered, Shields attacked through heavy mud and swamp in the direction of the highway, and after a long and hot fight, his men fought their way to the road. The Mexicans wavered and when Shields ordered his men to charge, the enemy broke and scattered. Shields reached the road just as Worth's advance came up from the captured bridgehead. He joined in the pursuit, until Harney's cavalry galloped by to follow the retreating Mexicans up to the city gate of San Antonio Abad.

Impetuously, Captain Phil Kearny and Lieutenant Richard S. Ewell and a small detachment of Dragoons, oblivious that Harney had sounded the recall, dashed into furious musket and artillery fire. Kearny called on the Dragoons to dismount and assault the entrenchment, and in the brief fighting he lost an arm. Ewell, to his "horror . . . found the Dragoons retiring" in response to the recall. "We were engaged while the rear was retreating," Ewell wrote. With difficulty, including having two horses shot from under him, Lieutenant Ewell extricated the Dragoons and galloped back to the main body, and the Battle of Churubusco was over.

The "butcher's list" was indeed long on August 20, American losses amounting to nearly fifteen percent of the troops engaged—137 killed, 879 wounded, and 40 missing, for the staggering total of 1,056. Mexican prisoners, taken at Padierna and Churubusco were tabulated by Inspector General Hitchcock at 2,637, of which 205 were officers, including eight generals, two of them former presidents of Mexico, Generals Salas and Anaya. Among the Mexican prisoners was the San Patricio Battalion of American deserters, sixty-nine of whom were captured at the bridgehead and in the convent. General Scott estimated the Mexican dead and wounded at 4,000. Great supplies of ammunition were taken.

"These great results have overwhelmed the enemy," wrote Scott. A Mexican source agreed: "The unfortunate day of the 20th of August had terminated . . . the sanguinary battles of Padierna and Churubusco had passed, and the invading army triumphed at the gates of the city. The spirits were worn out, the remains of our troops demoralized and lost, and confusion and disorder had overcome all classes of society . . . General Santa Anna retired to the palace, possessed of a black despair . . ."

In a conference of ministers, Santa Anna announced that a truce was indispensable to the Mexicans, and it was agreed that Foreign Minister J. R. Pacheco should request British Consul-General

Mackintosh and the Spanish minister to open communications with General Scott. The Spanish minister excused himself, but Mackintosh and Edward Thornton of the British Legation drove to San Agustín on the evening of the 20th to see Scott. Hitchcock, discerning the truth, noted in his journal that the purpose of the visit was "ostensibly to ask for a safeguard for . . . British subjects, but really to prepare the way for peace." Hitchcock reported the Englishmen saying "the city was perfectly astounded at our success—that the greatest consternation pervades the capital."

Scott, intending to march on Mexico City on the 21st and peremptorily demand its surrender, moved his headquarters to Coyoacán and gave marching orders to the troops. At about noon, General Ignacio Mora y Villamil, Mexican Chief of Engineers, drove to Coyoacán and delivered a sealed packet to General Scott. It contained a note from British Minister Charles Bankhead and a note from Foreign Minister Pacheco to Secretary of State Buchanan, the latter a belated answer to the Buchanan note which Trist had so much difficulty in delivering, several months earlier.

Pacheco's note stated that the justice of a cause is not always a guarantee of success in battle and that Santa Anna had fought the Americans up to the gates of the capital. Now other than military obligations commanded his duty, and he, Pacheco, under constitutional powers to receive ministers, would hear Mr. Nicholas Trist's proposals, if they were consistent with Mexican honor. He suggested a year's truce while a permanent peace was negotiated.

Scott and Trist read Pacheco's note and agreed to immediate rejection of the idea of a year's truce. The General then addressed a letter to Santa Anna, but omitted the demand for surrender. Scott, to whom the pen, if not mightier than the sword, was at least more dangerous, produced one of his better inept phrases when he told Santa Anna: "Too much blood has already been shed in this unnatural war between the two great republics of this continent." *Unnatural* was exactly how the Mexicans, from the beginning, had designated the struggle. "I am willing to sign, on reasonable terms, a short armistice," Scott wrote, although he intended to "seize and occupy such positions . . . necessary to the shelter and comfort of this army." The General told Santa Anna he awaited "with impatience . . . a direct answer" on the morning of the 22nd.

George Wilkins Kendall of the New Orleans *Picayune,* when he saw Mackintosh with Scott the previous day, bluntly exclaimed:

"It's no use, we're humbugged—Mackintosh is among them!" Kendall had known Mackintosh when he was a prisoner in Mexico after the abortive Santa Fé expedition.

Mexican Minister of War L. I. Alcorta replied for Santa Anna, couching his note as if Scott had requested an armistice and that Santa Anna had graciously agreed to grant one. The import of the message was for the American general, the language was for the Mexico City press. Generals Mora y Villamil and Benito Quijano met with Generals Quitman, Smith, and Pierce—three brilliant lawyers before becoming soldiers—on August 22 at Mackintosh's home in Tacubaya. They sat up all night haggling over phraseology but finally reached agreement and submitted the armistice document to both generals, who after slight changes in it then accepted it.

On August 24, the military armistice became effective within ninety miles of Mexico City, "for the purpose of enabling the government of Mexico to take under consideration the propositions which the commissioner for the President of the United States has to make." Either party, on forty-eight hours notice, could terminate the truce, and during its existence, no fortifications were to be built or improved, neither army was to advance or receive reinforcements. Supplies, but not arms and ammunition, could pass into the city, and Scott could draw on the city for supplies.

"After so many victories, we might, with but little additional loss, have occupied the capital . . ." Scott reported. But he and Trist had been warned "by the best friends of peace" that "by wantonly driving away the government and others—dishonored—we might scatter the elements of peace, excite a spirit of national desperation, and thus indefinitely postpone the hope of accommodation."

29

To the Halls of Montezuma

"We are in a strange situation—a conquering army on a hill over-looking an enemy's capital, which is perfectly at our mercy, yet not permitted to enter it, and compelled to submit to all manner of insults from its corrupt inhabitants."

So wrote Captain Ephraim Kirby Smith, a faithful diarist with both Zachary Taylor and Winfield Scott, on August 29, 1847, voicing five days after the armistice went into effect the almost universal feeling of the officers and men of the American army.

Scott's decision not to enter Mexico City at once was based on his fear of destroying any responsible Mexican Government with which to treat, and so leave his woefully small army within a hostile city and Santa Anna at large to rally new troops.

Irritating incidents jeopardized the armistice from the beginning. On the first day, an American wagon train, going into the city for supplies, was turned back at the gate. This was hastily rectified with apologies. Later a wagon train was attacked by a Mexican mob which hurled stones and insults at the American teamsters and their Mexican escorts.

"*Mueran los Yankees!*" shouted the mob, which did not stop at calling down death upon the invaders. "*Muera el General Santa Anna, por traidor!*" Many Mexicans, of all degrees and classes, felt that Santa Anna was, indeed, a traitor and that he had sold out to the despised Yankees.

These difficulties, however, were smoothed over, and General Scott continued scrupulously to observe the terms of the truce, although many of his officers were convinced that the Mexicans were not. "During the armistice," wrote Lieutenant Beauregard, "no reconnaissance was permitted by the General-in-Chief, although it was a notorious fact that the enemy was violating it day and night." Other officers thought as did Beauregard. "He has been flattering us with the hopes of peace [but] he has been actively collecting his scattered force, and with all his energies preparing to renew the combat," said Kirby Smith. "We hear that the fragments of Santa Anna's army brought together make a force of some 18,000 men, more than double our army," Colonel Ethan Allen Hitchcock noted.

The end of negotiations between Trist and the Mexicans on September 6 was Scott's signal to inform Santa Anna that he would consider the armistice terminated as of noon on September 7, unless he received "explanation, apology and reparation" for "direct breaches of faith" by the Mexicans. Santa Anna replied indignantly that he had remained silent when told that Americans had violated churches, stolen sacred vessels, and profaned images, and that he had endured "the complaints of fathers and husbands of the violence offered to their daughters and wives." Santa Anna said he did not wish to hinder negotiations to conclude the war, which Scott had "justly characterized as unnatural," and he charged that Scott's threat stemmed from the Mexican's refusal to dismember and dishonor his nation. He was, Santa Anna declared, ready "to repel force by force" to save "the first city of the American continent . . . of the horrors of war."

Among the reports of violations that Scott had received was one that Santa Anna was collecting church bells in the city and sending them to a foundry in a complex of low stone buildings known as El Molino del Rey (the King's Mill), to be cast into cannon. Molino del Rey was about a mile from Scott's headquarters in the town of Tacubaya, and stood at the foot of the western slope of Chapultepec, whose fortified castle's guns covered the mill effectively. About 500 yards west of the northern end of the nearly quarter-mile-long Molino del Rey was a square stone structure, also fortified, known as Casa Mata, which served as a powder magazine.

Movement of Mexican troops to Molino del Rey seemed to Scott to confirm the rumor that cannon were being cast there. "I resolved at once to drive [the enemy] early the next morning, to seize the powder, and to destroy the foundry," Scott reported.

For this raid, which developed into perhaps the bloodiest battle of the war for the number of American troops engaged, Scott assigned Worth's division, to which were added Cadwalader's brigade, a battery of three six-pounders under Captain Simon H. Drum, two twenty-four-pounder battery guns under Captain Benjamin

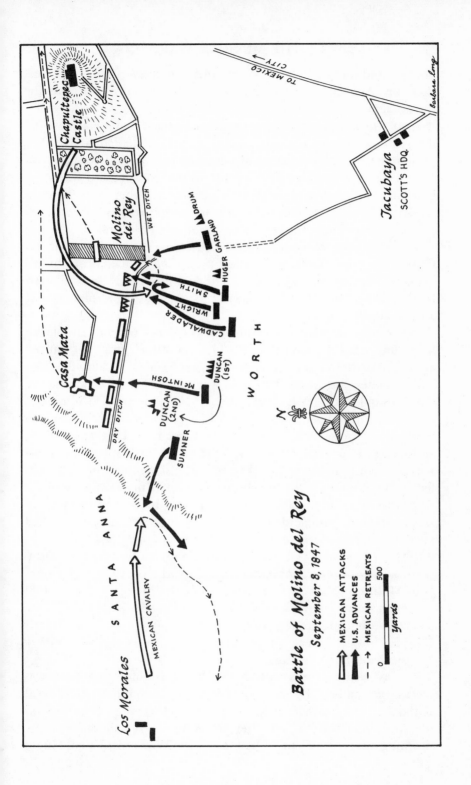

TO MEXICO CITY →

Chapultepec Castle

WET DITCH

Molino del Rey

DRUM

GARLAND

HUGER

SMITH

WRIGHT

CADWALADER

Casa Mata

DRY DITCH

MCINTOSH

DUNCAN (1ST)

DUNCAN (2ND)

W O R T H

SUMNER

S A N T A   A N N A

Los Morales

MEXICAN CAVALRY

N

Tacubaya
SCOTT'S HDQ.

Battle of Molino del Rey
September 8, 1847

⇨ MEXICAN ATTACKS
➧ U.S. ADVANCES
- -➤ MEXICAN RETREATS

0   500
Yards

Barbara Long

Huger, and Major Edwin V. Sumner's cavalry, numbering less than 300. Worth reported he had only 3,100 men of all arms for the mission.

Scott's original order for a midnight attack was delayed until daybreak, at Worth's request. Scott, however, denied his further plea that Chapultepec be assaulted after the Molino was carried. At 3 A.M., on September 8, the columns moved out "and when the gray of the morning enabled them to be seen, they were as accurately in position as if posted in midday for review," Worth reported. "The enemy was in a position of immense strength," wrote Lieutenant Isaac Stevens of the Engineers, "their left resting on Chapultepec and the foundry, their right on a ravine, a continuous breastwork covering their front." The Mexican line, also supported by the Casa Mata, was about a mile in length, and formed almost a right angle.

On his extreme right, Worth placed Garland's brigade, supported by Drum's two six-pounders—the "Buena Vista" guns, recaptured at Padierna—not only to cover the southern end of Molino del Rey, but to contest any attempt to reinforce the mill from Chapultepec. To Garland's left on a ridge, about 500 yards from Molino del Rey, Captain Huger's two twenty-four-pounders were placed to soften the defenses for the assault. In support of Huger was C. F. Smith's battalion, commanded for the attack by Captain Ephraim Kirby Smith ("Tomorrow will be a day of slaughter," he had written in his diary, and during the battle he fell mortally wounded.) The storming party, made up of 500 picked men from the various regiments and commanded by Major George Wright, was posted on the same ridge to the left of Huger's battering guns to charge the Mexican center. Clarke's brigade, with Colonel James Duncan's battery of four guns, commanded for the occasion by Colonel J. S. McIntosh, took a position opposite the Mexican right, while Sumner's cavalry, covering Worth's extreme left, was "to repel or attack, as the commander's judgment might suggest." Cadwalader's brigade, posted in reserve, could move to the support of either McIntosh or Huger's guns.

At daybreak, all was still in the Mexican lines and there was speculation among the Americans as to whether the Mexicans had abandoned the position. About 5 o'clock, Huger's guns opened on the Molino del Rey, and after ten rounds, Worth ordered the storming party to advance. In his report, Worth said that Huger had "sensibly shaken" the Mexican lines when "the assaulting party dashed gallantly forward." Critics of Worth's tactics at Molino del Rey feel he attacked with insufficient artillery preparation.

As the Americans advanced, the Mexican lines suddenly blazed with a withering fire. A shower of canister and musketry converged upon the storming party, but it rushed into the Mexican battery on its front, putting the bayonet to the cannoneers and supporting infantry, and seizing the pieces. The captured guns were turned upon the retreating enemy, but before they could be fired the Mexicans rallied and, supported by a galling fire from the infantry on the rooftops of the Molino del Rey, came surging back. The Americans were caught in a devastating concentration of musketry, which struck down eleven of the fourteen officers and did frightful damage to the troops. "This severe shock," wrote Worth, "staggered, for a moment, that gallant band."

Huger's guns, masked by the advance of the storming party, could not cover the attack, but Worth ordered Captain Smith forward and also part of Cadwalader's brigade to support the sagging and severely punished attackers. The fresh troops dashed down upon the enemy with determination and in the face of this assault, the Mexicans broke again and the center of their line was now fully possessed by the Americans.

Meanwhile, on the right, Garland's brigade and Drum's "Buena Vista" six-pounders were engaged in "an obstinate and very severe contest" with the Mexican left but, steadily advancing, they drove the enemy from his seemingly impregnable position under the guns of Chapultepec. Storming into the Mexican line, Drum and Huger turned the enemy pieces on their fleeing troops as long as they were in range.

At the other end of the American line, McIntosh moved his brigade forward as Duncan's four guns fired over the troops' heads at the Mexican right. McIntosh's advance, however, soon masked Duncan's guns and the battery ceased fire. Resolutely, McIntosh drove on toward the Casa Mata. This work, Worth reported, instead of being "an ordinary field entrenchment, as was supposed, proved to be a strong stone citadel, surrounded by bastioned entrenchments and impassable ditches." When McIntosh's men came into musket range, a frightful fire swept their ranks. The deadly torrent rained steadily upon them, cutting a dreadful path of death through the column. For a few brief moments, the rapidly thinning remnant pushed on to reach the slope of the parapet of the outer works of the Casa Mata. Then, with the three ranking officers—McIntosh, Lieutenant Colonel Martin Scott, and Major Carlos A. Waite—all stricken down and a large proportion of the troops either killed or wounded, the command fell into disorder and broke. Reaching Duncan's guns, they rallied.

Meanwhile Duncan had been busily engaged with Mexican cavalry and infantry advancing from across the ravine on the American left. When McIntosh masked Duncan's guns, the latter shifted position to bring his pieces to bear on this new Mexican threat. As the cavalry rode up boldly, all of Duncan's guns greeted the enemy with a blast of canister which cleared many saddles and killed many horses. Soon, the Mexican squadrons broke and fell back in disorder. Major Sumner now moved forward, despite "a most appalling fire" from the Casa Mata, and crossed the ravine. Although tremendously outnumbered by eight or nine to one by the Mexican cavalry, Sumner, reported Worth, "remained, doing noble service, until the close of the action."

Duncan now concentrated his guns on the Casa Mata with "well-directed fire," and the enemy soon abandoned the position. Duncan then played his pieces upon the retreating column until it fell back out of range. The Mexicans had now been driven from every portion of the field. "His strong lines, which had certainly been defended well," reported Worth, "were in our possession."

The occupation of the Molino del Rey had been achieved in an atmosphere of utter confusion. Some Americans battered in a gate at the southern end of the complex of buildings, while another force drove into the northern end. Many small fights were waged within the enclosure, by individuals and by groups, as the Mexicans were rounded up or driven from the roofs. Among the first to enter Molino del Rey were Captain Robert Anderson and Lieutenant U. S. Grant. Years later, the one would yield Fort Sumter to start the Civil War, the other would win Appomattox to end it.

General Worth discovered that no cannon were being cast at Molino del Rey ("Strange to say," wrote Colonel Hitchcock, "our information turned out to be false"), and "the unfortunate and bloody battle," as Beauregard called it, proved a needless one. Worth blew up the Casa Mata, destroyed a couple of old cannon molds, and returned to Tacubaya with a casualty list of 787—116 killed, 9 of them officers; 658 wounded, 49 of them officers; and

18 missing. The Fifth Infantry, in McIntosh's brigade, had thirty-eight percent casualties, while the entire command's percentage of loss, in a fight of only two hours' duration, was 25.4 percent. No wonder, Colonel Hitchcock wrote in his journal: "On Sept. 8th, we were like Pyrrhus after the fight with Fabricius—a few more such victories and this army would be destroyed." Naval Lieutenant Raphael Semmes, attached to Worth's staff, was perhaps Scott's severest critic for ordering the needless attack on Molino del Rey: ". . . He had originated it in error, and caused it to be fought, with inadequate forces, for an object that had no existence . . ."

Before the battle of Molino del Rey, and for three days after the costly fight, Scott kept his Engineer officers reconnoitering the southern and southwestern approaches to the city. They discovered that Santa Anna had strengthened and extended the fortifications at the gates, emplaced more guns, and had flooded the low ground between the causeways. Scott accompanied the Engineers on September 9, and again on the 11th, and that afternoon in a church in the village of Piedad, half a mile directly south of the Belén Garita, or gate, the General held a council of his generals, with the Engineers present. The general opinion, in which Captain Lee of the Engineers concurred, was that the attack on Mexico City should be made from the south. Lieutenant Beauregard, although urged by Nicholas Trist and Colonel Hitchcock to give his views, remained silent. Then General Scott said to Beauregard: "You, young man, in that corner, what have you to say on the subject?"

Beauregard rose, and in a well-prepared statement argued against the southern approach, pointing out that the Mexicans were expecting the attack there and had strengthened their positions considerably. He recommended a demonstration from the south and the assault on Chapultepec. Beauregard said that when he finished, General Franklin Pierce rose and "begged that he would be permitted to change his views, after what he had just heard—for he was now in favor of the attack by Chapultepec."

Such, indeed, was Scott's idea from the beginning. The General declared: "Gentlemen, we will attack by the western gates. The general officers present here will remain for further orders—the meeting is dissolved."

Quitman was ordered to march by daylight to reinforce Pillow at Piedad. Then, under cover of night, Pillow and Quitman would march to join Worth at Tacubaya, while Twiggs moved into Piedad. The latter's orders were to maintain the threat of an imminent attack up the causeway from Piedad.

To attack Mexico City from the west, Scott first had to seize Chapultepec Hill and its "castle," once the summer home of the viceroys of Mexico, but since 1833, the Mexican Military College. This building stood on the narrow crest of the 200-foot hill, the highest point and steepest slopes of which were toward the city. The hill, with its gardens and a grove of ancient cypress trees at its western end, was enclosed by walls of more than twelve feet which extended east and west for almost a mile, terminating at the Molino del Rey. There was a narrow gateway in the south wall, defended by an earthwork, and another fortified gateway on the southeast. Thirteen guns and a force of less than 1,000 men, plus the cadets of the Military College, defended Chapultepec, under the command of General Nicolás Bravo.

With Captain Lee locating the batteries, and Captain Huger emplacing the guns, Scott's arrangements for the bombardment of the palace were completed by 7 A.M. on September 12. Battery No. 1, under Captain Drum, was placed on the road from Tacubaya to the southeastern corner of the hill. It consisted of two sixteen-pounders and an eight-inch howitzer. Battery No. 2, to the left of the Tacubaya-Molino del Rey road, was just outside Tacubaya. Under Lieutenant P. V. Hagner, this battery consisted of one twenty-four-pounder and one eight-inch howitzer. Battery No. 3, halfway between Tacubaya and Molino del Rey on the road, ultimately consisted of a sixteen-pounder and an eight-inch howitzer, which its commander, Captain W. T. H. Walker could bring into service only after the fire from Chapultepec had slackened. Battery No. 4, on the road, close to the Molino, consisted of a ten-inch mortar under Lieutenant C. P. Stone.

Quitman's division was posted at Tacubaya to make his attack up the road to the southeast edge of Chapultepec. The divisions of Pillow and Worth were in position at the Molino del Rey to attack the western slope. Scott was determined there would not be insufficient artillery preparations as at Molino del Rey. "To prepare for an assault," he wrote, "it was foreseen that the play of the batteries might run into the second day . . . I was, therefore, in no haste in ordering an assault before the works were well crippled by our missiles."

Shortly after daybreak, Scott opened the bombardment. At first,

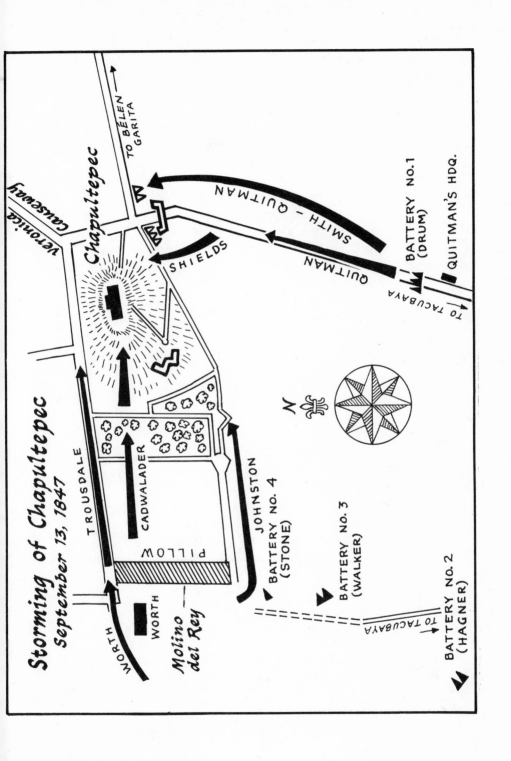

Storming of Chapultepec
September 13, 1847

the American guns took little effect. Soon, states a Mexican source, "the walls of the building commenced to be pierced by balls in all directions, experiencing great ravages also in the roofs, caused by the bombs which the mortar threw." Many of the defenders were killed or wounded as Scott's gunners for "fourteen hours . . . maintained a projectile in the air." General Bravo called on Santa Anna for reinforcements in vain. The latter, whether intimidated by the American bombardment or deceived by Twiggs's demonstration on the south, sent no relief to Bravo's support.

Darkness brought an end to the day-long bombardment, and Scott prepared for the assault early on the morning of the 13th. Quitman, supported by Persifor Smith's brigade from Twiggs's division, was to attack the hill from the south and southeast. Pillow, who was to attack from the west, would be supported by Worth. Worth and Twiggs were each to provide assault parties of 250 veteran regulars, respectively, for Pillow and Quitman.

That night the shadow of Molino del Rey seemed to fall upon American confidence. At a council at headquarters, General Worth told Colonel Hitchcock: "We shall be defeated." When all had left, Scott turned to Hitchcock: "I have my misgivings."

On September 13, the bombardment resumed with the dawn. The signal for the assault was to be the cessation of fire by the heavy batteries. Shortly after eight o'clock, the guns were silent. Pillow on the west and Quitman and Persifor Smith on the south and southeast moved to the attack with scaling ladders, pickaxes, and crowbars provided for the assaulting parties.

Pillow advanced in three columns. One, under Lieutenant Colonel Joseph E. Johnston, pushed forward outside the enclosure's south wall. Colonel William B. Trousdale, with two new regular regiments and a section of artillery under Lieutenant Thomas Jonathan Jackson, moved outside the north wall. Inside the enclosure, Cadwalader advanced from the Molino del Rey. General Pillow advanced with this force. Marshy ground, boulders, and the large cypress trees all tended to slow the advance along a 500-yard front within the enclosure.

Captain Sam MacKenzie, who led Pillow's storming party, was held up, too, but his command swarmed into the lower works protecting the gate in the south wall so rapidly and so close on the Mexicans' heels that the latter were unable to light the powder trains, to fire the land mines, which were expected to blow the attackers to bits. The storming party, now supported by Johnston's Voltigeurs, followed the Mexicans halfway up the slope to a ditch at the base of the massive retaining wall for the terraces above, where they halted while waiting for the scaling ladders.

Meanwhile, Quitman had encountered Mexican infantry, supported by artillery, across the road, and the advance was held up. General Smith, striking off across the marshy terrain to the right of the road, moved to take the Mexicans in the rear. Shields's brigade, augmented by the Second Pennsylvania Regiment, veered to the left of the road, in the face of heavy fire from the Mexican batteries. His men marched to the south wall and began breaching it with pickaxes and crowbars. Two of Shield's regiments moved through the unguarded gate and fought the rest of the battle under Pillow.

By now, MacKenzie's scaling ladders had arrived, and Pillow, who had been wounded in the foot, called on Worth "to bring up his whole division, and make great haste, or he feared it would be too late." Worth sent Clarke's brigade forward, and Pillow's men moved ahead again up the western slope. As fast as the scaling ladders were in place, troops scampered up, and in their eagerness, they lost all semblance of organization as they swarmed over the crest. Lieutenant Lewis A. Armistead was wounded immediately; so too was Lieutenant James Longstreet, who was "advancing, color in hand." As Longstreet fell, the colors were caught by a new young West Pointer, Lieutenant George E. Pickett. Years later, Armistead, Longstreet, and Pickett would be involved in a much bloodier assault.

The regimental colors of the Voltigeurs were the first planted on Chapultepec, Captain Moses Barnard, although twice wounded, gaining the honor.

Even as the palace of Chapultepec was won from the west, and south, Quitman was still fighting furiously against courageous Mexican troops at the eastern end of the enclosure. Bitter hand-to-hand fighting ensued, but when the silence of the guns of the castle indicated that it had fallen, the defenders at the base broke and retreated. Chapultepec was now entirely in American hands.

The actual storming of the hill had taken just an hour. It was a long hour for the Americans engaged in the hot fight, a short one for twenty-nine of the San Patricio deserters, taken at Churubusco, who waited with ropes around their necks for the American flag to fly over Chapultepec before they swung to death. The hapless American deserters, who had fought, as it were, with their heads in nooses at Churubusco, were all given fair trials at Scott's insistence. Of the more than sixty taken, less than half were meted the death sentence. The scaffolds were so prepared that the condemned men, the ropes knotted around their necks, stood in wagons facing Chapultepec. As the flag broke out, the drivers lashed their horses and the wagons drove away, leaving twenty-nine bodies bobbing in their death throes.

The fall of Chapultepec was accompanied by valorous deeds on both sides, and out of the debacle for Mexico came the gallant legend of the *Niños Héroes,* the brave little cadets, fifty-one strong, who fought courageously to the last, some preferring to die rather than surrender.

Even after Chapultepec was captured, heavy fighting outside the north wall of the enclosure continued, with Colonel William Trousdale's two regiments engaged with large reinforcements from the city. Trousdale was wounded and his outnumbered force held on until support arrived only because of the "highest qualities of a soldier—devotion, industry, talent, and gallantry," with which Lieutenant Thomas Jonathan Jackson manned his one remaining gun, after men and horses were killed or wounded and his other piece knocked out of action.

From Chapultepec there were two avenues of approach to the halls of the Montezumas. One, the Tacubaya (or Chapultepec) Causeway, ran to the Belén Gate, about a mile and three-quarters away. The other route was over the Verónica Causeway, which extended generally north for about the same distance to the Tacuba Causeway, which it joined at right angles. The Tacuba Causeway, over which Cortés retreated on the famous *noche triste,* led to the San Cosme Gate, Mexico City's point of entry from the west. Each causeway had double roadways divided by massive arched aqueducts, which afforded cover for both attack and defense.

It was not much after 9 A.M. that Garland's brigade of Worth's division, after rushing to Trousdale's support outside the north wall of Chapultepec, was in motion up the Verónica Causeway, with the San Cosme gate as its destination. About the same time Quitman's division, to which many mixed commands attached themselves, pushed up the Tacubaya Causeway.

General Scott ordered the brigades of Clarke and Cadwalader to support Worth in the San Cosme attack, while he directed Pierce's brigade and a number of the heavy guns to follow in Quitman's wake. After garrisoning Chapultepec with the Fifteenth Infantry, Scott rode on to join Worth's column.

Expecting resistance from a strong point at the junction of the causeways, Worth's advance to its surprise found the works abandoned, without a gun in place. Worth turned on the Tacuba Causeway, but here the forward progress of the column was arrested by stout Mexican opposition.

Meanwhile, Quitman had made good progress on the Tacubaya Causeway. His men filled the ditches the Mexicans had dug on the roadway, and leveled breastworks, so that a clear path was ready for the artillery. From arch to arch of the aqueduct, Quitman's men worked their way, firing and seeking cover to reload and advance. After advancing more than halfway to the Belén Gate, Quitman encountered "the enemy in considerable force," who offered "obstinate resistance" at a strong point. Well-directed fire by Captain Drum with an eight-pound howitzer, softened the defense and a bold charge with the bayonet carried it. Quitman pushed on steadily, his men moving in small groups, some along the road, some in ditches, some ducking in and out of the arches. A stand was made by the Mexicans at the Insurgentes Bridge, but not for long, and Quitman's command swept up to the Belén Gate, and within the barrier. It was 1:20 P.M. Less than a quarter of a mile ahead was the formidable stone Citadel and the Belén prison, both of which bristled with men and guns.

Quitman's advance was over; moreover, he was now hard-pressed to hold his position as the Mexicans launched a massive counterattack. There was furious fighting. The dashing Captain Drum and Lieutenant Calvin Benjamin, turning the Mexican guns on the enemy, were killed as they blazed away. The withering Mexican fire at the Belén Gate wounded a number of men who would become generals in blue or gray later—Fitz-John Porter, John Brannan, and Zealous B. Tower on one side, and P. G. T. Beauregard, A. H. Gladden, Mansfield Lovell, Earl Van Dorn, and W. W. Loring on the other. But Quitman grimly hung on to his "bridgehead" in the city of the Montezumas.

A mile across the swampy soil, Worth had brushed aside indifferent opposition until he approached the built-up portion on the outskirts of the city. Here Mexican resistance stiffened and Worth's progress was slowed throughout the afternoon and into the night. The tools and techniques which Worth had used so successfully

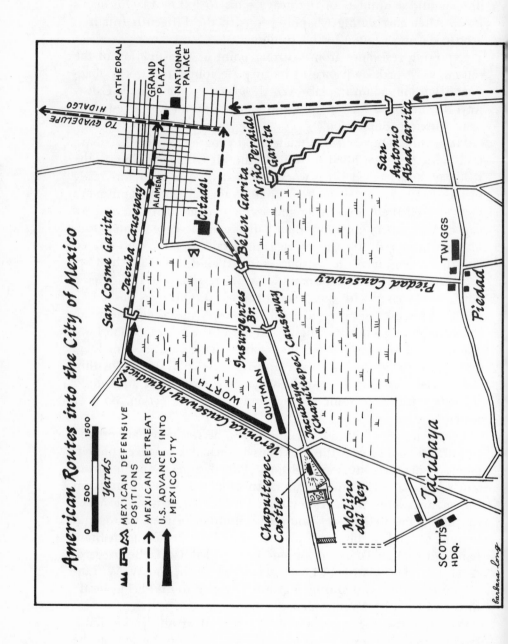

American Routes into the City of Mexico

Yards

0   500   1500

▨▨▨ MEXICAN DEFENSIVE
      POSITIONS

→ → → MEXICAN RETREAT

➤ U.S. ADVANCE INTO
   MEXICO CITY

San Cosme Garita

Tacuba Causeway

San Antonio Abad Garita

Niño Perdido Garita

Belén Garita

Citadel

ALAMEDA

CATHEDRAL

GRAND PLAZA

NATIONAL PALACE

TO GUADELUPE
HIDALGO

Insurgentes Br.

Veronica Causeway–Aquaduct

WORTH

QUITMAN

Tacubaya (Chapultepec) Causeway

Piedad Causeway

TWIGGS

Piedad

Chapultepec Castle

Molino del Rey

Tacubaya

SCOTT'S HDQ.

barbara long

at Monterrey were now called into use. With pickax and crowbar, the infantry knocked down walls between houses and burrowed from building to building on both sides of the roadway. When Lieutenant Jesse Reno came up with his light guns, they were hoisted to the roofs of houses from which their sweeping fire proved effective. Lieutenant U. S. Grant, while reconnoitering, discovered a church, south of the road, whose belfry commanded the ground back of the San Cosme Gate. "I got an officer of the Voltigeurs, with a mountain howitzer and men to work it, to go with me," Grant wrote. The howitzer was dismantled and carried to the belfry and Grant was soon blazing away with great effect. "We were not more than two or three hundred yards from San Cosme," Grant wrote. "The shots from our little gun dropped in upon the enemy and created great confusion. Why they did not send out a small party and capture us, I do not know."

One of the little ironies of the war, in the light of distant events, occurred when General Worth, having observed the operation, sent Lieutenant John C. Pemberton to the church tower to bring the officer in charge of the gun to him. Pemberton and Grant met again on a battlefield sixteen years later when the former surrendered Vicksburg.

By late afternoon, aided by a "brilliant exhibition of courage and conduct" by Lieutenant Henry Hunt, who pushed his gun through the fireswept street up to the enemy's breastworks, Worth finally carried the San Cosme Gate and his men burst through the barrier. Desultory fighting continued throughout the night, but in reality, Santa Anna was through. The city was breached at two gates, and Twiggs, whose feinting pinned down large Mexican forces throughout the day, threatened a third. At 1 A.M., on September 14, amid great confusion, Santa Anna and about 9,000 troops evacuated the capital and retired to the suburban town of Guadelupe Hidalgo.

A deputation from the *ayuntamiento* called on Worth at about this time, and it was sent to Scott's headquarters at Tacubaya. Scott replied peremptorily, to the request for terms of capitulation, that the American army would enter Mexico City "under no terms not *self*-imposed." At 4 A.M., orders were sent to Worth and Quitman to advance cautiously to the center of the city.

Before Captain Lee delivered Scott's order to Quitman, a white flag came out from the Citadel with the message that Santa Anna had left the city and the request for the Americans to march in. Lieutenants Beauregard and Mansfield Lovell, although wounded, volunteered to go into the city as scouts. From the Citadel, the two signaled to Quitman to enter, and the Americans advanced into the city. Leaving garrisons at both the Belén Gate and the Citadel, Quitman marched to the Grand Plaza, entered the National Palace, and ordered Captain Benjamin Roberts to raise the American flag.

Then he left Lieutenant Colonel S. E. Watson's battalion of Marines as a garrison for the halls of Montezuma and thereby wrote a line in the fighting song of the corps.

General Quitman sent Beauregard to tell Scott of his occupation of the Grand Plaza, and the Lieutenant encountered the head of Worth's column at the handsome Alemeda or public garden. "They appeared as astonished to see me coming from that direction as I was to find them . . ." wrote Beauregard. "When I told them of our having occupied the Palace, they appeared considerably vexed at our temerity and success." Beauregard went in search of Scott, whose first question was, "Whether we had been in any hurry to forestall General Worth in the occupation of the Palace."

About 9 o'clock General Scott, "Old Fuss and Feathers" in his most resplendent finery, rode with his staff into the plaza at the head of Worth's troops, as the drums rolled and the Dragoon band played "Yankee Doodle," and a salute was fired.

Scott promptly named Quitman civil and military governor of Mexico City, and totaled up the recent casualties at Chapultepec and the gates as 130 killed and 704 wounded. The General imposed a contribution of $150,000 upon the city of Mexico, the amount to be paid within four weeks. One-third of this amount Scott used for the benefit of his troops, the sick, wounded, and those in need of shoes and blankets. He sent $100,000 to the United States with the suggestion that it be used to establish a soldiers' home at Washington.

Today the Soldiers' Home is a monument to Winfield Scott's brilliant campaign from the beach at Vera Cruz to the halls of the Montezumas.

Scott summed up this campaign in a single sentence in his report, which he dated, "National Palace of Mexico": "This glorious army hoisted on the morning of the 14th, the colors of the United States on the walls of this palace."

30

Peace Without Authority

Making peace with Mexico proved a longer process than the military operations that brought that nation at last to the peace table.

From the landing at Vera Cruz on March 9, 1847, to September 14, when General Scott marched into the ancient capital of the Montezumas, six months and five days elapsed.

But it took eight and a half hectic months after the American flag flew over the National Palace for a formal exchange of ratifications of the treaty of Guadelupe Hidalgo.

During that period, a responsible government had to be established in Mexico to deal with Nicholas P. Trist, while Trist himself negotiated without authority, having peremptorily been ordered home by President Polk.

The military front, after the nearly month-long siege of Puebla was raised on October 12 by the arrival of General Joseph Lane with 4,000 troops from Zachary Taylor's army and several new commands, quieted down to guerrilla raids on Scott's long communication line to the coast.

But inside Scott's military family, victory was marked, not by amity but by discord, the sounds of which reached all the way to Washington. In mid-November Scott removed Generals Worth and Pillow from their commands, and on January 13, President Polk relieved Scott as commander-in-chief and ordered him, Worth, and Pillow before a court of inquiry. This extraordinary removal of a victorious general in the field and its consequences will be treated subsequently.

Two days after Scott entered Mexico City, on September 16, Santa Anna renounced the presidency of Mexico, but continued as the head of the army. Manuel de la Peña y Peña, who had reluctantly rebuffed John Slidell's peace mission early in 1846, was finally persuaded, as President of the Supreme Court, to assume the interim presidency of Mexico. Peña y Peña took office on September 26 at Querétaro. Then his provisional government deposed Santa Anna and placed him on summons before a military court.

The status of Peña y Peña's government was provisional in fact as well as name. He was to hold office only until Congress convened and elected a new provisional president who would hold office only until January 8, 1848. By then a new Congress was expected to be elected and to choose a chief executive for a full presidential term.

Trist waited a month to let the new government stabilize itself before sending word to Peña y Peña that he was prepared to reopen peace negotiations. The American Commissioner got no formal answer, for Peña y Peña was waiting for the existing Congress to gather at Querétaro before acting on a treaty. On November 2, a quorum of the Congress was finally assembled and after more than a week of internal struggle between the peace party and war party, General Pedro María Anaya, former Interim President, was elected President of Mexico.

Meanwhile, in Washington, President Polk decided on October 4 to recall Trist "because his remaining longer with the army could not, probably, accomplish the object of his mission, and . . . might, and probably would, impress the Mexican Government with the belief the United States were so anxious for peace that they would ultimately conclude one upon the Mexican terms."

By October 21, Trist's dispatches concerning the armistice had been read by the President with considerable disgust. Polk's diary for the next few days reflects this: "Mr. Trist has exceeded his instructions . . . Mr. Trist . . . departed from his instructions . . . He had no right to depart from his instructions, and I disapprove his conduct in doing so . . . His course is much to be regretted . . . Mr. Trist has managed the negotiations very bunglingly and with no ability . . . I expressed [to the cabinet] in strong and decided terms my disapprobation of his conduct . . . I directed Mr. Buchanan to prepare a dispatch expressing in strong terms my disapprobation, and to repeat his order of the 6th instant for his immediate recall."

It was not until November 16 that Trist learned of his recall, when both of Buchanan's dispatches reached him on the same day. Trist's first thought was to advise the Mexican Government of the "inutility of pursuing their intention to appoint commissioners" to meet with him. On reflection, he felt that an official communication would have a "depressing influence . . . upon the peace party." When he gave out informally the news of his recall, one official eager to negotiate a treaty could not disguise his disappointment. "His countenance fell, and flat despair succeeded to the cheeriness with which he had accosted me," Trist reported. When Peña y Peña, Minister of Foreign Affairs for the recently elected President Anaya, sent a note to Trist stating he had appointed commissioners to treat with him, the American envoy, now without portfolio, reluctantly replied that "the powers conferred upon him . . . have been revoked" and that he was returning to the United States as soon as possible. On December 4, however, Trist, conscious that the fate of negotiations hung on the immediacy of the moment, suddenly changed his mind. "What is my line of duty to my government and my country, in this most extraordinary position in which I find myself?" he wrote a friend, probably the Englishman Thornton. "Knowing, as I do, that peace is the earnest wish of both, is it, can it be my duty to allow this last chance for peace to be lost . . . ?"

Trist concluded that it was "now or never," and, violating his instructions to negotiate no further with the Mexicans and to leave the country immediately, he remained and went to work with the Mexican commissioners, declaring his determination "to carry home a treaty of peace."

Having cast the die, "for good or for evil," Trist then wrote a most extraordinary letter to Buchanan for length—it requires thirty five printed pages—as well as for its contemptuous tone, regarding President Polk's censures. This letter, which also set forth Trist' reasons for ignoring his instructions, fell on President Polk's desk like a bombshell. The President's diary reveals Polk's state of mind when, through a British source, he learned of Trist's renewal of negotiations:

January 4, 1848—This information is most surprising. Mr. Trist has acknowledged the receipt of his letter of recall, and he possesses no diplomatic powers. He is acting, no doubt, upon General Scott's advice. He has become a perfect tool of Scott. He is, in this measure, defying the authority of his Government . . . He seems to have entered into all Scott's hatred of the administration, and to be lending himself to Scott's evil purposes."

January 5, 1848— [Trist's] conduct astonished both the Secretary of State and myself . . . I fear he may greatly embarrass the Government.

January 15, 1848— . . . A very long dispatch from Mr. Trist . . . is the most extraordinary document I have ever heard from a diplomatic representative . . . His dispatch is arrogant, impudent, and very insulting to his government, and even personally offensive to the President . . . If there is any legal provision for his punishment he ought to be severely handled. He has acted worse than any man in the public employ whom I have known. His dispatch proves that he is destitute of honour or principle, and that he has proved himself to be a very base man. I was deceived in him.

While the President in Washington was recording his anger against Nicholas Trist, that gentleman had begun the peace negotiations on January 2. The three Mexican commissioners, Bernardo Couto, Miguel Atristaín, and Luis Gonzago Cuevas—the first two had participated in the armistice negotiations—resisted, as best they could, some of the conditions contained in the draft treaty which Trist had brought from the United States. Trist emphasized his "Now or never" belief about peace, and the Mexicans, faced with a reality, overcame their initial reluctance and worked resolutely to bring the conflict to an end. Moreover, on January 8, when Anaya's temporary term ended, Peña y Peña, a true friend of peace, in the failure of a congressional quorum to elect Anaya's successor, again moved into the office.

Under Peña y Peña's encouragement the progress of the negotiators was steady. On February 2, the treaty of peace was signed at the suburban village of Guadelupe Hidalgo, last-minute Mexican objections having been overcome. The treaty fixed the present boundaries between Mexico and the United States (except for later modifications by the Gadsden Purchase), and our country agreed to pay Mexico $15,000,000 and assumed the claims of American citizens against that nation, up to $3,250,000. In substance, Trist achieved a treaty with Mexico which conformed to Polk's original ideas and one which the President, despite his fulminations against the unauthorized negotiator, could not possibly refuse to submit to Congress without opening himself to criticism of the Whigs who still inveighed against "Mr. Polk's War."

One of the Mexican negotiators, Bernardo Couto, justified the loss of Mexican territory as a "compulsory and inevitable" consequence of hostilities. "It was in the war, and not in the treaty, that the territory which now remains in the possession of the enemy was lost," he wrote. "The present treaty does not merely prevent an increase of our losses by a continuance of the war; but it serves to recover the better part of that which was already under the control of the conquering army of the United States; it is more exactly an agreement of recovery than an agreement of session."

Trist delegated James L. Freaner, correspondent of the New Orleans *Delta* to carry the treaty to Washington, and Freaner, whose war dispatches were signed "Mustang," galloped out of Mexico City early on February 3. Right on his trail rode the courier for the New Orleans *Picayune,* with George Wilkins Kendall's story and the text of the treaty. At Vera Cruz, the naval steamer *Iris* was waiting to rush Freaner across the Gulf of Mexico to Mobile. Also waiting to depart was the *Picayune's* chartered steamer, *New Orleans,* but to keep Kendall from "scooping" the President of the United States, the *New Orleans* was held in port for two days after the *Iris* left. Nevertheless, Kendall's dispatch reached New Orleans about the time Freaner reached Mobile and started his journey north. The *Picayune* Extra was no sooner off the press than its pony express rider, his saddlebags stuffed with copies of the edition, gave spur to his horse and hurried east with the thrilling news of peace.

Before Freaner reached Washington and delivered the treaty to Secretary of State Buchanan after dark on February 19, the details of the treaty, taken from the *Picayune,* were telegraphed from Petersburg, Virginia, to the Baltimore, Philadelphia, and New York newspapers, which, it being a Saturday, were compelled to defer publication until Monday.

At 9 P.M., Buchanan called at the White House with the treaty which, Polk grudgingly admitted to his diary, was within Trist's "instructions which he took out in April last, upon the important question of boundary and limits." Despite the fact that Trist "acted very badly," Polk wrote that "if on further examination the treaty is one that can be accepted, it should not be rejected on account of his bad conduct."

While Polk still considered Trist "an impudent and unqualified scoundrel," and the cabinet was unanimous in condemnation of the envoy's disregard of orders, the President nonetheless sent Trist's treaty to the Senate on February 23. The Senate immediately went into executive session to consider it, but action was delayed by the death of former President John Quincy Adams, stricken at his seat in the House of Representatives.

Early the next week, on February 28, Chairman Ambrose H. Sevier of the Senate Foreign Affairs Committee called on Polk and stated his committee had resolved to recommend rejection of the treaty by the Senate. Sevier, alone of the committee, was for the treaty. Daniel Webster was for no acquisition of territory, while Senator Edward A. Hannegan was for taking all Mexico. ". . . For opposite reasons," noted Polk, "they will oppose the Treaty." Thomas Hart Benton, still fuming over the treatment of his son-in-law, Frémont, and Senator W. P. Mangum, also opposed the treaty and wanted the President to send a nonpartisan commission to Mexico to negotiate a new treaty.

Debate in the Senate continued for nearly two weeks. Finally, shortly before 10 P.M. on March 10—a year and a day after the American landings at Vera Cruz—the Senate ratified the treaty by a vote of 38 to 14, with four Senators not voting. There had been thirty-eight roll-call votes on suggested amendments and deletions, but in the end, with only minor changes, the treaty was ratified essentially in the form that Trist had submitted it. Senator Sevier and Attorney General Nathan Clifford were named commissioners to take the modified treaty to Mexico. They reached Mexico City in mid-April, but nothing could be done until a quorum of the Mexican Congress could be assembled. Such a quorum was obtained on May 3, and the debate on ratification began. On May 19, the Chamber of Deputies, by a fairly narrow 51 to 35 vote, approved the treaty, and on May 25, the Senate ratified it, 34 to 4.

Formal exchange of ratifications took place on May 30, and the next day the movement of American troops out of Mexico City began. On June 12, General Worth's division marched out of the capital and newly elected President José Joaquín Herrera entered and the Mexican War was over. The last American troops sailed from Vera Cruz on July 31.

31

"... As an Old Horse to Die"

There was not the slightest doubt in the mind of Captain Robert E. Lee as to why the United States brought the Mexican War to a successful conclusion.

"The great cause of our success was in our leader," Lee wrote his brother Sidney Smith Lee. "It was his stout heart that cast us on the shore of Vera Cruz; his bold self-reliance that forced us through the pass at Cerro Gordo; his indomitable courage that, amidst all the doubts and difficulties that surrounded us at Puebla, pressed us forward to this capital, and finally brought us within its gates . . ."

As Lee wrote those lines, General Winfield Scott, who had hailed General Pillow and General Worth before a military court of inquiry, was removed from command of the army by President Polk, and himself ordered before a court of inquiry.

Captain Lee deplored "the dissensions in camp [that] have clouded a bright campaign," but, by implication, he was sharply critical of President Polk: ". . . To suspend a successful general in command of an army in the heart of an enemy's country; to try the judge in place of the accused, is to upset all discipline; to jeopardize the safety of the army and the honor of the country, and to violate justice." In another letter to his brother, Lee again implied criticism of Polk: "General Scott . . . having crushed the enemy and conquered a peace, can now be dismissed, and turned out as an old horse to die."

General Worth, ever since Scott had reproved him at Puebla, had nourished ill-feelings for the Commanding General, despite the ties of friendship, both personal and professional, that had existed between them for thirty-five years. He was "ripe" for an open break with Scott when the occasion was presented to him. A modern biographer of Worth suggests that Scott, not having "enjoyed a convenient qarrel" for some time, went out of his way to pick a quarrel with Worth and General Gideon Pillow, Polk's old law partner.

It was the latter, a military nonentity, who provoked the *cause célèbre*, perhaps the most disgraceful controversy in the military history of the United States. It all began with General Pillow's reports on the battles of Padierna-Churubusco and the storming of Chapultepec, in each of which there was no attempt to conceal the military genius, inspired leadership, and intrepid bravery of Gideon Pillow. Scott might have indulged Pillow's excessive "deployment" of the first personal pronoun, had not that worthy, in so doing, trod on Scott's own vanity. Even fulsome praise that Pillow bestowed on Scott was inadmissible, because the General wrote Pillow on October 2, "if the right of a junior to praise be admitted, it would carry with it the correlative right of the junior to censure." Scott requested certain changes in the report in "several passages . . . which seem to require correction."

Concerning Chapultepec, Scott wrote: "General S. is sorry to perceive, in General P.'s report, of September 18th, a seeming effort, no doubt unintentional, to leave General S. entirely out of the operations of September 13." (Scott and his pen! How could "a seeming effort" possibly be "unintentional"?). To Pillow's assertion that "having carried Chapultepec, and being unable to proceed with my command, *I* ordered it forward under Generals Quitman and Worth, etc., etc.," Scott offered this rebuttal: "General S. . . . thinks, from what he personally saw, that General P., after receiving an agonizing wound . . . was not in a condition, unfortunately, to command; and . . . General S. *knows* that he, himself, gave reiterated orders . . . to support, etc., etc."

Pillow, still confined to bed by his wound received at Chapultepec, replied with exaggerated politeness, concluding with the avowal that he had no hesitation in correcting anything "deemed erroneous" and he requested "a few minutes' call, as I am unable to call upon you," for a personal discussion of the matter.

Scott brushed aside the request: "I am occupied and fatigued," and then, in the same note, took Pillow to task again for claiming to have conceived "the joint attack on San Antonio, in front and rear." "That part of your report, therefore, is unjust to me, and seems, without intending it, I am sure, to make you control the operations of the whole army, including my own views and acts."

Pillow's reply was as unctuous as his first note, as he pointed out that he had altered his reports in conformity to all of Scott's suggestions, except that concerning Chapultepec. On October 4, Scott terminated the correspondence:

The discrepancies between your memory and mine . . . are so many and so material, that I regret that you have made any alteration in either report at my suggestion . . . I shall . . . forward them to the War Department, with my two notes to you and your two in reply; and here, I suppose, all further correspondence between us on the subject ought to cease.

The breach between Scott and Pillow widened several weeks later when the former intimated that the latter had appropriated as personal trophies two small howitzers taken at Chapultepec. Pillow demanded a court of inquiry, which ironically in the light of developments, was presided over by General Worth. The court concluded that while the howitzers were taken and placed in General Pillow's baggage wagon "without the previous knowledge, authority or consent" of Pillow, the latter did not express surprise when told they were there, nor had "he then evinced any desire or determination to have the howitzers returned to their proper places." When General Scott approved the findings of the court of inquiry, which were announced on October 27, Pillow appealed to the Secretary of War.

Meanwhile, the *American Star,* one of two newspapers published in Mexico City immediately after the occupation by United States troops, printed a letter on October 23, which it had obtained from the New Orleans *Picayune* of September 16. This letter, which the *Picayune* had lifted from the *Delta* of September 9, was signed "Leonidas" and was devoted to extolling Gideon Pillow's military prowess and how he had planned and executed virtually all the successful operations in the Valley of Mexico. Pillow, "Leonidas" wrote, "evinced on this, as he has done on other occasions, that masterly military genius and profound knowledge of war, which has astonished so much the mere martinets of the profession." It was further claimed that during the two-day Padierna-Churubusco battles, "General Pillow was in command of all the forces engaged, except General Worth's . . . and . . . General Scott gave but one order . . ."

In reprinting the piece, the *Picayune* presented in italics two amazing paragraphs stressing Pillow's military skill, judgment, and personal bravery, which it claimed the *Delta* had deleted. Both made absurdly exaggerated claims, especially the second insert which described a hand-to-hand clash between Pillow and a Mexican Lancer, whom he slew as "both the American and Mexican armies witnessed this splendid effort." It developed later that the

Picayune had faked the inserted paragraphs to hold the unpopular Pillow up to ridicule.

Shortly after this, an American newspaper in Tampico reprinted a letter written from the army which the Pittsburgh *Post* had published on September 25. This letter gave General Worth credit for choosing the route south of Lake Chalco for the attack on Mexico City. The two letters set Scott's blood to boiling, and on November 12 he issued General Order No. 349 couched in the most intemperate language and aimed directly at Pillow and Worth. After reminding "certain officers of this army" of regulations against writing letters about campaigns for publication, Scott dipped his pen in vitriol and wrote:

> As yet, but two echoes from home, of the brilliant operations of our arms in this basin, have reached us . . .
>
> It requires not a little charity to believe that the principal heroes of the scandalous letters alluded to, did not write them, or specifically procure them to be written, and the intelligent can be at no loss in conjecturing the authors—chiefs, partizans, and pet familiars . . .

General Worth was completely innocent of the "Tampico letter," neither writing it, nor causing it to be written, nor even knowing about it being written. His resentment to having "scandalous" conduct imputed to him was reflected in his letter of November 13 to Scott. He inquired "whether, in any sense or degree, he [Scott] condescended to apply, or designed to have applied, the epithets contain in that order, to myself . . ." On November 14, Scott replied that he referred to "the authors, aiders, and abettors of these letters —be they who they may."

Meanwhile the now Brevet Colonel James Duncan, who had made the Chalco reconnaissance, had written the previous day to the *North American,* the anti-Scott paper in Mexico City, that he was the author of the "Tampico letter." Absolving Worth of any responsibility, he added: "The statements in the letter are known by very many officers of this army to be true."

Scott's evasive note of the 14th drew from Worth on the same day the desire, "as an act of simple justice," to "know, distinctly, and with a view to further measures to protect myself, if, as is supposed, I was one of the persons referred to." Scott, replying through his adjutant, said "that he cannot be more explicit than in his reply . . .

already given," that he had no positive information as to the authorship of the letters and that if he had "valid information," he would institute general court-martial proceedings immediately. Still unsatisfied, Worth replied at once—the 14th must have been spent in writing and reading letters—that having no satisfactory answer to his "just and rightful inquiries," his only recourse, as he scorned "to wear 'honors not earned,'" was "to appeal . . . through the prescribed channels, to the constitutional commander-in-chief."

Two days later, General Worth wrote the Secretary of War his letter of grievance beginning as follows:

> From the arbitrary and illegal conduct—the malice and gross injustice practiced by the general officer, commanding-in-chief this army—Major-General Winfield Scott—I appeal, as is my right and privilege to the constitutional commander-in-chief— the President of the United States. I accuse Major-General Winfield Scott of having acted in a manner *unbecoming an officer, and a gentleman.*

Worth added that he didn't expect immediate action, because of the inconvenience to the service at the time, but he asked that President Polk examine the case. It was not until November 24 that Worth submitted the letter to Scott for forwarding through channels. The Commander-in-Chief removed Worth from his command and placed him under arrest for "behaving with contempt and disrespect toward his superior and commanding officer." About the same time, General Pillow had made his appeal to the Secretary of War on the matter of the howitzers, and had voiced "contempt and disrespect" for Scott in the letter, a copy of which he had forwarded directly to the Secretary of War "to guard against the hazards of miscarriage." For such insubordination, Pillow was stripped of his command and placed under arrest. Scott, by now having learned that Duncan had written the "Tampico letter," had him also placed under arrest.

When all the documents reached Washington, Polk, as might be expected, blamed everything on General Scott's "vanity and tyrannical temper . . . and his want of prudence and common sense." In his diary on December 30, 1847, the President wrote: "I deplore the unfortunate collisions which have arisen between the generals in Mexico, as they must prove highly prejudicial to the public service . . . The whole difficulty has grown out of letters written from the army and published in the newspapers of the United States, in which General Scott is not made the exclusive hero of the war."

For two weeks, the President discussed with his cabinet and party leaders the "embarrassing state of things . . . in the army, all produced by General Scott's bad temper, dictatorial spirit, and extreme jealousy," and wound up by directing Secretary of War Marcy to relieve Scott of command of the army in Mexico and replace him by General William O. Butler. On January 13, 1848, Marcy wrote twice to Scott. One dispatch, in effect, stated:

1. That the President disapproved Scott's action against General Worth, and that a court-martial was denied.

2. That a court of inquiry was ordered to sit in Mexico to examine charges against Worth, Pillow, and Duncan, and Worth's charges against Scott.

3. That the President directed the release from arrest of Worth, Pillow, and Duncan.

The second dispatch removed Scott from command, and ordered him to hold himself at the disposal of the court of inquiry. A third document, also bearing the date of January 13, set up the court.

Word of Scott's removal reached Mexico City in time to appear in an extra edition of the *American Star* on February 7. However, the General did not receive the official order until February 18. Meanwhile, noting that from "unofficial announcements" he had learned of his impending removal, Scott wrote Marcy on February 9, expressing approval of his successor, General Butler, and stating that the President had ordered him before a court "for daring to enforce necessary discipline in this army against certain of its high officers!" His brief note to the Secretary of War concluded with a mild blast at the administration: "My poor services with this most gallant army are at length to be requited as I have long been led to expect they would be."

Before the court of inquiry, composed of General Nathan Towson, paymaster general, General Caleb Cushing, and Colonel William G. Belknap, assembled on March 13 in the National Palace in Mexico City, behind-the-scenes efforts of peacemakers bore considerable fruit. General Worth wrote a note to the court, stating that as the President had done him "ample justice" he asked that his charge against General Scott be withdrawn. Scott agreed to lay over the cases of Worth and Duncan until orders from the President were received. The court then concerned itself with General Pillow's case.

In his opening address before the court, General Scott on March 16 declared that he had asked a court-martial and the court of inquiry was the result. "I am stricken down from my high command," Scott read from the prepared paper. "One of the arrested generals is pre-acquitted and rewarded—and the other parties—the judge and his prisoners, the innocent and the guilty, are, with that strange exception, all thrown before you, to scramble for justice as we may."

Scott then announced he would decline prosecuting the charges against Pillow for a number of cogent reasons: some witnesses had returned to the United States; the court would be compelled to adjourn to the United States to complete its work; the approaching yellow fever season would endanger judges, prosecutor, and accused alike when they passed through Vera Cruz; peace was close at hand and Pillow, as a civilian appointee, would pass back to civilian life out of the military jurisdiction; should the court of inquiry, on sifting the evidence, deem a court-martial justified, then the whole dreary business had to be repeated. Scott's final reason for dropping the case was "that the time has probably gone by for benefitting the service by a conviction and punishment" and that he would not prosecute Pillow before "this *preliminary* court, without its special orders, or the further orders of the President of the United States."

The next day, Pillow presented a paper in which he insisted on a full hearing: "I am now here, ready and anxious to go on with the proceedings, should such be the pleasure of the court." When the court suggested that it write Washington for instructions, which meant a certain delay of more than a month, Scott changed his mind and stated he was ready to proceed.

Testimony began on March 21, and the "Leonidas" letter was first investigated. J. L. Freaner, back from delivering the Treaty of Peace in Washington, was the first witness and he gave damning testimony to the effect that Pillow had given him virtually the same text as the "Leonidas" piece and he had not forwarded it to the *Delta*. He could not state how a copy got into his packet of dispatches to the *Delta*. Nicholas P. Trist, who suspected Pillow had influenced the President to recall him, and who hated him with a passion, also gave damaging testimony. (Trist, in his incredible dispatch of December 6, had described Pillow's character as "such as to qualify him for shining at a country court bar, in the defense of a fellow charged with horse-stealing; particularly if the case were a bad one and required dexterous tampering with the witnesses.")

Dozens of witnesses of all ranks testified to the charges against

Pillow. The court on orders from the Secretary of War also sought to question General Scott regarding an alleged attempt to bribe Santa Anna, when the army was at Puebla. To this request, Scott flatly refused to answer on the grounds that it involved the conduct of certain foreign diplomats (the British Legation), and he was bound to say nothing about it "except to the President and *perhaps* the Sec't of War."

On April 21, the court adjourned to meet again in the United States, leaving "reflecting men," wrote a Mexican historian, "to admire the moral force of the American Government, which by a single slip of paper, written at a distance of two thousand leagues, could humble a proud and victorious soldier and make him descend from his exalted position."

Scott did not tarry with the adjournment of the court. On April 22, he rode out of Mexico City, having refused all military and civic honors and farewell meetings. Nonetheless, a great crowd of officers assembled, many with their horses, to escort him out of the city, and as "Old Fuss and Feathers" climbed into his mule-drawn carriage, all joined in the cry: "God bless you, General!"

On May 20, General Scott landed at Elizabeth, New Jersey, and he soon was reunited with his wife and three daughters. From them he doubtless learned that on March 9, a Congress, more grateful than the President of the United States, had passed a joint resolution thanking him and his entire army for "uniform gallantry and good conduct," and requesting the President to have struck a medal to be presented, along with the resolution, to General Winfield Scott, "as a testimony of the high senses entertained by Congress of his valor, skill, and judicious conduct in the memorable campaign of 1847."

Thus the Mexican War—Mr. Polk's War—ended on what must have been a sour note for the President, with the nation, the impartial press, and the Congress honoring the victorious general who was anathema to James Knox Polk.

However, there was some solace for the President. The court of inquiry, reconvening at Frederick, Maryland, on June 7 delivered its findings on July 1, which amounted to almost a complete whitewash of Polk's one-time law partner, Gideon J. Pillow.

And President Polk had what he set out to get at the start of his term—California.

Appendix
Postscript to Victory

Zachary Taylor, who had never voted in a Presidential election, was swept into the White House in 1848 by his unbroken string of victories in the Mexican War.

After Palo Alto and Resaca de la Palma, Thurlow Weed, editor of the Albany *Evening Journal,* and an important voice in the Whig party, boomed Old Zach for the Presidency.

Taylor at first thought the idea utterly ridiculous, declaring in June, 1846, "that high office . . . I would decline if proffered." A month later he stated he was not then, and never would be, an aspirant for the Presidency. "My opinion has always been against the elevation of a Military Chief to that position," he wrote. And in August he was still determined "to have nothing to do with that high office."

With the victory of Monterrey, Old Zach's already widespread popularity soared and he began to backtrack a little on his avowed disinterest in going to the White House. "I will not say I would not serve if the good people were to be so inprudent as to elect me," he confessed to his son-in-law in December.

By July, 1847, Old Zach's mind was made up and he told Dr. Wood: "I am satisfied if the election was to come off now or during the present year, that nothing could prevent my election to that high office."

And so, by easy stages, paced to his Mexican War victories and to his growing distrust of President Polk and General Scott and their "plot" against him, Zachary Taylor moved to the Presidency. Nominated on the fourth ballot by the Whigs, Taylor took no active part in the 1848 campaign, remaining in Louisiana, and leaving the managing to the Whig politicians. He defeated Lewis Cass, the Democratic candidate, receiving 163 electoral votes to Cass's 127. The popular vote also gave Old Zach the edge: Taylor 1,360,-099; Cass, 1,220,544; Martin Van Buren, 291,263.

How successful a President Zachary Taylor would have been will never be known for he died at the White House on July 9, 1850, after serving barely sixteen months.

The Mexican War also created three other Presidents—two from the field and one from Polk's cabinet. Brigadier General Franklin Pierce, a political soldier to whom Polk had offered the post of attorney general before making him a brigadier general, served under Winfield Scott in Mexico and then defeated him for the Presidency in 1852. In 1856, James Buchanan, Polk's Secretary of State, followed Franklin Pierce into the White House. The fourth American President to emerge from the Mexican War was the Mississippi colonel, whose celebrated "V" saved the day at Buena Vista, Jefferson Davis, later President of the Confederate States of America.

President Polk went into office in 1845 with one dominating ambition, and that was to acquire California, peaceably for a price, if possible, or, if war with Mexico came, by right of conquest. That Polk provoked the war to gain his end, many contended then and have since. Nevertheless, by the acquisition of California and New Mexico, the United States completed its march to the Pacific, an inevitable march, say some, the fruit of Manifest Destiny, say others.

The Mexican War fed, rather than extinguished, the flames of Manifest Destiny and the filibustering projects of Narciso López in Cuba and William Walker in Nicaragua found ready support in both the North and South, but for different reasons. Although deeprooted in "a national or sectional superiority complex," Manifest Destiny was, nevertheless, a land-grabbing scheme, pure and simple, no matter how eloquently or altruistically it appeared in public under the auspices of editors, politicians, business and professional leaders, and ministers of the Gospel.

None was more explicit in charting the course of empire through Manifest Destiny than the influential southern editor, J. D. B. DeBow, writing at the close of the Mexican War in 1848:

> The North Americans *will* spread out far beyond their present bounds. They *will* encroach again and again on their neighbors. New territories *will* be planted, declare their independence and be annexed! We have new Mexico and California! We will have Old Mexico and Cuba! The isthmus can not arrest—not even the St. Lawrence. Time has all this in her womb.

Out of the Mexican War came one of the last of many "wedges of separation" that split the sections apart and thus brought on the Civil War. This was the Wilmot Proviso, which although it never passed the Senate, was a constant irritant to the South during the decade before the election of Abraham Lincoln.

The most significant consequence of the Mexican War from the point of view of national defense was the "proving" of West Point. At the start of the war, about 500 of the Military Academy graduates were on active duty. Approximately the same number of West Point alumni were in civilian life, but were available to fill officer cadres in the volunteer regiments and divisions.

And yet Congress, on the very eve of the war, was debating whether to abolish the United States Military Academy! In toasting West Point after the capture of Mexico City, General Scott paid tribute to the graduates of the Military Academy, stating that without their science "this army multiplied by four, could not have entered the capital of Mexico."

In his *Memoirs,* General U. S. Grant recalled that the seven classes of cadets with which he was in contact during his West Point days, and which sent young officers into the Mexican War, produced "more than fifty officers who became generals on one side or the other in the rebellion." Older graduates of West Point with whom Grant served under Winfield Scott "became conspicuous in the rebellion," and he listed among them Robert E. Lee, Joseph Eggleston Johnston, and Albert Sidney Johnston.

One has only to run over the list of General Scott's brilliant young Engineers to realize what West Point contributed to the victory in Mexico. And provided, too, the leadership in the bitter four-year struggle which, coming in 1861 because the Nation was split apart, actually brought the divided country together again.

Colonel Joseph G. Totten, commanding the Engineer Corps in Mexico, won a brevet to brigadier general at Vera Cruz and in the Civil War, as a brigadier general, he was Chief Engineer of the Union Army.

Only three of Totten's seven captains lived to serve in the Civil War:

Robert E. Lee, commander of the Army of Northern Virginia and, briefly, Confederate Commander-in-chief.

John G. Barnard, who, breveted major general in the Union Army, became Grant's chief engineer in the field.

Joseph K. F. Mansfield, who, attached to Zachary Taylor's army, won brevets of major, lieutenant colonel and colonel, and, as a Union major general, died of wounds received at Antietam.

Six of the seven first lieutenants among the engineers with Scott —one died in the 1850's—all became general officers in the Civil War:

P. G. T. Beauregard (CSA); Henry W. Benham (USV); Jeremy F. Gilmer (CSA); Henry W. Halleck (USA); Isaac I. Stevens (USA); Zealous B. Tower (USA).

Likewise, all three second lieutenants became Civil War generals: John G. Foster (USA); George B. McClellan; and Gustavus W. Smith (CSA).

Turning to the Topographical Engineers, one finds no fewer than eight Civil War generals among the officers who served in the Mexican War, most of them with Scott: Captain Joseph E. Johnston (CSA); First Lieutenants William H. Emory (USA) and Eliakim P. Scammon (USA); Second Lieutenants William B. Franklin (USA), George G. Meade (USA), John Pope (USA), Martin L. Smith (CSA), and Thomas J. Wood (USV).

Thus, the two groups of Engineers in Mexico produced between them twenty-one Civil War generals. But this impressive figure was almost doubled by the Artillery and tripled by the Infantry. The following shows other Civil War generals who were both West Pointers and Mexican War veterans in the branch of service indicated:

Assistant Adjutant Generals: Edward R. S. Canby (USV), Joseph Hooker (USA), William W. Mackall (CSA), Irvin W. McDowell (USV).

Quartermaster Corps: Thomas Jordon (CSA), James G. Martin (CSA), Justus McKinstry (USV), Henry C. Wayne (CSA).

Commissary: Amos B. Eaton (USA), John B. Grayson (CSA).

Paymasters: David Hunter (USV).

Ordnance: Alexander B. Dyer (USA), Josiah Gorgas (CSA), Benjamin Huger (CSA), George D. Ramsey (USA), Charles P. Stone (USV).

Dragoons: John Adams (CSA), Richard Anderson (CSA), Abraham Buford (CSA), Robert M. Chilton (CSA), Philip St. George Cooke (USA), John W. Davidson (USV), Richard S. Ewell (CSA), William J. Hardee (CSA), James M. Hawes (CSA), Rufus Ingalls (USV), Philip Kearny (USV), Alfred Pleasanton (USV), Daniel

Rucker (USV), Henry H. Sibley (CSA), Andrew J. Smith (USV), William D. Smith (USV), William Steele (CSA), George Stoneman (USV), and Samuel D. Sturgis (USV).

Mounted Rifles: George B. Crittenden (CSA), Daniel M. Frost (CSA), Alfred Gibbs (USV), George H. Gordon (USV), Gordon Granger (USV), John P. Hatch (USV), Dabney Maury (CSA), Innis N. Palmer (USV), Andrew Porter (USV), and Benjamin S. Roberts (USV).

Artillery: Robert Anderson (USA), William F. Barry (USV), Braxton Bragg (CSA), John M. Brannan (USV), Ambrose E. Burnside (USV), Darius N. Couch (USV), Gustavus A. DeRussy (USV), Abner Doubleday (USV), Arnold Elzey (CSA), Samuel G. French (CSA), William H. French (USV), Robert S. Garnett (CSA), George M. Getty (USV), John Gibbon (USV), William Hays (USV), A. P. Hill (CSA), Daniel H. Hill (CSA), Henry J. Hunt (USV), Thomas Jonathan Jackson (CSA), Mansfield Lovell (CSA), John B. Magruder (CSA), John S. Mason (USV), John P. McCown (CSA), Edward O. C. Ord (USV), John J. Peck (USV), John C. Pemberton (CSA), John W. Phelps (USV), Fitz-John Porter (USV), John P. Reynolds (USV), James B. Ricketts (USV), Roswell S. Ripley (CSA), John Sedgwick (USV), Thomas W. Sherman (USV), Charles P. Smith (USV), George H. Thomas (USA), James Totten (USV), Stewart Van Vleit (USV), Seth Williams (USV), Thomas Williams (USV), John H. Winder (CSA).

Infantry: Benjamin Alvord (USV), Lewis A. Armistead (CSA), Christopher C. Augur (USV), Barnard E. Bee (CSA), Albert G. Blanchard (CSA), William T. H. Brooks (USV), Robert C. Buchanan (USV), Don Carlos Buell (USV), Simon B. Buckner (CSA), Silas Casey (USV), Napoleon J. T. Dana (USV), Frederick T. Dent (USV), Franklin Gardner (CSA), William M. Gardner (CSA), Theophilus T. Garrard (USV), Charles C. Gilbert (USV), Maxcy Gregg (CSA), U. S. Grant (USA), Charles S. Hamilton (USV), Winfield S. Hancock (USA), Alexander Hays (USV), Samuel P. Heintzelman (USV), Paul O. Hébert (CSA), Ethan Allen Hitchcock (USV), Theophilus H. Holmes (CSA), Bushrod R. Johnson (CSA), Edward Johnson (CSA), David R. Jones (CSA), Henry M. Judah (USV), James Longstreet (CSA), Nathaniel Lyon (USV), Robert P. Maclay (CSA), Randolph B. Marcy (USV), Samuel B. Maxey (CSA), Lafayette McLaws (CSA), William R. Montgomery (USV), George W. Morgan (USV), Marsena R. Patrick (USV), Gabriel R. Paul (USV),

George E. Pickett (CSA), Thomas G. Pitcher (USV), Joseph B. Plummer (USV), Joseph H. Porter (USV), Henry Prince (USV), Israel B. Richardson (USV), John C. Robinson (USV), Daniel Ruggles (CSA), David A. Russell (USV), Edmund Kirby Smith (CSA), Frederick Steele (USV), Carter L. Stevenson (CSA), George Sykes (USV), John B. S. Todd (USV), Earl Van Dorn (CSA), Egbert L. Viele (USV), William H. T. Walker (CSA), Henry W. Wessells (USV), Cadmus M. Wilcox (CSA), James M. Withers (CSA), and George Wright (USV).

The above lists 166 West Point graduates who fought as young officers in Mexico and became Union or Confederate generals. It is no wonder that Captain William S. Henry, writing in 1847 in the full flush of Old Zach's victories at Palo Alto, Resaca de la Palma, Monterrey and Buena Vista, exclaimed with enthusiastic pride and confident prescience:

> By far the great majority of the officers were graduates of the Military Academy; all did their duty, and many distinguished themselves by their skill and thorough knowledge of their profession. All arises from their instruction received at that best of institutions, the West Point Military Academy. In the hour of our country's danger she will always prove her usefulness, and her graduates will show to their country and the world that the money expended in the education of so talented a corps of officers has not been thrown away; richly will she be repaid for every cent expended. Our Alma Mater may be proud of her sons; conspicuously have they shown themselves soldiers upon *the field of battle*.

In the closing years of the 1960's, almost a century and a quarter after those words were written, the American people, living in a world of dangerous unrest, may prayerfully add: "Amen."

Bibliography

Books

Balbutin, Manuel. *La Invasion Americana, 1846 a 1848.* Mexico City, 1888.

Ballantine, George. *Autobiography of an English Soldier in the United States Army.* New York, 1853.

Bassett, John Spencer. *Correspondence of Andrew Jackson.* 6 vols. Washington, 1926–35.

Beauregard, P. G. T. *With Beauregard in Mexico.* T. Harry Williams, ed. Baton Rouge, Louisiana, Louisiana State University Press, 1956.

Bill, Alfred Hoyt. *Rehearsal for Conflict, The War with Mexico, 1846–1848.* New York, Alfred Knopf, 1947.

Bosch Garcia, Carlos. *Material Para la Historia Diplomatica de Mexico y los Estados Unidos, 1820–1848.* Mexico City, Escuela nacional de ciencias politicas y sociales, 1957.

Brooks, Nathan C. *A Complete History of the Mexican War.* Philadelphia, Grigg, Elliot & Co.; and Baltimore, Hutchinson & Seebold, 1849.

Callcott, Wilfrid Hardy. *Santa Anna; The Story of an Enigma Who Was Mexico.* Norman, Okla., Univ. of Oklahoma Press, 1936.

Capers, Gerald M. *John C. Calhoun, Opportunist: A Reappraisal.* Gainesville, Fla., Univ. of Florida Press, 1960.

Carleton, James Henry. *The Battle of Buena Vista.* New York, Harper & Bros., 1848.

Chamberlain, S. E. *My Confession.* New York, Harper & Bros., 1956.

Claiborne, J. F. H. *Life and Correspondence of John A. Quitman.* New York, Harper & Bros., 1860.

Connelley, William Elsey. *War with Mexico, 1846–1847: Doniphan's Expedition.* Topeka, 1907. Published by the author.

Conner, Philip Syng Physick. *The Home Squadron Under Commodore Conner in the War with Mexico.* Philadelphia, 1896. Privately printed.

Copeland, Fayette. *Kendall of the Picayune.* Norman, Okla., Univ. of Oklahoma Press, 1943.

Davis, Matthew L. *Memoirs of Aaron Burr.* 2 vols. New York, Harper & Bros., 1837. Vol. II.

Davis, Varina Howell. *Jefferson Davis, Ex-president of the Confederate States of America: A Memoir by His Wife.* 2 vols. New York, Belford Co., 1890.

Doubleday, Rhoda van Bibber (ed.) *Journals of the Late Brevet-Major Philip Norbourne Barbour . . . and His Wife Martha Isabella Hopkins Barbour.* New York and London, G. P. Putnam's Sons, 1901.

Dufour, Charles L. *Gentle Tiger: The Gallant Life of Roberdeau Wheat.* Baton Rouge, La., Louisiana State Univ. Press, 1957.

Dupuy, R. Ernest. *Men of West Point: The First 150 Years of the United States Military Academy.* New York, W. Sloane Associates, 1951.

Dyer, Brainerd. *Zachary Taylor.* Baton Rouge, La., Louisiana State Univ. Press, 1946.

Edwards, Marcellus Ball. *Journal.* Edited by Ralph B. Beiber, in *Southwest Historical Series,* IV. Glendale, Calif., 1936.

Elliott, Charles W. *Winfield Scott.* New York, 1937.

Ferguson, Philip Gooch. *Journal.* Edited by Ralph B. Beiber in *Southwest Historical Series,* IV. Glendale, Calif., 1936.

Freeman, Douglas S. *R. E. Lee; A Biography.* 4 vols. New York, Charles Scribner's Sons, 1934.

French, Gen. Samuel G. *Two Wars: An Autobiography of Gen. Samuel G. French.* Nashville, 1901.

Fuentes, Maria José. *Santa Anna, Aurora y Ocaso de un Comediate.* Mexico City, 1956.

Gibson, George Rutledge. *Journal of a Soldier Under Kearny and Doniphan.* Edited by Ralph B. Beiber, in *Southwest Historical Series,* III. Glendale, Calif., 1936.

Giddings, Luther. *Sketches of the Campaign in Northern Mexico, in Eighteen Hundred Forty-six and Seven.* New York, 1853. Published by the author.

Graebner, Norman A. *Empire on the Pacific: A Study in American Continental Expansion.* New York, Ronald Press, 1955.

Grant, U. S. (E. B. Long, ed.) *Personal Memoirs of U. S. Grant.* 2 vols. Cleveland and New York, 1885.

Gregg, Josiah. *Diary and Letters of Josiah Gregg.* M. G. Fulton, ed., 2 vols. Norman, Okla., Univ. of Oklahoma Press, 1941–1944.

Hamilton, Holman. *Zachary Taylor, Soldier of the Republic.* 2 vols. Indianapolis and New York, Bobbs-Merrill, 1941. Vol. I.

Hanighan, Frank C. *Santa Anna, the Napoleon of the West.* New York, Coward-McCann, 1934.

Henry, Robert S. *The Story of the Mexican War.* Indianapolis, 1950.

Henry, Capt. W. S. *Campaign Sketches of the War with Mexico.* New York, 1847.

Hitchcock, Ethan Allen. *Fifty Years in Camp and Field: Diary of Major General Ethan Allen Hitchcock, USA.* Ed. by W. A. Croffut. New York, G. P. Putnam, 1909.

Hogan, William Ransom. *The Texas Republic.* Norman, Okla., Univ. of Oklahoma Press, 1946.

Hollon, W. Eugene and Ruth Lapham Butler, eds. *William Bollaert's Texas.* Norman, Okla., Univ. of Oklahoma Press, 1956.

Hughes, John Taylor. *Doniphan's Expedition.* Cincinnati, J. A. & V. P. James, 1848.

Johnston, Abraham Robinson. *Journal.* Edited by Ralph B. Beiber in *Southwest Historical Series,* IV. Glendale, Calif., 1936.

Jones, Robert L. *History of the Foreign Policy of the United States.* New York, G. P. Putnam, 1933.

Kendall, George W., and Carl Nebel (artist). *The War Between the United States and Mexico, Illustrated.* New York, D. Appleton & Co., 1851.

Lewis, Lloyd. *Captain Sam Grant.* Boston, Little, Brown, 1950.

McEniry, Sister Blanche Marie. *American Catholics in the War with Mexico.* Washington, Catholic Univ. of America, 1937. Published Ph.D. thesis.

Mansfield, Edward D. *The Mexican War.* New York, A. S. Barnes, 1852.

Meade, George Gordon. *Life and Letters of George Gordon Meade, Major General, United States Army.* 2 vols. New York, Charles Scribner's Sons, 1913.

Merk, Frederick. *Manifest Destiny and Mission in American History, A reinterpretation.* New York, Alfred Knopf, 1963.

Meyers, William Starr. *The Mexican War Diary of George B. McClellan.* Princeton, N. J., 1917.

Nevins, Allen, ed. *Polk—The Dairy of a President, 1845–1849.* New York, Longmans, Green & Co., 1952.

Nichols, Edward J. *Zach Taylor's Little Army.* Garden City, N. Y., 1963.

Parker, Capt. William Harwar. *Recollections of a Naval Officer.* New York, Charles Scribner's Sons, 1883.

Quaife, Milo Milton, ed. *The Diary of James K. Polk During His Presidency, 1845–1849.* 4 vols. Chicago, A. C. McClurg & Co., 1910.

Ramsey, Albert C. *The Other Side: Or Notes for the History of the War Between Mexico and the United States.* New York, J. Wiley, 1850.

Ripley, Roswell S. *The War with Mexico.* 2 vols. New York, 1849.

Rives, George L. *The United States and Mexico, 1821–1848.* New York, Charles Scribner's Sons, 1913.

Roa Barcena, José Maria. *Recuerdos de la Invasion Norte Americana.* Antonio Castro Leal, ed. 1947. Vol. II.

Rose, Victor M. *The Life and Services of Gen. Ben McCulloch.* Philadelphia, Pictorial Bureau of the Press, 1888.

Ruiz, Ramon Eduardo. *The Mexican War: Was It Manifest Destiny?* New York, Holt, Rinehart & Winston, 1963.

Scott, Winfield. *Memoirs of Lieut. Gen'l Scott*. New York, Sheldon & Co., 1864.

Semmes, Raphael. *Service Afloat and Ashore During the Mexican War*. Cincinnati, 1851.

Singletary, Otis. *The Mexican War*. Chicago, Univ. of Chicago Press, 1960.

Smith, Ephraim Kirby. *To Mexico with Scott: Letters of Capt. E. Kirby Smith to His Wife*. Cambridge, Mass.; Harvard Univ. Press, 1917.

Smith, Justin H. *The War with Mexico*. 2 vols. New York, The Macmillan Co., 1919.

Stevens, Hazard. *Life of Isaac Ingalls Stevens, by His Son*. Boston, Houghton, Mifflin & Co., 1901.

Taylor, Zachary. *Letters of Zachary Taylor from the Battlefields of the Mexican War*. Rochester, N. Y., The Genesee Press, 1908.

Wallace, Edward S. *General William Jenkins Worth, Monterey's Forgotten Hero*. Dallas, Southern Methodist Univ. Press, 1953.

Warner, Ezra J. *Generals in Blue: Lives of the Union Commanders*. Baton Rouge, La., Louisiana State Univ. Press, 1964.

Wilcox, Cadmus M. *History of the Mexican War*. Washington, 1892.

Articles

Military Affairs, Vol. XIII, No. 3. Fall, 1949.

Ramirez, José Fernando. *Mexico During the War with the United States*. Walter V. Scholes, ed. Translated by Elliott B. Scherr. *Univ. of Missouri Studies*, Vol. XXIII, No. 1, 1950.

Sears, Louis Martin. "Nichols P. Trist, A Diplomat With Ideals." In *Mississippi Valley Historical Review*, Vol. XI, No. 1.

Documents

Allis, S. D., Letter, dated Sept. 28, 1846, in *The New Orleans Picayune* (New Orleans, La.), Oct. 22, 1846.

Congressional Globe, 29th Congress, 1st Session (May 11, 1846).

Executive Document No. 4, House of Representatives, 29th Congress, 2nd Session.

Public Document No. 378, Senate, 29th Congress, 1st Session.

Public Document No. 388, Senate, 29th Congress, 1st Session.

Ex. Doc. No. 1, Senate, 30th Congress, 1st Session.

Ex. Doc. No. 33, Senate, 30th Congress, 1st Session.

Ex. Doc. No. 41, H.R., 30th Congress, 1st Session.

Ex. Doc. No. 50, H.R., 30th Congress, 1st Session.

Ex. Doc. No. 52, Senate, 30th Congress, 1st Session.

Ex. Doc. No. 60, H.R., 30th Congress, 1st Session.

Ex. Doc. No. 65, Senate, 30th Congress, 1st Session.

Letters of Sergeant John B. Duncan, in *Journal of Illinois State Historical Society*, Dec., 1948.

The New Orleans Picayune, March 25, 1847.

The New Orleans Picayune, May 1–6, 1847.

Worth, William Jenkins. Manuscript Letters in Chicago Historical Society.

Index

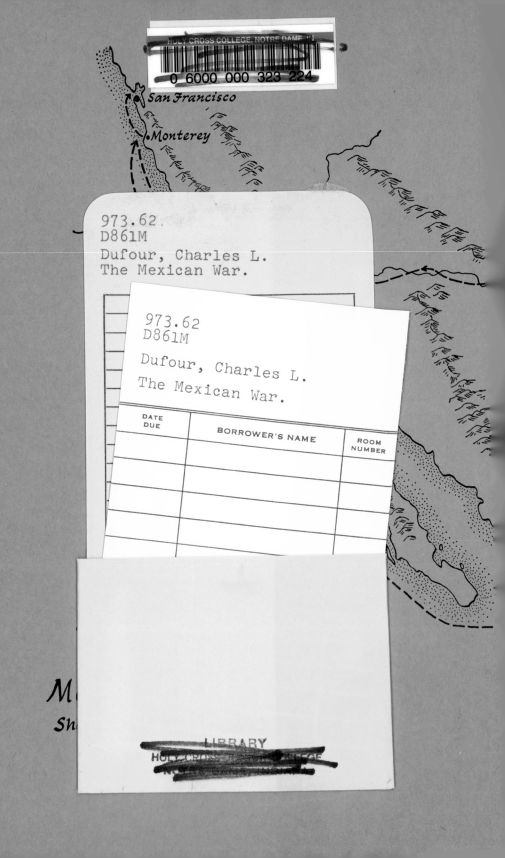